Chinese Enough

Chinese Enough

**Homestyle Recipes for Noodles,
Dumplings, Stir-Fries, and More**

Kristina Cho

ARTISAN

NEW YORK

Names: Cho, Kristina, author.
Title: Chinese enough : homestyle recipes for noodles, dumplings, stir-fries, and more / Kristina Cho.
Description: New York, NY : Artisan, 2024. | Includes index.
Identifiers: LCCN 2023058395 | ISBN 9781648293429 (hardback)
Subjects: LCSH: Cooking, Chinese. | LCGFT: Cookbooks.
Classification: LCC TX724.5.C5 C5655 2024 | DDC 641.5951–dc23
/eng/20231220
LC record available at https://lccn.loc.gov/2023058395

Design by Suet Chong

Artisan books may be purchased in bulk for business, educational, or promotional use. For information, please contact your local bookseller or the Hachette Book Group Special Markets Department at special.markets@hbgusa.com.

The publisher is not responsible for websites (or their content) that are not owned by the publisher.

The Hachette Speakers Bureau provides a wide range of authors for speaking events. To find out more, go to hachettespeakersbureau.com or email HachetteSpeakers@hbgusa.com.

Published by Artisan,
an imprint of Workman Publishing,
a division of Hachette Book Group, Inc.
1290 Avenue of the Americas
New York, NY 10104
artisanbooks.com

The Artisan name and logo are registered trademarks of Hachette Book Group, Inc.

Printed in Malaysia on responsibly sourced paper
First printing, August 2024

10 9 8 7 6 5 4 3 2 1

For my family.
I'm so lucky to cook for you all.

CONTENTS

INTRODUCTION

A few years ago, I was going about my Sunday-morning ritual of shopping at the Clement St. Farmers Market in the Inner Richmond District of San Francisco, admiring the first stone fruits of the season, when all of a sudden, a little girl ran past me yelling "Goong Goong, Goong Goong!" I watched as she joyfully ran into the arms of a sweet-looking elderly man. I immediately teared up. It took me a few moments to realize I was crying in public while holding a fistful of peaches. *Goong goong* is the Cantonese term for maternal grandpa. My goong goong passed away when I was eighteen, so it had been a good amount of time since I had affectionately called out to him in the same way.

I had been living in San Francisco for about five years at that point, many miles away from my childhood home just outside Cleveland, Ohio. Until then, I hadn't quite considered the impact of growing up in such a homogeneous place, where I was ethnically different from nearly everyone except my family members. My goong goong and pau pau (maternal grandmother) immigrated to the United States from Hong Kong in the late 1960s. After settling in Cleveland, they worked in restaurants and factories until they had saved enough money to open their own business, Dragon House. This was their first Chinese restaurant, where my mom and her siblings all helped out, at least part-time. They eventually opened a restaurant (their last) in the suburb I grew up in, and I spent my afternoons there as a kid zooming around the kitchen and all four corners of the dining room on roller skates. We visited my grandparents weekly in Cleveland's Chinatown (now officially called Asiatown) for family dinners and Sunday-morning dim sum. I loved eating Chinese food, and it felt nice to be part of a small community. But I went to a predominantly white school, and most of my friends were white. My lack of fluency in Cantonese, the way I dressed, and the occasional comment from an aunty made me feel not quite Chinese enough at times.

Within my suburban bubble growing up, I often felt not American enough, too. I could count on one hand the number of Asian students in my grade. Once, during elementary school,

I accidentally said something in Cantonese instead of English. I was immediately embarrassed as my classmates and teacher looked at me, perplexed. I rejected going to Chinese school on weekends (something I now regret) and asked my mom to pack me more "normal" ham and cheese sandwiches for lunch instead of a steamed bun or leftover stir-fried noodles, so I could at least hide the nonphysical aspects of myself that made me stand out.

I answer to two names. With my family, I am Yee (short for Cho Wing Yee, my Chinese name), but to everyone else, I am Kristina (my legal and birth name). Both are true names, neither one more valid than the other. Being a child of immigrants (or any combination of disparate identities) is a complicated and often uncomfortable feeling. You're constantly going back and forth between feeling othered and wanting to fit in. When you feel proud of your culture, there's always someone asking you to prove your authenticity (sometimes causing you to question it yourself). When you have a foot planted firmly in two seemingly disconnected worlds, there's this deep longing for true community, one that sees you, embraces you, and uplifts you for all the things that make you different.

FINDING MY WAY BACK TO CHINESE FOOD

I had an early interest in cooking, though not in cooking Chinese food. I would plop down in front of the TV on weekends to watch Food Network and PBS reruns of Julia Child's series. It was thrilling to see a chicken get trussed and enlightening to learn that ingredients should be at room temperature when making a cheesecake. My mom shared my enthusiasm for learning about non-Chinese food, and watching those shows together became a routine for us. When I asked if I could start baking and making dinner on occasion, she gave me the space and encouragement to do so. Soon I was feeding our family macaroni and cheese with herby breadcrumbs for dinner, followed by rich, dense chocolate chip blondies for dessert. They loved every bite, and seeing their satisfied faces made me feel proud that there was something I could do to take care of them.

I've always been drawn to creating space, places that are beautiful, comforting, and safe. This was initially why I studied architecture in college. I carried a love for cooking with me as

I went to architecture school and later moved to California. As I welcomed new people into my life, it was probably no coincidence that many shared similar experiences of growing up with a blended identity. It was refreshing to find people who appreciated a creative lifestyle and a good meal as much as I did (the prime example being my husband, Reuben, a fellow architect and lover of all cuisines). Friends soon felt like family as we formed bonds at the dinner table, and my world started to look and feel much more diverse. I was learning that creating space, community, and a meal were one and the same.

I began to tackle recipes from my childhood to connect to a past that I had once tried to distance myself from. Cooking Chinese food started to feel more empowering, less intimidating. In time, I developed my own style of cooking, an amalgamation of all my culinary influences to date. It was distinctly Chinese, with generous Midwestern hospitality and practicality, and a sunny Californian approach to ingredients. As I cooked more and more, the contrast that I had once felt between being Chinese and being American slowly softened.

YOU ARE ENOUGH

Minorities in America often get asked insidious questions like "Where are you *really* from?" and "How Asian [or insert your own ethnic background] are you?" The former feels more annoying than anything, and I always answer "Cleveland." I used to absolutely dread the latter. I've been asked the question many times, by acquaintances, Asian people, non-Asian people, and even an employer. Each time, I know that what they are implying has nothing to do with my 23andMe results and more to do with how assimilated my family and I are. I curtly answer "Enough" and leave it at that, reminding myself to avoid saying much to that person in the future. Any question about my identity used to linger with me and make me feel sensitive to how others perceived me. But through cooking, I've been able to fortify my own sense of self. I hope the food within these pages will do just that for you.

The recipes in this book highlight the multiple facets of what it means to be Chinese American through my personal lived experience. There are old-world recipes that have been passed down to me, like my pau pau's Hom Chi (page 251), which she was taught to make when she was a young girl. Other recipes, like Mom's Spaghetti (page 89), give a taste of what it was like to grow up in Cleveland in the 1990s, or, like the best Pineapple Sweet-and-Sour Sauce (page 307), offer a glimpse into my life as a restaurant kid. Still others, like San Francisco Garlic Noodles (page 90) and Steamed Dungeness Crabs with Tomato Butter (page 216), are informed by the beauty of cooking in the bountiful Bay Area. Recipes like Smashed Ranch Cucumbers (page 115) and Whitefish Rangoon (page 258) are playful ways I serve up the combination of my Midwestern upbringing and new and old familial influences in my life. These are the recipes I've introduced to my family's and friends' critical palates and woven into my everyday meal rotation.

My hope for this book is to offer a fresh take on Chinese American recipes, one that isn't often represented in the food culture at large. The recipes illustrate the intricacies of a life bridging cultures. They highlight the nuances of Chinese food, help me understand the perspective of generations that came before me, and allow me (and, in turn, you) to create new traditions. Whether you share my background or not, you may

share the sentiment of sometimes not feeling enough of one thing or another. I want you to know that in your own special way, you are more than enough.

Looking back on that unexpectedly emotional Sunday morning at the farmers' market, I also remember walking to my apartment and thinking about my newfound home. I was living in a place where a lot of people looked like me, spoke a language that I knew intimately (even without speaking it fluently), and understood the food that I grew up with. I was no longer seen as other. Most importantly, this world existed in such an everyday context. The Richmond District is one of a few neighborhoods in San Francisco where many Chinese families moved when the city's main Chinatown got too expensive or crowded. These areas are filled with Asian restaurants and grocery stores, but they lack the traditional visual vernacular of a more instantly recognizable Chinatown. I wasn't explicitly looking for all this when I was searching for an apartment in the city, but living in the Inner Richmond healed me in ways I didn't know I needed.

I think about that little girl at the farmers' market and how I wish I had had the courage when I was younger to shout "Goong Goong, Goong Goong!" at the top of my lungs in public, to feel unapologetically Chinese. It has taken a long time, some deep self-reflection, and, honestly, writing about my food and culture to get to this point. Now I can happily say I am proud to be Chinese, and particularly to be Chinese American. No matter what anyone thinks, I am Chinese enough, and so is my food.

HOW TO USE THIS BOOK

I want you to turn to this book to feed your family, partner, roommates, and friends on a weekly basis. Invite your pals over on a Wednesday night for big bowls of Creamy Tomato Udon (page 74). Dinner can be special, but you don't need to wait for a special occasion to feed people well. Over the past few years, I've gotten into a really good rhythm of having casual weeknight dinners with friends. Take advantage of the smaller moments in the kitchen and save your energy for the bigger productions, like a celebratory dinner party, Lunar New Year, or a backyard barbecue. Events of both scales are equally meaningful and memorable. Remember that cooking for others doesn't need to be an elaborate spectacle. It can (and should) be fun, joyous, loud, and spontaneous—anything but stressful.

Each recipe in this book has been developed with flexibility in mind. I'll let you know when it's okay to substitute an ingredient and when it's better that you don't. I do my best to break down the recipes to the fundamentals, describe steps clearly, and anticipate any questions or mishaps you might encounter along the way. I also recognize that specialty equipment and counter space can be limited in many kitchens. I want you to spend more time enjoying food with your favorite people than doing dishes or wiping down countertops.

CHAPTER ORGANIZATION

Rather than divide the recipes into traditional cookbook chapters (chicken, fish, sides, and the like), I've organized thematically into chapters inspired by the way I like to serve and enjoy a meal. The recipes from the Best with Rice chapter, for example, are designed to take as long to prepare as a pot of rice takes to steam, making them excellent options for weeknight dinners. Take It Outside is perfect for cookouts, and the dumplings and rolls of It Takes a Village benefit from having a few extra sets of helpful hands around to get in on the action. The recipes from every chapter can be mixed and matched, however. You can pick one or two recipes to make for an intimate meal, or compose a celebratory menu for a crowd. The Menu Sets on pages 354–355 will give you some good ideas.

SERVING SIZES

All the recipes are designed to feed at least four, and most will feed four to six people family-style, but I find that serving sizes are a little arbitrary—there have been moments in my life when I could have easily consumed multiple servings of San Francisco Garlic Noodles (page 90) and felt no regrets about it. You know your people best, so keep in mind that these recipes make a generous portion but are often meant to be shared and paired with another dish or two. If you're cooking for yourself, don't feel intimated by the amount of food. After all, what's better than leftover Chinese food?

COOK WITH YOUR SENSES

There are so many inconsistencies when it comes to kitchens and even kitchen equipment. Your oven is different from my oven. Your burners are different from my burners. The recipes are written to instruct you to cook to a visual indicator or cue first, before a time measurement. That means if your sauce thickens and looks glossy in 2 minutes instead of the 3 to 4 minutes written, you don't need to keep it simmering for those additional minutes. Indicators are important, so pay attention to your food! It'll often tell you when it's ready.

WEIGHING INGREDIENTS

All these recipes include both volume and weight measurements (with the exception of liquid measurements) for ingredients in quantities of ¼ cup or more. An extra 25 grams of tomato will not ruin your Hot-and-Sour Soup (page 298), but there's so much variety in the size of tomatoes and other produce that I encourage you to use your kitchen scale for better accuracy. Getting in the habit of using a kitchen scale when you cook can also help streamline the entire cooking process and reduce the number of dirty measuring cups and spoons you'll have to wash later. And when you're baking, using grams instead of cups will ensure you get the most consistent and successful results.

You got this!

STOCK UP

This is a thorough guide to the essential ingredients in my kitchen, the ones I use most in my cooking. I've listed the most frequently used ingredients at the top of each section. Most are staples in any Chinese kitchen, though a few might surprise you. You could turn this into a grocery list and stock up on them all, but even with only a few of these items, you'll be able to cook your way through this book.

SAUCES AND PASTES

Oyster Sauce | This is a fundamental ingredient in Cantonese cooking. Despite its name, it doesn't actually make food taste overly seafood-y, just sweet and briny! My mom considers oyster sauce her secret ingredient, sneaking it into her potato salad (page 167) and spaghetti sauce (see page 89) for an extra punch of umami. Lee Kum Kee premium oyster sauce is worth seeking out (see Resources, page 358)—it's the absolute best and the only one I use.

Soy Sauce | Not all soy sauces are created equal. The best ones are more than simply salty, with additional flavor notes of caramel, coffee, or even mushroom. Some soy sauces are lighter (less viscous) and sweeter, too. Most conventional grocery stores carry one or two brands of soy sauce, but if you go to an Asian grocery store, the options may extend from floor to ceiling. Experiment with varieties and brands of soy sauces to experience the full range of flavors. Refrigerate your soy sauce so it retains its freshness for as long as possible.

Dark Soy Sauce | This is darker and thicker than regular soy sauce. The flavor leans more sweet than salty, but not overly so. I use dark soy sauce in recipes that need a deeper color and more caramelized flavor. Its inky color can easily overpower a dish, so use it sparingly.

Ketchup | An all-American condiment that's good for more than french fries, ketchup is used surprisingly often in Chinese American cooking. Its sweet-sour flavor profile complements many Cantonese-style dishes. When it's the offseason for tomatoes, a squirt of ketchup in Tomato Egg (page 30) can be just what you need to amp up the flavor.

Hoisin | The name means "seafood sauce" in Cantonese, but it's not derived from seafood. Similar to soy sauce, hoisin is made from fermented soybeans, but it also incorporates garlic, chilis, and vinegar, giving it an almost sweet, barbecue-like flavor.

Fish Sauce | This kitchen staple, which is made from salted fermented anchovies, is unapologetically bold and in-your-face. It is most used in Southeast Asian cooking, adding a pungent funk to complement

all things spicy, sour, and sweet. Different brands of fish sauce vary in saltiness and fishiness, but I prefer those with a little sweetness, too. My favorite brands are Squid and Red Boat (see Resources, page 358).

Sesame Paste | Chinese sesame paste and tahini can be used interchangeably most of the time, but they have their differences. Chinese sesame paste is made with toasted sesame seeds, giving it a more roasted flavor, and it tends to be thicker. Tahini is made with raw sesame seeds, so the nutty flavor is a little lighter; it's also a bit more runny. Black sesame paste is made with black sesame seeds and tends to be crunchier and have a slightly more bitter flavor.

Shrimp Paste | This is a popular ingredient in Chinese and Southeast Asian cooking that doesn't get nearly the attention it deserves. It's salty, briny, sweet, and not at all fishy. Use shrimp paste as a way to add instant flavor to fried rice (page 65). It pairs well with flavors beyond the realm of seafood, like Shacha Roast Chicken (page 193). Look for jarred shrimp paste in soybean oil, which tends to have a brighter red color.

Doubanjiang | This spicy broad bean paste is a staple in Sichuan-style cooking and a fundamental ingredient for mapo tofu. A spoonful will add an intensely salty and fiery heat to any dish. It also has a strong fermented undertone, so prepare yourself for a little funk.

OILS

Olive Oil | My everyday cooking oil is extra-virgin olive oil. It's great for sautéing, but I don't deep-fry with it. Good-quality olive oil has a relatively high smoke point of 410°F (210°C), which makes it a good fat for roasting at higher temperatures. Standout olive oil is flavorful; depending on the variety, it can be fruity, grassy, and peppery, so keep that in mind as you incorporate it into dishes.

Neutral Oil | When it comes to frying or cooking at higher temperatures, use a neutral oil with a high smoke point. Grapeseed oil and avocado oil are my preferences, but sunflower, canola, and vegetable oils are perfectly fine alternatives.

Toasted Sesame Oil | A little goes a long way with this ingredient. When added to a recipe, it provides a lovely unctuousness and intoxicating smell. Look for toasted sesame oil; untoasted sesame oil is essentially a neutral oil and lacks the flavor you need.

Chili Crunch | "Chili oil," "chili crunch," and "chili crisp" are labels used interchangeably for this spicy, oily jarred condiment; crunches and crisps tend to have a higher ratio of aromatic bits (like garlic, chilis, and seeds) to oil. Whether you make it yourself (see page 302) or grow a collection of store-bought varieties, chili crunch is an essential ingredient that instantly adds heat, smokiness, and fattiness to a dish. Some of my favorite brands are Lao Gan Ma (with the black beans) and Fly By Jing (see Resources, page 358).

VINEGARS AND COOKING WINE

Rice Vinegar | While not the most acidic vinegar, rice vinegar is refreshing and crisp. Its clean, neutral flavor prevents it from overpowering other ingredients while still adding a sharp tartness. It's the perfect vinegar for Party Pickles (page 309).

Chinkiang Vinegar | Also known as Chinese black vinegar, this is most similar to balsamic vinegar, but not quite as thick or acidic. It has a complex malty flavor, and I love to mix this vinegar with Chili Crunch (page 302) for an easy sauce to toss with crisp vegetables or noodles.

Shaoxing Wine | If you take a sip of this rice-based cooking wine, you'll experience a delicate sweetness and a robust warmth on your palate. I use it to deglaze my pans and to add complexity to long, slow braises and simmering soups. If you don't have Shaoxing wine, bourbon is a great substitute in a pinch!

SEASONINGS

Salt | For everyday cooking, I use Diamond Crystal kosher salt. It has a coarse texture with slightly larger granules. If you're using Morton kosher salt or a finer table salt, use about half the quantity listed in the recipe (their finer crystals allow more salt to fit in a measuring spoon, making your food taste saltier). Everyone has different preferences regarding saltiness, so remember to taste your food along the way and adjust as needed. I consider my preference nicely situated in the middle of the salt spectrum, meaning appropriately seasoned but not aggressively so (unless we're talking about cookies—I like my cookies salty).

White Pepper | White pepper is used more commonly than black pepper in Chinese cooking. It has a finer texture and a more floral heat that tends to linger and grow on your palate. White pepper is made from fermented ripe peppercorn berries (black pepper uses unripe green berries) and the outer layer is removed, leaving the lighter-colored seed inside. Due to its fine powdery consistency, it tends to go airborne when you cook with it. If you start sneezing in the kitchen, it might be because you just used some white pepper. I mainly use preground white pepper for convenience, but on occasion I'll grind whole white peppercorns with a spice grinder at home.

Chinese Five Spice Powder | The five spices typically used in this blend are cinnamon, star anise, clove, Sichuan peppercorns, and fennel. Sometimes dried orange peel or ginger is incorporated into the mix. I use five spice in both savory and sweet recipes. The warm spices bring out the best in Chop Shop Pork Belly (page 195) and can be used as an elevated version of pumpkin spice for fall-centric desserts like Soy Caramel Apple Crisp (page 342).

Sichuan Peppercorns | The tingly sensation on your tongue that results from eating Sichuan peppercorns is something that grows on you. I find it enjoyable, as if the spice is waking up my taste buds. The flavor of these dainty peppercorns is citrusy, floral, and not necessarily spicy. When combined with chilis, it creates mala spice, a pillar of Sichuan and Northern Chinese cooking.

Chicken Bouillon Powder | Homemade chicken stock (see page 300) is liquid gold, but chicken bouillon powder is a convenient flavor enhancer that delivers deep and pure chicken flavor for soups, grains, and jook.

It's a workhorse in a Chinese pantry. I prefer bouillon powder over cubes because it's easier to integrate into recipes, and bouillon cubes often have a yellow coloring that I don't necessarily want to add to my food.

SWEETENERS

Sugar | A canister of granulated sugar is always sitting on the shelf next to my oils, salt, and pepper. A pinch of sugar in a stir-fry or marinade is often what you need to balance the heat and savoriness of a dish. Some recipes call for rock sugar, which is a light-amber-colored crystallized sugar sold in chunks. Rock sugar is ideal for braises and gives them a caramel undertone, but if you don't have it on hand, brown sugar is a fine substitute.

Honey and Maple Syrup | Reach for these unrefined sugars when a recipe needs sweetness with a little more complexity. Honey can range vastly in flavor, often leaning in a more botanical direction, while maple syrup is more caramel-like in flavor and naturally works well with Chinese five spice. Honey and maple syrup both also tend to be sweeter than granulated sugar, so you can add smaller amounts to a recipe and still achieve the sweetness you want.

DRIED AND PRESERVED GOODS

Fermented Black Beans | These are not the kind of beans you'll find tucked into your burrito. Fermented black beans are actually salted soybeans. Out of the package, they are dry and almost raisin-like. They have a distinctly salty and intensely savory flavor, like a highly concentrated pill of soy sauce. You can find packages of fermented black beans in the dried or preserved foods aisle. I like Yang Jiang brand in the iconic yellow tube (see Resources, page 358).

Dried Seafood | Preserving seafood is an art form among the islands and enclaves surrounding Hong Kong (and in other Asian countries). Salting and drying fish, shrimp, and scallops concentrates their flavors, bringing their natural sweetness to the surface. Dried shrimp and scallops are integral for XO Sauce (page 303) and add immense flavor when stir-fried with noodles or rehydrated in anything brothy. Dried shrimp and fish can normally be found in the refrigerated section of a Chinese grocery. Dried scallops are more expensive and will most likely be stored in a jar behind a counter somewhere, so you'll have to ask an employee for a scoop or two.

Lap Cheong | These Chinese cured pork sausages are sweet, salty, and very fatty. When you cook rice and vegetables with lap cheong, the fat within the sausage renders and perfumes the dish with its distinctive porky richness. I love KamYenJan brand lap cheong (see Resources, page 358).

Dried Mushrooms | Rehydrated shiitake mushrooms have a meaty chew and more concentrated earthy flavor than fresh mushrooms, making them exceptional

for soups and braises. Dried wood ear mushrooms rehydrate quickly and maintain a springy, crunchy texture that's great for salads and soups.

Kombu | A type of kelp, kombu is the ocean's version of MSG, lending sweet and savory brininess and many nutritious minerals. Following the lead of Japanese dashi, I add a sheet of kombu whenever I make a stock or broth.

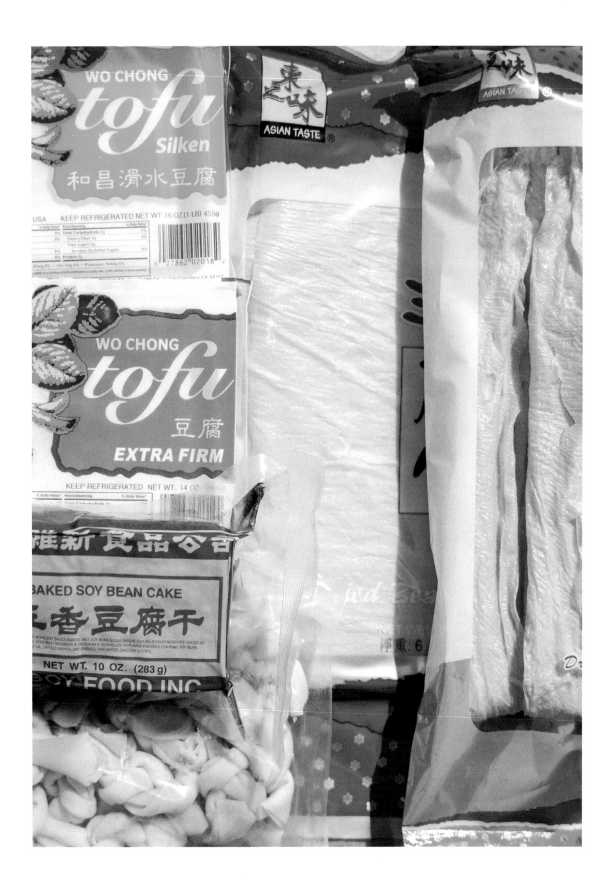

TOFU

I'm not a vegetarian—no one in my family is—but tofu is fundamental to our diet. Every time I open a package of tofu, I'll trim off a small piece for my husband and me to have as a snack. I can't help but roll my eyes whenever I hear someone describe a recipe as "a way to make tofu taste good." Good tofu tastes great simply on its own.

Tofu comes in many different forms, but they are all made from soy milk—either by pressing soy milk curds to form blocks of tofu or simmering the milk and forming thin layers of bean curd.

Firm or Extra-Firm Tofu | Pressed curds of soy milk form this denser variety of tofu. The sturdy texture of firm or extra-firm tofu is perfect for searing, stir-frying, and frying. It is packed in water, so before cooking with it, drain the tofu and then press out the excess water with some paper towels. House Foods, Wo Chong, and Hodo make some of my favorites (see Resources, page 358).

Silken Tofu | As the name implies, this tofu is silky and custardy and doesn't require any pressing. It makes an instant refreshing meal with a simple chili crunch and Chinkiang vinegar dressing, and you can add scoops of it to soup for additional protein. Silken tofu comes in a package similar to firm tofu (in water and refrigerated), but it can also come in a shelf-stable cardboard box.

Pressed Tofu | I love the texture of pressed tofu—imagine extra-firm tofu, but about twice as dense. It's chewy, almost like a sliced rice cake, and holds up much better in a stir-fry, with no fear of breaking. It comes vacuum-packed in sets of four or eight smaller blocks. Pressed tofu can come unflavored, but it's very common to find spiced pressed tofu, which has been marinated in soy sauce and Chinese five (or more) spice, as well as smoked pressed tofu.

Bean Curd | This is the thin layer that forms on top of soy milk when you simmer it without stirring. The sheet of curd is swiftly lifted away and dried to form bean curd sheets (also called tofu skin). The curd can also be gathered into ripples before drying to form bean curd sticks (or bean sticks). These can be added to soups, where they will return to their original softness, and also make a hearty addition to braises.

Tofu Knots | These are ribbons of pressed tofu that have been tied into knots. I like to grab a bag of them to throw into soups. Their denser texture allows them to hold up well in braises, too. They're also just visually fun to include in dishes.

ESSENTIAL TOOLS

Whether you have a tiny studio kitchen or a dream kitchen with a 16-foot island, you'll be able to create an incredible meal with these recipes. Tools are important, but I have a less-is-more mindset when it comes to equipment. You don't need every fancy kitchen gadget to be a good cook—you just need the right ones. Here are a few trusty tools that will make your experience in the kitchen much more fun and get delicious food on the table faster.

Cast-Iron Skillet | Cast iron is so versatile, and I use my cast-iron pan nearly every day. It has exceptional heat retention and achieves the closest level of sear to a really hot wok. When it's well seasoned, cast iron is more nonstick than any nonstick pan, and it'll last forever.

Dutch Oven | I deep-fry in a Dutch oven because it holds the oil temperature steady and the higher walls help prevent splatter. You can also use it to boil noodles, steam clams, and braise lamb or oxtails for hours. It doesn't hurt that Dutch ovens are beautiful things to display in the kitchen.

Saucepan | A 3-quart saucepan is perfect for steaming rice, hard-boiling eggs, cooking a packet of instant ramen, or making a creamy custard.

Good Knives | A sharp knife is one of my favorite gifts to give, because not only is a dull knife dangerous, it also makes cooking less fun. If you only have space for two knives, get a good-quality santoku and nakiri. Both are Japanese-style knives. A santoku is a classic chef's knife with a pointy end and is useful in nearly every occasion for cutting. A nakiri has a flat rectangular blade and feels like a scaled-down version of a cleaver. It's excellent for chopping vegetables and smashing aromatics.

NOTE ON GIFTING KNIVES: *In the Chinese culture, gifting a knife to someone is actually bad luck (it represents severed relations). To repel all bad vibes, tape a coin to the blade of the knife before presenting it as a gift.*

Spider | Essentially a handheld strainer, a spider makes removing everything from dumplings to noodles from hot oil or water a breeze. I'll also set a spider over a plate or baking sheet and use it as a makeshift wire rack to cool fried chicken or anything crispy.

Tongs | Tongs create distance between your hand and hot food and can maneuver food with more precision than a spatula. If you're on expert level with chopsticks, a sturdy pair of extra-long chopsticks is just as useful and operates in the same way.

Quarter Sheet Pans | A quarter sheet pan is half the size of a standard baking sheet (or half sheet pan), measuring 9 by

13 inches (23 by 33 cm). Include a few in your arsenal, because they're incredibly handy. Fill a quarter sheet pan with all the prepped ingredients for a recipe and feel extra organized. A quarter sheet pan packed with dumplings will fit much better in the freezer than a half sheet pan, and they're the perfect size for baking a small batch of cookies or toasting nuts in the oven.

Kitchen Scale | When I bake, I always whip out the kitchen scale. It's the only way to accurately measure flour, and simply streamlines the overall baking process. For savory cooking, there's more wiggle room, but it's still practical to have a kitchen scale on hand to confirm the weight of an ingredient.

Bamboo Steamer | I prefer to use a bamboo steamer because moisture won't condense on the lid and drip back down into your food (which happens with metal steamers). There's often confusion about how to use a bamboo steamer, but all you need besides the steamer itself is a pot that matches its diameter. This could be a deep pan or a Dutch oven (my go-to)—really any vessel that fits below the steamer and prevents steam from escaping. To set up a bamboo steamer, fill the pot with 3 inches (7.5 cm) of water and bring to a simmer over medium heat. Place the food in the steamer, cover, and set the steamer over the simmering water. If you're steaming dumplings directly on the bamboo, make sure to brush it with neutral oil.

Food Processor | My life before a food processor involved a lot more chopping and crushing graham crackers in a zip-top bag with a rolling pin. Now I use my food processor all the time to blitz a bulk amount of garlic or make pie dough in under a minute. You can live without a food processor, but life is a little easier with one.

WHERE'S THE WOK?

Wok cooking is a beautiful thing to watch and gives food a distinctly charred and smoky flavor (called wok hei). The back wall of the kitchen at my grandparents' restaurant was lined with wok stations, and the chefs wielded the giant woks effortlessly over flames similar to those from jet engines.

You might be wondering why a wok is not listed under "essential tools" in a Chinese cookbook. I do own a carbon-steel wok and use it on occasion, but I simply don't think it's necessary for cooking these recipes. It's difficult to replicate restaurant results at home because home stovetops don't reach temperatures nearly as hot. My parents have a few of the original restaurant woks in their basement, but even they never cook with a wok at home. If you do own a wok and want to use it, by all means do so. Make sure to get it as hot as possible so food doesn't stick to it.

Woks are also wonderfully multipurpose. Their tapered widemouthed shape makes them great for deep-frying, boiling noodles, and steaming big batches of dumplings. But a cast-iron pan will give you a wonderful sear and caramelized edges, and a bamboo steamer works just the same set over a deep pan or pot. Wok or don't wok, it's up to you.

KNIFE CUTS

As soon as I showed interest in cooking, my mom took the time to teach me some basic knife skills. We used a Chinese cleaver because that's essentially all she uses in the kitchen, apart from a paring knife that is older than me! You don't need a cleaver, though; a sturdy and sharp chef's knife is perfect for making these dishes. Knowing how to break down your ingredients makes cooking so much easier. Understanding *why* you want to smash garlic as opposed to thinly slicing it for a specific recipe is a game changer as well.

Smash | Smashing aromatics like ginger and garlic instantly damages their structure, releasing their moisture and flavor. A piece of smashed ginger will release much more flavor than a chunk or thick slice. For ginger, cut it into 1-inch (2.5 cm) pieces across the grain and place on a cutting board so the grain or internal fibers are facing upward, then firmly smack it with the flat face of the knife blade. A clove of garlic easily flattens with a firm smack. For cucumbers, I find it much easier and less messy to cut smaller chunks first, then set them skin-side up and firmly press down on them with the blade (as if you're giving CPR or a chiropractic adjustment) until they break.

Mince | After a good smash, ginger and garlic are only a few back-and-forths of the blade away from minced. This size is great for a general stir-fry or if you're making something light and crispy, like typhoon breadcrumbs (see page 157) or Chili Crunch (page 302). You can create a paste by rocking the blade back and forth even more and smearing the garlic or ginger against the cutting board. This is a good alternative to using a Microplane or grater if you don't have one.

Bias Cut | This is a fancy way of saying you want to cut something at a steep angle, about 60 degrees. Bias-cut green onions feel special because they look like a restaurant-quality garnish. Cutting thicker vegetables like carrots and zucchini at a steep angle creates more surface area for the vegetable to make contact with the pan, which allows it to brown and cook faster.

Matchsticks | Delicate strips of vegetables are great for hot-and-fast cooking, when you want to retain their texture but don't want them to taste raw, or if you're making a filling for something long like a spring roll or an egg roll. For ginger or hearty vegetables, cut ¼-inch-thick (6 mm) slices at an angle to get 2- to 3-inch-long (5 to 7.5 cm) pieces. Stack the slices and then cut into ¼-inch-wide (6 mm) pieces. For thicker matchsticks (batons), it's the same mechanics, but you want closer to ½- to ¾-inch-thick (1 to 2 cm) slices and then ½- to ¾-inch-wide (1 to 2 cm) batons.

Roll Cut | It may be a lesser-known cut, but you'll see vegetables prepared this way in Chinese recipes as a method to increase surface area and reduce cooking time. For example, cut off the very end of a carrot at a 45-degree angle. Keep the knife at the same angle, but roll the carrot about a half turn with your non-knife hand and cut about an inch down from the end. This creates a triangular shape with two angled sides. Repeat the rolling-and-cutting process all the way down the vegetable.

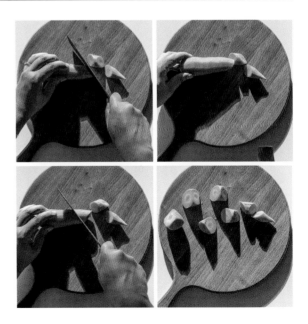

Best with Rice

A typical dinner in my house (and many Asian households) follows this very basic formula: steamed rice + a quick protein + a vegetable. Dinner for me begins with getting the rice started (and putting on the nightly news in the living room for background noise—a sign I am clearly turning into my parents!). After that, garlic gets smashed and vegetables get trimmed for a dish to go best with rice. Some nights, dinner is a saucy tomato egg, and others, it's a seared oyster sauce–marinated steak with savory pan sauce. The recipes in this chapter are trusty standbys that are easy to execute Monday through Thursday (but still feel special enough for Friday through Sunday), because when you time them just right, they take as long to prepare as a pot of rice takes to steam.

To accompany these dishes, turn to Perfect Steamed Jasmine Rice (page 286) and the other delicious grains in the More Than Sides chapter (page 284).

Tomato Egg

Serves 4

2 tablespoons extra-virgin olive oil

1 (2-inch/5 cm) knob fresh ginger, peeled and cut into thin matchsticks

10 medium tomatoes (681 g), preferably Roma (see headnote), roughly chopped

⅓ cup (80 ml) oyster sauce

1 tablespoon toasted sesame oil

1½ teaspoons kosher salt

1½ teaspoons ground white pepper

1½ teaspoons crushed red chili flakes

1 cup (240 ml) water

1 tablespoon cornstarch

6 large eggs, whisked

⅓ cup (15 g) chopped green onions

Steamed rice (any kind, see pages 286–291), for serving

Tomatoes and eggs belong together in dishes from eggs in purgatory to scrambled eggs and ketchup, and definitely in this Chinese tomato egg. There are many ways to make tomato egg, and because it can be such a personal recipe, there are some *very strong* opinions about the best version. The typical Chinese tomato egg looks like scrambled eggs with big chunks of stir-fried tomatoes. This almost gravy-like tomato egg leans more in the Cantonese direction, which favors silky sauces thickened with cornstarch. The tomatoes are cooked down until jammy and whisked eggs are then gently stirred into the tomato sauce (like in egg drop soup), leaving curds of egg in the wake of the spoon. When it's peak tomato season, make this with the ripest tomatoes you can find; I love Early Girl tomatoes and heirloom varieties. But even if it's the dead of winter and all you have are grocery store Romas, the sauce is flavorful enough to bring out the best in them.

COOK THE TOMATOES: In a large skillet, heat the olive oil over medium-high heat. Add the ginger and cook until fragrant and just starting to brown, 1 to 2 minutes. Add the tomatoes, oyster sauce, sesame oil, salt, white pepper, and chili flakes. Toss to combine and cook, stirring occasionally with a wooden spoon or spatula, until the tomatoes are jammy, 8 to 10 minutes. If the tomatoes aren't breaking down as quickly as you'd like, gently smash them with the back of the spoon or spatula.

In a small bowl, whisk together the water and cornstarch to make a slurry. Pour the slurry into the pan and stir. Cook until the tomatoes have broken down and the sauce thickens, 2 to 3 minutes.

STIR IN THE EGGS: Reduce the heat to maintain a simmer. Drizzle the eggs over the tomatoes, but do not stir. Let the eggs gently cook in the tomatoes until just barely set, 1 to 2 minutes. Add most of the green onions (set some aside for garnish) and gently stir to break up the egg. Take care not to overstir; you want to maintain some larger curds of egg.

Serve with rice and garnish with the reserved green onions.

Green Steamed Egg

Serves 4

⅔ cup (30 g) fresh Thai basil or cilantro (or a blend of the two)

1 cup (240 ml) water

4 large eggs

1 teaspoon chicken bouillon powder

¼ teaspoon kosher salt

Soy sauce

Chili Crunch (page 302, or store-bought)

Steamed rice (any kind, see pages 286–291), for serving

If you're like me, you probably have a bundle of tender herbs slowly wilting somewhere in the fridge. This recipe is a great opportunity to make use of an abundance of basil (you should actually keep cut basil in some water on your counter instead of in the fridge) or cilantro. Blending the herbs into Chinese steamed eggs lends the egg a lovely herbaceous flavor and stunning green color. The texture of steamed eggs is luxuriously silky and akin to custard. The trick to achieving a smooth texture is to strain the mixture through a mesh sieve and then carefully scoop off any foam from the top once it's in the bowl. These extra measures are purely for aesthetics, so if you don't want to do this, don't. The steamed egg will taste delicious regardless.

BLEND THE HERBS AND EGGS: Puree the basil and water in a blender until smooth, then pour into a medium bowl. Add the eggs, bouillon, and salt and whisk to combine. Strain the mixture through a sieve (this is optional, but the top won't be smooth otherwise) into a heatproof shallow bowl (that fits in your steamer). Scoop away the foamy egg on top with a spoon and discard.

STEAM AND SERVE: Set up a bamboo steamer (see page 25). Bring the water to a boil over medium heat. When the water is boiling, place the bowl of eggs in the steamer and cover with the lid. Reduce the heat to medium-low and steam until the eggs are mostly set, about 10 minutes. Turn off the heat and allow the eggs to fully set in the residual steam, another 5 minutes (they will still have a slight jiggle). Let cool slightly and then lightly score the surface. Drizzle with soy sauce and chili crunch and serve with steamed rice.

VARIATION

ADD THOUSAND-YEAR-OLD EGGS: Peel and quarter 2 thousand-year-old eggs (see page 38). Place them in the bowl with the egg mixture after straining and continue the recipe as directed.

Chilly Silken Tofu with Tomato Salad

Serves 4

1 (16-ounce/454 g) block
silken tofu

2 cups (250 g) cherry
tomatoes, cut in half

2 tablespoons Chili
Crunch (page 302,
or store-bought)

2 tablespoons Chinkiang
vinegar

2 garlic cloves, grated

1 teaspoon toasted
sesame oil

½ teaspoon kosher salt

¼ teaspoon ground white
pepper

2 green onions, thinly
sliced

Steamed rice (any kind,
see pages 286–291),
for serving

When it's so hot that you can't fathom turning on your oven or burners, make a meal out of silken tofu to help beat the heat. This recipe is more assembly than actual cooking. The vinaigrette that forms at the base of the bowl along with the juice of the tomatoes is perfect mixed into rice (the one thing you will have to actually cook).

ARRANGE THE TOFU: Slice the tofu into ½-inch (1 cm) slices. Transfer to a serving plate and gently press the tofu so the slices angle back.

MIX THE TOMATOES: In a medium bowl, stir together the tomatoes, chili crunch, vinegar, garlic, sesame oil, salt, and white pepper to combine.

SERVE: Pour the tomato mixture over the tofu. Top with the green onions and serve with rice.

VARIATION

ADD THOUSAND-YEAR-OLD EGGS: Peel and quarter 2 thousand-year-old eggs (see page 38). Arrange the eggs around the tofu and tomatoes.

Don't Be Afraid of Thousand-Year-Old Eggs

You will always find a package of thousand-year-old eggs in my fridge next to the carton of regular eggs, an arrangement you'll find in many other Chinese households as well. Thousand-year-old eggs (or century eggs) are not actually aged for a thousand years—more like a few weeks or months. The eggs are cured in an alkaline solution, which turns the egg white a translucent brown color with a firm and jiggly texture, the yolks green and creamy, and the shells a speckled gray. They taste like extra-savory eggs. When my mom was growing up, my pau pau used them very sparingly, for special occasions, because they were expensive. It was considered quite a luxury if you got just one bite of thousand-year-old egg at dinner. And when I was a kid, it felt like a treat when my mom added thousand-year-old-egg wedges to her jook or steamed eggs.

You can purchase thousand-year-old eggs at Chinese grocery stores, and they can be eaten without any additional cooking. They are delicious peeled and cracked just like a hard-boiled egg. If you're going to incorporate them into other dishes, cut them into quarters or wedges first. Arrange them on a platter with cold silken tofu (see page 36), stir them into a creamy jook (page 210) during the last 10 minutes of cooking, or add them to a silky steamed egg (page 35).

Seared Egg Tofu with Honey and Soy

Serves 4

2 tablespoons soy sauce

1 tablespoon mirin

½ teaspoon sugar

2 tablespoons extra-virgin olive oil

2 (8-ounce/454 g) tubes egg tofu, cut into ¾-inch-thick (2 cm) slices

1 Fresno chili, thinly sliced

2 teaspoons honey

Steamed rice (any kind, see pages 286–291), for serving

Introducing people to egg tofu is so much fun. Typically sold in tube form at Asian grocery stores, egg tofu has the same consistency as a silken tofu but with a rich, eggy flavor. It's a little slippery to handle, but you can prepare it in a multitude of ways. It fries beautifully with a light coating of cornstarch, and scoops of it make for soft egg clouds in a brothy soup. One of the best and simplest ways to highlight egg tofu is to sear thick rounds of it (almost resembling scallops) in a little olive oil until crisp and dress them with not-too-spicy chilis, slightly sweet soy sauce, and honey. In less than 10 minutes, you'll have a light and refined dish that everyone will love.

MIX THE SAUCE: In a medium bowl, whisk together the soy sauce, mirin, and sugar. Set aside.

SEAR THE EGG TOFU: In a large skillet, heat the olive oil over medium-high heat. Add the egg tofu in a single layer (work in batches if there isn't enough room in the pan) and fry until golden brown, 3 minutes on each side. Transfer the egg tofu to a serving platter and top with the chili.

SERVE: Pour the sauce over the egg tofu and drizzle on the honey. Serve with rice.

Sticky Maple Tofu Sticks

Serves 4 to 6

2 (16-ounce/454 g) blocks
firm tofu

For the sauce

⅓ cup (80 ml) maple syrup

3 tablespoons rice vinegar

2 tablespoons soy sauce

1 teaspoon crushed red
chili flakes

½ teaspoon ground white
pepper

½ teaspoon kosher salt

½ teaspoon Chinese five
spice powder

Neutral oil, such as
grapeseed, for frying

½ cup (60 g) cornstarch

1 tablespoon toasted
sesame seeds

Green onions, thinly sliced
on a bias, for garnish

Steamed rice (any kind,
see pages 286–291),
for serving

Frying tofu is one of the best ways to prepare it. Coating thick sticks of fried tofu in a sticky, sweet, tangy, and spicy sauce? Even better. The maple syrup that forms the base of this sauce caramelizes and reduces into a beautiful glaze in the pan.

Frying something until it reaches crunchy perfection only to soak it in a sauce so it loses that crunch might sound counterintuitive. But this technique is common in a lot of Chinese cooking. The batter is meant to act like a sponge, especially helpful when you're cooking tofu because its inherent flavor is pretty mild. Pressing the tofu before battering it helps you achieve a crispier texture after frying, which allows the coating to hold up better and retain more flavor.

PRESS THE TOFU: Cut each block of tofu into 8 sticks so you have 16 sticks total. Line a cutting board or baking sheet with a clean kitchen towel and arrange the tofu sticks on top. Cover with another clean kitchen towel and place another cutting board on top. Set something heavy, like a cast-iron pan, on top and let stand for 15 minutes to press as much moisture from the tofu as possible.

MIX THE SAUCE: In a medium bowl, whisk together the maple syrup, vinegar, soy sauce, chili flakes, white pepper, salt, and five spice.

FRY THE TOFU: In a large skillet, heat 1 inch (2.5 cm) of oil over medium-high heat to 360°F (182°C). (If you don't have a thermometer, test the temperature by dipping a wooden chopstick into the oil: if many tiny bubbles appear around the chopstick, the oil is hot enough; if not, it needs to continue warming up.) Set a wire rack over a rimmed baking sheet and place the cornstarch in a shallow bowl.

Working in batches of 8 sticks to avoid overcrowding the pan, coat a piece of tofu in cornstarch, shake off any excess, and add it to the hot oil. Fry until crispy and golden brown on each side, 3 to 4 minutes per side. Transfer the tofu sticks to the rack and repeat with the remaining tofu, adding more oil to the pot if needed and letting it come to temperature between batches.

When you have finished frying the tofu, drain the oil into a heatproof container and wipe the pan clean with a paper towel.

ADD THE SAUCE: Allow the pan to cool for about a minute. Pour the sauce into the pan and set it over medium heat. Cook, stirring continuously with a flexible spatula, until thickened, 2 to 3 minutes. Return the tofu to the pan and toss to coat in the sauce. Continue to simmer and reduce for a few more minutes until the tofu is well coated in the sticky maple sauce.

SERVE: Transfer to a serving platter and garnish with the sesame seeds and green onions. Serve with rice.

Orange Pepper Popcorn Chicken

Serves 4

1 pound (454 g) boneless, skinless chicken thighs, cut into 1½-inch (4 cm) pieces

¼ cup (30 g) cornstarch

1½ tablespoons orange zest, plus more for topping

2 tablespoons freshly squeezed orange juice

1 tablespoon soy sauce

1½ teaspoons freshly ground black pepper

3 garlic cloves, grated

1 teaspoon kosher salt

1 teaspoon toasted sesame oil

Neutral oil, such as grapeseed, for frying

¾ cup (90 g) sweet potato starch

Steamed rice (any kind, see pages 286–291), for serving

Everyone should have a casual fried chicken recipe in their back pocket. Casual in that you don't need to heat a big pot of oil for deep-frying, so the dish feels doable on a Tuesday night. This orange pepper chicken is just that. Juicy chicken thighs marinated in a lively blend of soy sauce, orange juice, and black pepper get a dusting of sweet potato starch, the secret to the lightest, crispiest coating. (I'm a dark meat person, but you could use chicken breast instead; to make the dish gluten-free, replace the soy sauce with tamari.) And since the pieces are small, the chicken cooks through in a matter of minutes. They are delicious in a simple rice bowl, add a little indulgence to a salad, and make an amazing appetizer for a crowd with some Kewpie mayo for dunking.

MARINATE THE CHICKEN: Place the chicken in a medium bowl. Add the cornstarch, orange zest, orange juice, soy sauce, black pepper, garlic, salt, and sesame oil. Mix until evenly combined. Cover and let the chicken marinate at room temperature for 30 minutes.

WARM UP THE OIL: In a medium saucepan, heat about 1 inch (2.5 cm) of neutral oil over medium-high heat to 360°F (182°C). (If you don't have a thermometer, test the temperature by dipping a wooden chopstick into the oil: if many tiny bubbles appear around the chopstick, the oil is hot enough; if not, it needs to continue warming up.) Set a wire rack over a rimmed baking sheet. Place the potato starch in a medium bowl.

FRY THE CHICKEN: Working in batches, remove a piece of chicken from the marinade, shake off any excess, and dip it in the potato starch to fully coat. Shake off any excess starch and carefully lower the chicken into the hot oil. Fry until golden brown and cooked through, 3 to 4 minutes. Transfer the chicken to the rack and repeat with the remaining chicken. Let cool for a few minutes before serving.

SERVE: Top with extra orange zest and serve with rice.

Crispy Chicken Thighs with Sticky Rice

Serves 4

4 bone-in, skin-on chicken thighs

1½ teaspoons kosher salt

2 teaspoons extra-virgin olive oil

2 lap cheong (Chinese sausages), thinly sliced

1½ cups (330 g) sticky rice

1½ cups (360 ml) water

1 tablespoon soy sauce

4 green onions, thinly sliced

½ teaspoon ground white pepper

Dark soy sauce, for serving

This dish is a one-pot wonder that takes flavor inspiration from one of my favorite dim sum staples: lo mai gai, a steamed bundle of lotus leaf stuffed with sticky rice and chicken. Make this using a cast-iron braiser with a fitted lid so you can move the dish from stove to oven to table (if you don't have one, any oven-safe pan will work just fine). Starting the chicken in a cold pan allows the fat to render more evenly, resulting in extra-crispy chicken skin; the fat from the chicken and the Chinese sausage is used to toast and flavor the sticky rice. A fitted lid traps the steam to fully cook the rice and chicken, and then the whole party goes under the broiler to give both the rice and chicken skin a crispy finish.

SEAR THE CHICKEN: Season the chicken skin with 1 teaspoon of the salt. Pour the olive oil into a large oven-safe skillet or braiser and set over medium heat. Immediately add the chicken thighs, skin-side down, and cook until the skin is golden brown and releases from the pan, 8 to 10 minutes. Transfer the chicken to a plate (skin-side up) and set aside.

STEAM THE STICKY RICE: Add the lap cheong to the pan and cook until crisp, 2 to 3 minutes. Add the rice and cook, stirring, in the rendered fat until the rice is lightly toasted, about 2 minutes. Add the water, soy sauce, green onions (save some for garnish), white pepper, and remaining ½ teaspoon salt. Stir to combine and bring to a simmer. Return the chicken to the pan, skin-side up, and reduce the heat to medium-low to maintain a gentle simmer. Cover and steam until the rice is cooked through, 15 to 20 minutes.

BROIL THE RICE: Heat the broiler. Remove the lid from the pan and transfer the pan to an upper rack in the oven. Broil until the rice and chicken skin are crispy, 8 to 10 minutes. Watch carefully as they broil to prevent them from burning. Let cool for a few minutes.

SERVE: Top with the reserved green onions and serve with dark soy sauce on the side.

Curry Chicken Wings and Potatoes

Serves 4

2 tablespoons extra-virgin olive oil

1½ pounds (681 g) chicken wings

1 pound (454 g) russet potatoes, peeled and cut into 2-inch (5 cm) pieces

1¾ cups (420 ml) water

2 tablespoons curry powder

1½ tablespoons oyster sauce

1 tablespoon sriracha

1 teaspoon kosher salt

½ teaspoon ground white pepper

½ cup (120 ml) full-fat canned coconut milk

2 teaspoons cornstarch

Thinly sliced green onions, for garnish

Steamed rice (any kind, see pages 286–291), for serving

Chicken wings don't always have to be crispy. I think the obsession for crispy chicken skin over non-crispy chicken skin is a clear difference between conventional Western and Eastern palates. The wings in this curry start off with a hard sear to render out the fat for flavor and so the chicken skin isn't flabby. You won't be able to resist licking the creamy sauce from the wings, which soak up the flavor from the yellow curry and sweetness from the coconut milk. Take a lesson from me and try smashing the curry potatoes into your steamed rice for a bite of delicious carb-on-carb action.

SEAR THE CHICKEN AND POTATOES: In a large skillet with a fitted lid, heat the olive oil over medium-high heat. Add the chicken wings in a single layer, skin-side down, and sear until golden brown, 4 to 5 minutes. Flip the chicken wings and sear the other side until golden brown, 3 to 4 minutes. Transfer the chicken to a plate. Add the potatoes to the pan and cook, tossing occasionally, until golden brown on most sides, 6 to 8 minutes. Return the chicken to the pan.

ADD THE SAUCE: In a medium bowl, whisk together 1½ cups (360 ml) of the water, the curry powder, oyster sauce, sriracha, salt, and white pepper. Pour into the pan, stir to combine, and bring to a simmer. Reduce the heat to medium-low, cover, and gently simmer until the potatoes are tender, 20 to 24 minutes. Remove the lid and increase the heat to medium-high. Cook until the sauce has reduced by half, about 5 minutes. In a medium bowl, whisk together the coconut milk, cornstarch, and remaining ¼ cup (60 ml) water to make a slurry. Pour the slurry into the pan and stir to combine. Simmer until the sauce is thickened and creamy, 2 minutes, then remove from the heat.

SERVE: Garnish with green onions and serve with rice.

Roasted Salmon with Sambal Vinaigrette

Serves 4 to 6

1½ pounds (681 g) salmon fillet, skin-on, scales and bones removed

1 teaspoon kosher salt

½ teaspoon ground white pepper

1 tablespoon extra-virgin olive oil

¼ cup (60 ml) freshly squeezed lime juice

2 tablespoons sambal oelek

1 tablespoon honey

2 cups (90 g) watercress

1½ cups (130 g) thinly sliced Persian cucumber

2 tablespoons Fried Garlic (page 310)

Steamed rice (any kind, see pages 286–291), for serving

A fillet of salmon, even in its simplest form, has a way of wowing a crowd, but it looks especially beautiful topped with a tangle of watercress and crisp cucumbers dressed in a sambal vinaigrette. Farm-raised salmon has a higher fat content than wild salmon, so it needs to cook longer. Because of the fat content and the thickness of a salmon fillet, you'll finish the salmon in the oven after the skin gets crispy so it's perfectly cooked through. If you only have smaller portions of salmon (individual fillets) or are using wild salmon, it will cook much faster, so consider omitting the step of finishing the salmon in the oven. Instead, after the skin is crispy, simply flip the fish over and cook until cooked through, which takes only 2 to 3 minutes more.

Instead of serving the salmon with rice (which is obviously a great option), you could serve it with thick slices of toasted bread for dipping into the spicy and tangy dressing or crafting the perfect bite with a pile of greens and a hearty piece of fish. There's also plenty of dressing if you want to enjoy the salmon on top of more leafy greens for a satisfying salad.

WARM UP: Preheat the oven to 400°F (204 °C).

SEAR THE SALMON: Season the salmon with the salt and white pepper. In a large oven-safe skillet, heat the olive oil over medium-high heat. Immediately (before the pan gets too hot) place the fish in the pan, skin-side down, and sear until the skin is crispy and naturally releases from the pan, 6 to 7 minutes. Transfer the pan to the oven and bake until the fish is cooked through, 8 to 10 minutes.

MEANWHILE, MAKE THE VINAIGRETTE: In a medium bowl, whisk together the lime juice, sambal, and honey.

PLATE AND SERVE: Transfer the fish to a serving platter and pour half the vinaigrette over the fish.

In a large bowl, combine the watercress and cucumber. Pour over the remaining vinaigrette and toss to combine. Place the greens over the salmon and sprinkle the fried garlic over the greens. Serve with rice.

Chili Oil Shrimp with Sizzled Onions

Serves 4 to 6

2 tablespoons oil from
Chili Crunch (page 302,
or store-bought)

½ white onion, thinly sliced
into crescents

1½ pounds (681 g) shell-on
large shrimp, deveined
(but not peeled) and
patted dry

1 teaspoon kosher salt

2 tablespoons unsalted
butter, cut into cubes

Steamed rice (any kind,
see pages 286–291),
for serving

For this hot-and-fast weeknight-friendly meal, thinly sliced onions and shrimp are cooked in chili oil. The onions get a head start in the pan, and by the time the shrimp are crispy, so are the wisps of onion. For this recipe, look for shell-on shrimp. Cooking the shrimp with their shells on makes the dish more aromatic, imparting the oil with shrimpy flavor. The shells also get extra crunchy, like a thin cracker, and if you're really hard-core, you can eat the shrimp shell and all.

Keep a bag of frozen shrimp in your freezer at all times; they defrost very quickly, in about 20 minutes when soaked in a bowl of cool water, making them handy in emergencies.

SIZZLE THE ONIONS: In a large pan, heat the chili oil over medium heat. Add the onions and toss to coat in the oil. Cook until they just start to lightly brown, 4 to 5 minutes.

SEAR THE SHRIMP: Increase the heat to medium-high. Make room in the pan for the shrimp and add them in a single layer, then season with the salt. Sear the shrimp until crisp and pink, 2 to 3 minutes. Flip and cook until the shrimp are crisp on the other side and the flesh is pink, 2 to 3 minutes. Add the butter and allow it to melt. Baste the shrimp by spooning the melted butter and chili oil over them for the last minute of cooking.

SERVE: Transfer the shrimp and onions to a platter and serve with rice.

Welcome Home Steak

Serves 4

1 pound (454 g) thick boneless rib eye (or 1½ pounds/681 g if bone-in)

1½ teaspoons kosher salt

½ teaspoon ground white pepper

3 tablespoons oyster sauce

2 tablespoons neutral oil, such as grapeseed

½ white onion, thinly sliced

½ teaspoon sugar

½ cup (120 ml) water

1 teaspoon cornstarch

Steamed rice (any kind, see pages 286–291), for serving

During my freshman year of architecture school, I inadvertently became a vegetarian. I hadn't intended to, but the meat at the dining hall on campus just looked . . . questionable. So I lived off various forms of potatoes, grilled cheese, and soft-serve ice cream. When I came home for the weekend or holiday breaks, my mom would prepare a steak the moment I arrived. Maybe it was a lack of iron in my system or the fact that I was living off carbs and dairy, but I could feel my energy restored whenever I ate that steak. Just like many Asian moms, when my mom realizes I like something, she remembers it forever. It's been well over ten years, and my mom *still* has a steak in the fridge ready to cook for me (and now my husband, too) whenever we arrive in Cleveland.

I do love a good steak, but I don't need to have a huge cut to myself. I'd much rather cook a large steak, slice it for the table, and serve it so everyone can take as much or as little as they please. While the steak is resting, take advantage of the beef fat and flavor that's still in the pan. The oniony, savory pan sauce is luscious and perfect for draping over the steak and soaking into the rice on your plate.

MARINATE THE STEAK: Place the rib eye in a shallow dish. Season both sides with the salt and white pepper, then brush 2 tablespoons of the oyster sauce onto both sides. Let the steak stand at room temperature for 30 minutes or cover and refrigerate for up to 12 hours (if refrigerated, let it sit out on the counter for 30 minutes before cooking).

SEAR THE STEAK: In a cast-iron skillet, heat 1 tablespoon of the oil over medium-high heat. Make sure to open a window or turn your exhaust fan on. When the oil is very hot, place the steak in the pan. Sear until deeply browned on the bottom and crisp around the edges, 3 to 4 minutes. Flip and sear until deeply browned on the other side and crisp around the edges, 2 to 3 minutes. Transfer the steak to a cutting board and allow it to rest for 15 minutes before slicing.

MEANWHILE, MAKE THE PAN SAUCE: Reduce the heat to medium and add the remaining 1 tablespoon oil, the onion, and the sugar and cook, tossing frequently, until the edges of the onion are starting to brown and have softened a little, 2 to 3 minutes.

In a small bowl, whisk together the water, cornstarch, and remaining 1 tablespoon oyster sauce to make a slurry. Add the slurry to the pan and stir until the sauce has thickened, about 1 minute, making sure to scrape the bottom of the pan to get all the steak flavor.

SLICE AND SERVE: Slice the steak against the grain and transfer to a serving platter. Pour the onions and pan sauce over the top and serve with rice.

Triple Pepper Beef

Serves 4 to 6

1 pound (454 g) skirt steak, thinly sliced against the grain

1½ teaspoons ground black pepper

1 teaspoon toasted sesame oil

½ teaspoon kosher salt

3 tablespoons neutral oil, such as grapeseed

½ white onion, thinly sliced

8 ounces (227 g) shishito peppers

2 tablespoons oyster sauce

1 tablespoon sambal oelek

1 teaspoon sugar

Green onions, thinly sliced on a bias

Toasted sesame seeds

Steamed rice (any kind, see pages 286–291), for serving

Instead of beef with green bell peppers, try it with shishitos. They're like a better-tasting miniature version of a green bell pepper—slightly vegetal and sweet—and every so often you'll get an extra-spicy one (about one in ten shishitos are hot!). For Chinese pepper beef stir-fry, you want some of the grassiness of the shishitos to complement the more aggressive black pepper (the second pepper). The third pepper here is Indonesian chili pepper in the form of sambal oelek, which delivers all the spice this dish needs.

SEAR THE BEEF: In a medium bowl, combine the steak, 1 teaspoon of the black pepper, the sesame oil, and the salt. Set aside to marinate at room temperature for 15 minutes.

In a large skillet, heat 2 tablespoons of the neutral oil over medium-high heat. When the oil is just barely starting to smoke, add the steak and spread the slices into an even layer in the pan. Beware of oil splattering. Sear until the slices are deeply brown on the bottom, 3 to 4 minutes. Flip and cook until no longer pink on the second side, about 1 minute. Transfer the steak to a plate and set aside.

STIR-FRY THE PEPPERS: Add the remaining 1 tablespoon neutral oil to the pan. Add the onion and shishitos and toss to coat in the oil. Cook, tossing occasionally, until the shishitos are blistered, 6 to 8 minutes. Return the steak to the pan and add the oyster sauce, sambal, sugar, and remaining ½ teaspoon black pepper. Toss to combine and stir-fry everything for a final minute to warm up the steak.

SERVE: Transfer to a platter and top with green onions and sesame seeds. Serve with rice.

Miso Pork Meatballs

Serves 4 to 6

2 tablespoons white miso paste, or any of your choosing

1 tablespoon grated fresh ginger

1 tablespoon soy sauce

1 teaspoon sugar

½ teaspoon kosher salt

½ teaspoon ground white pepper

1 pound (454 g) ground pork

3 green onions, thinly sliced

½ cup (35 g) panko breadcrumbs

1 large egg

2 tablespoons extra-virgin olive oil

Steamed rice (any kind, see pages 286–291), for serving

I'll admit, it's difficult to make a platter of sauceless meatballs into a showstopper. But what these miso pork meatballs lack in aesthetics they make up for in the enormous amount of flavor they pack. These crispy, golden brown spheres are juicy and tender, but with enough structural integrity to still feel meaty. Aside from a rice bowl, these meatballs go great in a salad or meatball sub situation. They would also be an excellent accompaniment to a bowl of Creamy Tomato Udon (page 74). I promise they really don't need any sauce, but if that doesn't sit well with you, try a drizzle of sriracha and Kewpie mayo.

MIX AND FORM THE MEATBALLS: In a large bowl, whisk together the miso, ginger, soy sauce, sugar, salt, and white pepper. Add the ground pork, green onions, panko, and egg. Mix by hand or with a flexible spatula until just combined. Scoop 2-tablespoon portions of the pork mixture and roll into meatballs, gently pressing the mixture together to pack it. Place the formed meatballs on a plate or quarter sheet pan as you go.

SEAR THE MEATBALLS: In a large skillet, heat the olive oil over medium-high heat. Add the meatballs in a single layer and sear, turning them every few minutes, until deeply golden brown on most sides, 10 to 12 minutes. Turn off the heat and place a fitted lid on top, leaving a small gap for steam to escape. Allow the residual heat of the pan to fully cook the meatballs through, 5 minutes.

SERVE: Transfer the meatballs to a platter and serve with rice.

Steamed Pork Cake with Chives and Cilantro

Serves 4

1 pound (454 g) ground pork

½ cup (50 g) finely chopped Chinese garlic chives

⅓ cup (27 g) chopped fresh cilantro leaves and tender stems, plus more for topping

2 tablespoons Shaoxing wine

1 tablespoon doubanjiang

2 teaspoons toasted sesame oil

1 teaspoon sugar

½ teaspoon ground white pepper

½ teaspoon kosher salt

Steamed rice (any kind, see pages 286–291), for serving

In the way that many Americans grew up eating meatloaf, I grew up eating pork cake (and meatloaf, too, actually). Steamed pork cake, or yuk beng, is one of the simplest Chinese recipes. You almost never see it on menus at Chinese American restaurants because it's such a humble and homey meal. When the patty of ground pork steams, the fat and moisture within the steamer pools around it, becoming an intensely rich and flavorful sauce to spoon over the pork and rice. You can make this recipe using ground beef, chicken, or turkey in addition to pork with great results. Fattier blends of meat will produce a richer sauce, of course.

FORM THE PORK CAKE: In a medium bowl, combine the pork, garlic chives, cilantro, Shaoxing wine, doubanjiang, sesame oil, sugar, white pepper, and salt. Transfer the mixture to a heatproof shallow bowl (that fits in your steamer) and press it into a 7-inch (18 cm) patty.

STEAM THE PORK CAKE: Set up a bamboo steamer (see page 25). Place the bowl in the steamer and cover with the lid. Set the steamer over the simmering water and steam the pork cake until fully cooked through, 10 to 12 minutes. Allow the pork cake to cool for a few minutes before serving.

SERVE: Top with cilantro and serve with rice.

Fried Pork Chops
with Sweet-and-Sour Sauce

Serves 4

½ cup (60 g) cornstarch

1 tablespoon oyster sauce

2 large eggs

1 teaspoon kosher salt

½ teaspoon ground white pepper

1½ pounds (681 g) thin bone-in pork chops (about 4)

¼ cup (30 g) rice flour

Neutral oil, such as grapeseed, for frying

Steamed rice (any kind, see pages 286–291), for serving

Pineapple Sweet-and-Sour Sauce (page 307), for serving

My brother, Tyler, is three years younger than me, and we are very similar, yet different in a multitude of ways. He's frugal, he's a doctor, and he doesn't get squeamish very easily. I, on the other hand, spend my days cooking and intensely studying the instant ramen aisle at the Asian grocery store. We even have different favorite recipes from our childhood: I have a deep love for making and eating Joong (page 279), while Tyler loves our mom's fried pork chops and makes them regularly. Her pork chops are, in fact, very craveable. The cornstarch and rice flour coating creates an amazing crunch, and the pork is especially spectacular dipped in a pineapple-centric sweet-and-sour sauce and served over rice.

MARINATE THE PORK CHOPS: In a large bowl, mix ¼ cup (30 g) of the cornstarch, the oyster sauce, eggs, salt, and white pepper to combine. Add the pork chops and toss to coat. Set aside to marinate at room temperature for 20 minutes or in the fridge for a few hours.

WARM UP THE OIL: In a large cast-iron skillet, heat about ½ inch (1 cm) of oil over medium-high heat. Set a wire rack over a rimmed baking sheet.

FRY THE PORK CHOPS: In a shallow bowl, combine the remaining ¼ cup (30 g) cornstarch and the rice flour. Remove a pork chop from the marinade, shake off the excess, and dip in the cornstarch mixture to fully coat. Shake off any excess cornstarch and carefully place the pork chop into the hot oil. Repeat with a second pork chop and fry until golden brown and crispy on the bottom, 5 to 6 minutes. Flip and cook until golden brown on the other side, 3 minutes. Transfer the pork chops to the wire rack to cool. Repeat with the remaining pork chops.

SLICE AND SERVE: Slice the pork chops, cutting around the bone, or leave whole. Spoon the sweet-and-sour sauce over top or serve on the side with rice.

Shrimpy Ketchup Fried Rice

Serves 4 to 6

4 tablespoons (60 ml) extra-virgin olive oil

6 green onions, whites and greens separated and thinly sliced

4 garlic cloves, minced

3 small bok choy (370 g), finely chopped

4 to 5 cups (520 to 650 g) cold leftover Perfect Steamed Jasmine Rice (page 286)

3 tablespoons ketchup

2 tablespoons shrimp paste

1 tablespoon soy sauce

1 teaspoon toasted sesame oil

½ teaspoon ground white pepper

4 large eggs

Kewpie mayo

Fried rice is a fridge-foraging kind of meal. Repurposing leftover rice is an opportunity to use up any green onions and bok choy in the crisper that are a little old and soft. Shrimp paste and ketchup are my sauces of choice to enhance a simple fried rice. I got the shrimp paste trick from my mom, who learned it from her grandmother. The sweetness and light acidity of the ketchup are a perfect complement to the brininess of the shrimp paste and give the rice a warm orange color.

Fried rice is best made with cold rice, which has had a chance to dry out a bit and let the starches emerge onto the surface of the grains. If you don't already have rice in the fridge, make the Perfect Steamed Jasmine Rice at least 2 hours before you want to make fried rice. Once it's fluffy, spread the hot rice over a large rimmed baking sheet lined with parchment paper. Fan the rice (I use a cutting board) until it is no longer steaming, or just leave it alone on the counter for 20 minutes. Then stick the pan in the fridge, uncovered, to chill and dry out the rice, 1 to 1½ hours, or pop it in the freezer for even faster chilling, 45 minutes.

SIZZLE THE AROMATICS: In a large skillet, heat 2 tablespoons of the olive oil over medium-high heat. When the oil just starts to shimmer, add the green onion whites and the garlic. Toss to combine and cook until aromatic and just starting to brown around the edges, 2 to 3 minutes. Add the bok choy, toss to combine, and cook until the bok choy is starting to soften and brown around the edges, 2 to 3 minutes.

FRY THE RICE: Break up the cold rice into smaller chunks and add it to the pan. Further break up the rice clumps by pressing down with the back of a spatula. Add another tablespoon of olive oil and the ketchup, shrimp paste, soy sauce, sesame oil, and white pepper. Toss to incorporate into the rice. Cook, tossing every 2 minutes or so, until the rice is crispy, 8 to 10 minutes.

ADD THE EGGS: Push the rice to the outer edge of the pan, making room for the eggs. Add the remaining 1 tablespoon olive oil to the center of the pan and let it warm up for a minute. Add

the eggs and cook until the whites are just starting to set, about 2 minutes, then scramble the eggs in the center and incorporate the scrambled eggs into the rice. Add the green onion greens (reserving 2 tablespoons for garnish) and toss to combine.

SERVE: Transfer to a platter, drizzle with mayo, and top with the reserved green onion greens, then serve.

Dear Kewpie,

You are the only mayo for me. My fridge door isn't full without your smooth silhouette and easily squeezable shape. Extra egg yolks and a dash of MSG make you truly stand out from the other mayos in the condiment aisle. Your delicate red nozzle creates the most artful parallel strands over fried rice and crispy noodles. Creamy salads and deviled eggs wouldn't be complete without your richness and subtle tang. Everything you touch, from popcorn chicken to crispy Brussels sprouts, becomes that much more flavorful in your presence. I'm so lucky to have a constant supply of you in my life.

Love,

Kristina

P.S. Please never change or go out of stock.

Cook Your Own Way

It's true what they say—you grow the most when you step out of your comfort zone. I didn't have an interest in cooking Chinese food until I left home. When your family is always making great food, why get in their way? When I moved to San Francisco, I was surrounded by excellent Asian food, too. I grew up on Cantonese and Toisanese flavors, but here I was immersed in a whole world of regional Chinese specialties, like Sichuan-style and Yunnan-style dishes, and also so much Vietnamese, Thai, Filipino, and Burmese food (to name just a few). I could stop for a small box of dim sum in the morning before hopping on the 38 MUNI bus to work, grab a sushi burrito in Chinatown for lunch, and then treat myself to excellent red duck curry in my neighborhood for dinner.

My original plan was to live in San Francisco for four months while I did an architecture internship for graduate school. But I was charmed by the city and by Reuben, my future husband, whom I'd met the first month I was in San Francisco, another architecture student a few years ahead of me. I eventually dropped out of graduate school because the draw of the Bay Area was too much for me to leave behind. Even then, I didn't think I was going to stay for long, but three years turned to six years turned to nine, and now, more than a decade later, Reuben and I have a dog and a house in the East Bay.

When I get bouts of homesickness, the best cure is making food that tastes like home. During my first few months living in San Francisco, I would call my parents and ask them to walk me through the steps of making their famous potstickers or to explain the secret to getting crispy fried rice without a wok. I spent time researching (from afar) how my family cooks and attempting to re-create flavors from memory. When I flew back to Ohio, I watched my parents cook, noting every palm's worth of salt or shake of oyster sauce so I could replicate their food back in San Francisco.

The truth is, cooking with my parents is not always easy. Parents in general can be set in their ways and incredibly particular about the proper method of preparing certain things. One of the biggest kitchen disagreements my mom and I have ever had was about washing chicken. She believes (passionately, in fact) that raw chicken must be washed before cooking, and when I tried to explain that it is not only unnecessary but can spread bacteria, the argument grew so heated that we needed a cooling-down period before I eventually yielded and allowed her to wash the chicken. (For the record, you don't need to wash chicken!)

One of the benefits of cooking on my own is that I have the freedom to stray from tradition. I don't have to stick to "how it's always been done." Instead, I can figure out methods that work for me. In some instances, I've improved upon family recipes that have been prepared the same

way for decades, by stir-frying the cabbage for Chicken and Cabbage Spring Rolls (page 263), for instance, to remove some of the moisture instead of salting and squeezing it by hand, which takes forever. Or including tomatoes in my Hot-and-Sour Soup (page 298), an addition initially met with heavy skepticism from my mom.

Ultimately, my move to San Francisco allowed me to develop confidence and to gain more independence in my life and in the kitchen. I wouldn't be the cook I am today if I hadn't had that opportunity. Just because your parents or your ancestors did something a certain way doesn't mean you have to follow in their footsteps exactly. Even now, after I have written an award-winning cookbook, my parents remain initially suspicious of my culinary interpretations of foods like Chrysanthemum Salad with Lap Cheong Vinaigrette (page 116) and Char Siu Mushrooms (page 172) and other dishes they've only ever eaten in a particular way . . . but then I catch them going back for seconds or thirds. That's typical parent behavior for you—always keeping you humble.

You'll Always Have Noodles

Through thick and thin, you can always count on a tangled pile of noodles to make a hearty and comforting meal. I've dedicated an entire cabinet to storing my noodle collection, with some overflow in my fridge for perishable varieties. These recipes take full advantage of the array of premade noodles found at your local Asian market (many can be found at your regular grocery store, too). No need to make noodles from scratch; instead, focus your attention on developing the most flavorful sauces and broths. Some noodles are ideal for a thick and creamy sauce, others are best for stir-frying until light and crispy, and still others are meant to be submerged in a nourishing soup. Try them all!

Tingly Instant Ramen Salad

Serves 4 to 6

3 (4-ounce/340 g) packages instant ramen (such as Shin Ramen brand), plus 1 tablespoon of the ramen seasoning mix

8 celery stalks (400 g), thinly sliced on a bias

2 Persian cucumbers, thinly sliced

¼ cup (60 ml) Chinkiang vinegar

2 tablespoons extra-virgin olive oil

2 teaspoons Sichuan peppercorns, ground

1 teaspoon kosher salt

¾ teaspoon ground white pepper

This salad is loosely inspired by instant ramen salad composed of bagged cabbage mix and broken ramen noodles, with dressing made from the seasoning packet that was really popular in the '90s. It's a salad I encountered a lot growing up in Ohio. I didn't love it, but I did think it was an innovative use of the ramen seasoning packet.

To make an updated version of that salad, cook the noodles (until *just* al dente). Instead of cabbage, use crisp cucumbers and crunchy celery for a boost of hydration and texture that would have otherwise come from the uncooked noodles. The dressing is amped up with some malty Chinkiang vinegar and tingly Sichuan peppercorns. Any leftover ramen seasoning can be stored in a small jar. This "soup dust" is essentially MSG, spices, and dehydrated aromatics, all things that are delicious sprinkled over popcorn or roasted vegetables, or mixed into a dressing.

BOIL THE NOODLES: Bring a large pot of water to a boil. Add the ramen and cook until al dente, about 3 minutes. Loosen the noodles with tongs or a pair of chopsticks as they cook (refer to the package for exact cooking directions). Drain the noodles and rinse under cold water. Transfer the noodles to a bowl and chill in the fridge for at least 20 minutes and up to 1 day.

TOSS THE NOODLES AND SERVE: In a large serving bowl, mix the celery, cucumber, vinegar, olive oil, ramen seasoning, Sichuan peppercorns, salt, and white pepper to combine. Allow the vegetables to sit for 10 minutes to bring out some of their moisture. Toss in the chilled noodles and serve, or cover and refrigerate for up to 4 days before serving. (The noodles tend to firm up after a while in the fridge, so allow the salad to sit on the counter for about 20 minutes, then give everything a toss before serving.)

Creamy Tomato Udon

Serves 4

2 pounds (908 g) frozen udon noodles (4 bundles; keep frozen or defrost)

2 tablespoons extra-virgin olive oil

4 garlic cloves, minced

1 yellow onion, diced

1 (1-inch/2.5 cm) piece fresh ginger, peeled and minced

¼ cup (65 g) tomato paste

1 teaspoon kosher salt

1 teaspoon sugar

½ teaspoon ground white pepper

½ teaspoon curry powder

½ teaspoon crushed red chili flakes

¾ cup (180 ml) full-fat canned coconut milk

2 tablespoons fish sauce

Thinly sliced green onions

Fried Garlic (page 310)

Udon is my Platonic ideal of a noodle: bouncy and slippery with a distinctive chew that's very craveable. It's a noodle that translates well when given the pasta treatment; save the starchy water it's cooked in to make a silky sauce with other pantry staples like canned coconut milk and tomato paste. This dish starts off similarly to an Italian vodka sauce, but fresh ginger, curry powder, and a splash of fish sauce take it in a Southeast Asian direction.

BOIL THE NOODLES: Bring a large pot of water to a boil. Add the noodles and blanch until loose and bouncy (frozen udon is already cooked), 45 to 60 seconds. Reserve ½ cup (120 ml) of the noodle water for the sauce, then drain the noodles and rinse under cold water.

SIMMER THE SAUCE: In a large skillet, heat the olive oil over medium heat. Add the garlic, onion, and ginger and cook, stirring occasionally, until tender and starting to brown around the edges, 5 to 6 minutes. Add the tomato paste, salt, sugar, white pepper, curry powder, and chili flakes. Stir to combine and cook for 1 minute to reduce the paste. Add the reserved noodle water, the coconut milk, and the fish sauce. Stir until smooth and combined and bring to a simmer. Add the udon and toss to evenly coat in the sauce.

SERVE: Transfer the noodles to a platter and top with green onions and fried garlic.

Pick Your Noodle

In most Asian grocery stores, there are two(!) noodle aisles: you have the dried noodle aisle, where there are endless instant ramen varieties, and then you have the fresh or semi-fresh noodle aisle, where you'll find thick egg noodles that need to be kept refrigerated. There are so many options that it can feel overwhelming. I've described the varieties here so you can learn what makes each type of noodle great and uniquely suited for the recipes in which it's used.

Fresh or Semi-Fresh Noodles

NOTE: All fresh and semi-fresh noodles can be stored in the freezer, so feel free to stock up if you have to make a long road trip to get to an Asian grocery store.

Chow Mein: Sometimes labeled "Hong Kong stir-fry noodles," these might look like wonton noodles or thin egg noodles but are not the same texturally. Packaged chow mein noodles are parboiled or precooked, so they can go directly into a hot pan for stir-frying or be blanched briefly in hot water. Parboiling gives them a crisper and lighter texture, which is why they are mainly designated for stir-fried situations. If you can't find chow mein, you can use thin egg noodles instead, but prepare for the noodles to be softer and more delicate.

Thick Egg Noodles: Made with only wheat flour and eggs (and sometimes water), these are simple noodles with a chew you can't help but want to sink your teeth into. Because their sturdy structure makes them less likely to break, they're ideal for stir-frying.

Wonton Noodles: These egg noodles made with the addition of lye water or an alkaline solution have a distinctively chewy texture even though they're super thin. The wonton noodles in Hong Kong are just barely cooked and have an al dente texture. These are best served in a soup.

Wheat Noodles: This is a broad category of noodle—you can find varieties that are thick or thin, but all should be made only with wheat flour and water. The lack of egg in the dough means wheat noodles have a more neutral flavor than egg noodles, which makes them great for dishes with extra-savory and rich sauces, where they won't compete with other flavors.

Udon: This Japanese noodle can be found refrigerated or frozen (and dried, yes, but I've never found a dried variety that has remotely the same consistency). Udon is considered a wheat noodle but has a more slippery and starchy texture than Chinese wheat noodles. Udon is versatile, working beautifully in both stir-fries and soups.

Fresh Rice Noodles: If you're lucky, your local Chinese grocery store will get a shipment of freshly steamed rice noodles every few days. Take advantage of this and grab them while they're still soft and bouncy. Fresh rice noodles can come in stacked sheets (great for chow fun), rolled up (cheong fun), or precut into thin or wide noodles. Rice noodle rolls and wider cuts are perfect for crisping up in a pan, while the more delicate precut noodles are best in noodle soups. Parcooked thin rice noodles are amazing and cook so fast, but are more challenging to find.

Nian Gao: Similar to their cylindrical Korean cousins, nian gao (sliced rice cakes) are oval shaped, dense, and deliciously chewy. Rice cakes need to be soaked in water for about 15 minutes before they're added to soups or stir-fries to rinse away the extra starch and reconstitute them slightly.

Dried Noodles

Dried Rice Noodles: You can get dried rice noodles in widths ranging from thin to thick, and all work wonderfully in noodle soups. Wider varieties are sturdy enough to stir-fry with minimal breakage, but if you want to stir-fry thinner rice noodles, remember to undercook them when you boil them (they will continue to cook and take on moisture in the pan). Three Ladies Brand dried rice noodles will always reign supreme (see Resources, page 358).

Fun See: Often labeled "glass noodles," "bean thread noodles," or "bean vermicelli," these noodles are made from mung bean starch. Starch-based noodles are gluten-free, translucent, and delightfully chewy when cooked. They don't require boiling, just a soak in hot water for a few minutes to hydrate. Fun see have the ability to continue hydrating without becoming mushy, so they're also used in dumpling and spring roll fillings to absorb moisture and prevent sogginess.

Instant Ramen: You know them, you love them. Instant ramen noodles can always feed you in a pinch. Nongshim, MAMA, and Sapporo Ichiban are some of my trusty standbys (see Resources, page 358), but I make a point of grabbing a new-to-me instant ramen whenever I go grocery shopping.

Sliced Noodles: You can distinguish sliced noodles by their ruffled edge. These thin dried wheat noodles are perfect for dishes with a thick, luscious sauce. You can also boil them to add to noodle soups.

Spaghetti and Macaroni: Spaghetti and macaroni are beloved by many Chinese people in the form of Hong Kong diner–inspired Spam and Mac Soup (page 100) and many Chinese-American hybrid pasta dishes.

Sizzle Sauce Noodles

Serves 4

1 pound (454 g) dried sliced noodles (or thick wheat noodles)

¾ cup (180 ml) Sizzle Sauce (page 305)

1½ tablespoons soy sauce

4 large egg yolks

Sliced noodles, with their squiggly ruffled edges, call for a creamy sauce to cling on to. The simple combination of sizzle sauce, with its holy trinity of Chinese aromatics (green onions, garlic, and ginger); soy sauce; and rich egg yolks emulsifies with a few tosses and transforms into a luscious coating. Much as it does in carbonara or Caesar dressing, the egg yolk acts as both a thickener and a binder in the dish. While you can serve these noodles family-style, consider serving them in individual bowls, with a yolk placed on top of each, so that each person has the satisfying experience of mixing their noodles and egg together.

BOIL THE NOODLES: Bring a large pot of water to a boil. Add the noodles and cook until al dente, 7 to 8 minutes (refer to the package for exact cooking directions). Loosen the noodles with tongs or a pair of chopsticks as they cook. Reserve ½ cup (120 ml) of the noodle cooking water, then drain the noodles (no need to rinse).

If serving individually: While the noodles are still warm, divide evenly among four bowls. Top the noodles in each bowl with 3 tablespoons of sizzle sauce, 2 teaspoons of soy sauce, 1 egg yolk, and 2 tablespoons of the noodle cooking water. Mix in the noodles until glossy and creamy. Serve immediately.

If serving family-style: In a large serving bowl, whisk together the sizzle sauce, soy sauce, and the reserved noodle cooking water. Whisk in 1 egg yolk at a time until the sauce is creamy. Add the warm noodles and toss to fully coat. Serve immediately.

Toisan-Style Fun See

Serves 4

1 cup (80 g) small dried shrimp

4 bundles (8 ounces/ 240 g) bean thread noodles (see page 79)

2 tablespoons extra-virgin olive oil

4 green onions, whites and greens separated and chopped

4 garlic cloves, minced

2 tablespoons soy sauce

1 tablespoon oyster sauce

1 tablespoon toasted sesame oil

1 teaspoon sugar

½ teaspoon kosher salt

½ teaspoon ground white pepper

2 teaspoons sesame seeds

Every dinner at my grandparents' house included a heaping bowl of fun see. It's a humble yet super-flavorful Toisan-style preparation of bean thread noodles cooked with dried shrimp. The use of dried seafood is intrinsic to Toisanese food. The tiny shrimp are salty and briny, with a highly concentrated seafood flavor. This is a lightning-fast dish to make because the noodles require only a quick soak in hot water to cook. During a big family dinner, this is always the last dish to be made and the first one everyone grabs a bundle of to add to their plate.

SOAK THE SHRIMP: Place the dried shrimp in a medium heatproof bowl. Pour very hot water over the shrimp to fully submerge and cover with a plate. Allow the shrimp to soak for 15 minutes. Drain the shrimp and set aside.

HYDRATE THE NOODLES: Place the bean thread noodles in a large heatproof bowl. Pour very hot water over the noodles to fully submerge and cover with a plate. Allow the noodles to soak until hydrated and bouncy, 5 to 10 minutes. Drain the noodles and set aside.

STIR-FRY THE NOODLES: In a large skillet, heat the olive oil over medium-high heat. Add the shrimp and cook until crisp and fragrant, 4 to 5 minutes. Add the green onion whites and the garlic. Toss to combine and cook until starting to brown around the edges, 2 to 3 minutes. Add the noodles, soy sauce, oyster sauce, sesame oil, sugar, salt, and white pepper. Toss to evenly combine and cook the noodles until warmed through, 3 to 4 minutes.

SERVE: Transfer the noodles to a large serving platter and top with the green onion greens and sesame seeds.

PB and Cheung Fun

Serves 4

1 pound (454 g) cheung fun, cut into 2½- to 3-inch (6 to 7.5 cm) pieces

3 tablespoons extra-virgin olive oil

2 teaspoons dark soy sauce

¼ cup (60 ml) water, plus more if needed

3 tablespoons creamy peanut butter, plus more if needed

2 tablespoons hoisin

1 tablespoon rice vinegar

2 teaspoons sriracha, plus more as needed

1½ teaspoons toasted sesame oil

½ teaspoon kosher salt

Green onions, sliced on a bias

My favorite after-school snack growing up was my dad's cheung fun. He would pan-fry the rice noodle rolls until blistered and crunchy on the outside and chewy in the middle, and serve them with a drizzle of oyster sauce and hoisin. This was a childhood snack of my dad's, too, when he was growing up in Hong Kong. There you can buy freshly made cheung fun from street vendors and top it with whatever your heart wants.

A lot of Chinese grocery stores sell freshly steamed cheung fun (and other forms of rice noodles). But if you can only find refrigerated cheung fun or need to refrigerate them to make later in the week, they quickly soften and return to their bouncy selves after a few minutes in the pan. This recipe doesn't stray too far from my dad's version. It's a little spicier and tangier, and uses peanut butter for nuttiness, but tastes every bit as nostalgic.

PAN-FRY THE CHEUNG FUN: Heat a large skillet over medium-high heat. In a large bowl, toss the cheung fun and 2 tablespoons of the olive oil to combine. Add the cheung fun to the pan in a single layer (work in batches if your pan isn't large enough) and fry until golden brown and crispy on the bottom, 6 to 8 minutes. Flip the cheung fun and fry until golden brown and crispy on the other side, 6 to 8 minutes. Add the dark soy sauce and give the pan a few shakes so the cheung fun takes on a light brown color.

MIX THE SAUCE: In a medium bowl, whisk together the water, peanut butter, hoisin, vinegar, remaining 1 tablespoon olive oil, sriracha, sesame oil, and salt. The sauce will seize up or curdle at first, but continue to whisk and it will eventually smooth out. If it's too loose, add a little more peanut butter; if it's too thick, add a little more water.

SERVE: Spread half the sauce on the bottom of a large serving platter and place the crispy cheung fun on top. Drizzle on the remaining sauce and additional sriracha, if you like. Or you can just toss the crispy cheung fun in a large bowl with the peanut sauce to fully coat. Top with green onions and serve.

Spiced Tofu Chow Fun

Serves 4

For the sauce

2 tablespoons dark soy sauce

2 tablespoons soy sauce

1 teaspoon sugar

1 teaspoon toasted sesame oil

½ teaspoon kosher salt

½ teaspoon ground white pepper

For the tofu and stir-fry

3 tablespoons neutral oil, such as grapeseed

1 pound (454 g) spiced pressed tofu, thinly sliced

½ white onion, thinly sliced

24 ounces (680 g) rice noodle sheets, cut into 1½ by 4-inch (4 by 10 cm) pieces

2 cups (100 g) bean sprouts

The wider the rice noodles, the better the chow fun. In order to make great chow fun at home, you need to locate freshly made rice noodle sheets and cut them into the ideal shape (1½ by 4 inches/4 by 10 cm). Most Chinese grocery stores stock freshly made rice noodle sheets, but if you can't find them, the next best thing is the widest dried rice noodles your store has available.

Beef is the most popular protein for this iconic Cantonese dish, but this spiced tofu version adds a Northern Chinese vegetarian spin. The tofu has a great dense texture to complement the rice noodles and gets extra crispy in a hot pan. The pieces of the rice noodle sheets that don't get a chance to totally separate in the stir-fry are extra chewy and satisfying to sink your teeth into. They are the best part!

MIX THE SAUCE: In a small bowl, mix the soy sauces, sugar, sesame oil, salt, and white pepper to combine.

SEAR THE TOFU: In a large skillet, heat 2 tablespoons of the neutral oil over medium-high heat. When the oil is hot, add the tofu and spread the slices into an even layer in the pan, cooking in batches if they all don't fit in the pan. Sear until deeply brown on the bottom, 3 to 4 minutes. Flip the tofu slices and cook until deeply browned on the other side, 2 to 3 minutes. Transfer the tofu to a quarter sheet pan or plate.

STIR-FRY THE NOODLES: Add the remaining 1 tablespoon neutral oil to the pan. Add the onion and cook, tossing occasionally, until browned around the edges, 5 to 7 minutes. Add the noodles, breaking up some of layers that are stuck together (the noodles will naturally separate as you stir-fry), and the sauce. Toss to combine and cook, tossing frequently, until the noodles are softened, 3 to 5 minutes. Return the tofu to the pan and add the bean sprouts. Toss to combine and stir-fry until the noodles have a nice char or are browning around the edges, 4 to 5 minutes.

SERVE: Transfer the noodles to a platter and serve.

Mom's Spaghetti

Serves 4

1 pound (454 g) spaghetti

2 tablespoons extra-virgin olive oil

1 pound (454 g) ground beef

3 tablespoons oyster sauce

1 teaspoon sugar

1 teaspoon kosher salt

1 teaspoon ground white pepper

½ cup (120 ml) ketchup

1 cup (240 ml) water

1 tablespoon cornstarch

Finely grated Parmesan cheese

I didn't realize that spaghetti sauce had actual tomatoes in it until I went over to a friend's house in middle school and was introduced to jars of Ragu and Prego. The way my mom makes spaghetti is a little unconventional, with ground beef and a sauce base consisting of oyster sauce, ketchup, and lots of white pepper. It's a recipe my mom first made up when she was twelve and wanted to try *American* food, and it's been going strong in our family for fifty years. What's interesting is that even though my mom seemingly made this dish in a cultural vacuum (Cleveland in the 1970s), there are so many similar recipes, like Filipino spaghetti with hot dogs, Japanese Neapolitan spaghetti, and Bay Area tomato chow mein. Convergent evolution of food is *so* cool.

BOIL THE NOODLES: Bring a large pot of water to a boil. Cook the spaghetti until al dente according to the package directions. Drain and rinse under cold water.

SIMMER THE SAUCE: Meanwhile, in a large skillet, heat the olive oil over medium-high heat. Add the ground beef and break it up with the back of a wooden spoon or flexible spatula. Cook until the beef starts to brown around the edges, 4 to 5 minutes. Stir in the oyster sauce, sugar, salt, and white pepper. Simmer until the beef is nearly cooked through, 5 to 6 minutes. Stir in the ketchup.

In a small bowl, whisk together the water and cornstarch to make a slurry. Stir the slurry into the pan and simmer until the sauce is thick and glossy, about 2 minutes.

SERVE: Add the spaghetti, tossing with tongs to coat in the sauce. Top with Parmesan and serve.

San Francisco Garlic Noodles

Serves 4

1 pound (454 g) fresh thick Chinese egg noodles

Olive oil or neutral oil, for the noodles

8 tablespoons (1 stick/ 113 g) unsalted butter, cut into cubes

⅓ cup (40 g) minced garlic (about 10 large cloves)

2 tablespoons oyster sauce

1 tablespoon fish sauce

2 teaspoons sugar

1 teaspoon kosher salt

½ teaspoon ground white pepper

Chopped fresh cilantro or green onions

My first home in the Bay Area was a big green house with Craigslist roommates in the Inner Sunset where I took advantage of all the incredible food that could be found within a few blocks. The most resonating meal was the garlic noodles from Perilla, a popular Vietnamese restaurant. I would stop by Perilla on my way home from work for a carton of them because they were insanely cheap, which made my low-paid-junior-architect bank account very happy.

San Francisco–style garlic noodles are not your average buttered noodle. It's a Vietnamese American dish said to have originated at Thanh Long in Outer Sunset in the early '70s. Now many Vietnamese and non-Vietnamese restaurants alike in the Bay Area make their own version, but Perilla's will always be the gold standard for me. It's important to take your time infusing the butter with way more garlic than you think you need. The key to crispy noodles is to leave them alone in the pan once they're coated in the butter. A few minutes of undisturbed contact with the pan will crisp up the bottom of the noodles, and then you can toss them and repeat the process until you're happy with the level of crispiness. You might be able to eat a whole platter of these on your own, but share the garlic noodle love with some friends.

BOIL THE NOODLES: Bring a large pot of water to a boil. Add the noodles and cook until al dente, 3 to 4 minutes for fresh noodles (refer to the package for exact cooking directions). Drain the noodles, rinse under cold water, and toss with a little bit of oil to prevent them from sticking.

MAKE THE SAUCE: In a large skillet, melt the butter over medium-low heat. Add the garlic and stir it into the butter. Cook, stirring frequently, until very lightly browned, 7 to 8 minutes. If the garlic is browning too quickly, reduce the heat. Add the oyster sauce, fish sauce, sugar, salt, and white pepper. Stir until the sugar dissolves into the sauce, 1 minute.

TOSS THE NOODLES AND SERVE: Add the noodles and toss with a pair of tongs to combine. Increase the heat to medium-high and cook, undisturbed, for a few minutes, then toss and cook until the noodles are crispy in spots, 6 to 8 minutes total. Transfer the noodles to a serving platter and top with cilantro.

Saucy Black Bean Noodles

Serves 4 to 6

2 pounds (908 g) thick wheat noodles (Shanghai-style noodles, sliced noodles, or udon)

3 tablespoons extra-virgin olive oil, plus more as needed

½ white onion, finely diced

1 large carrot, finely diced

1 large zucchini, finely diced

4 garlic cloves, minced

1 (1-inch/2.5 cm) piece fresh ginger, peeled and minced

1 pound (454 g) ground beef

1½ cups (360 ml) water

¼ cup (75 g) black bean paste

2 tablespoons hoisin

2 teaspoons cornstarch

1½ teaspoons sugar

1 teaspoon kosher salt

Cucumber matchsticks

Party Pickles (page 309)

Green onions, thinly sliced on a bias

Zhajiangmian (black bean noodles) is an irresistible noodle dish originating from Shandong, China. Composed of thick wheat-based noodles in an inky black bean sauce, it has an appeal similar to an Italian meat sauce or chili, just darker and more savory. Fermented black bean paste (not to be confused with black bean and garlic paste) is the workhorse of the sauce, giving it its dark brown color and salty bite. Hidden in the darkness of the sauce are tender ground beef, aromatics, and vegetables that simmer and meld together. The beauty of this recipe is its adaptability: Swap out the beef for another protein, such as ground chicken or crumbled firm tofu. Sneak in some more vegetables if you feel like it. Simmer the sauce for longer if you're still waiting for guests to arrive. Since the noodles are so savory, serve fresh cucumbers and Party Pickles on the side for a much-needed pop of brightness.

BOIL THE NOODLES: Bring a large pot of water to a boil. Add the noodles and cook according to the package directions. Drain the noodles and rinse under cold water. Toss the noodles with a little of the olive oil to prevent them from sticking.

SIMMER THE SAUCE: In a large skillet, heat 2 tablespoons of the olive oil over medium-high heat. Add the onion, carrot, zucchini, garlic, and ginger. Cook the vegetables, stirring occasionally, until starting to brown around the edges, 7 to 8 minutes. Move the vegetables to the perimeter of the pan and add the remaining 1 tablespoon olive oil to the center. Add the ground beef to the center of the pan and break it up into smaller pieces with the back of a flexible spatula. Cook the beef, continuing to break it into smaller pieces, until starting to brown, 3 to 4 minutes. Mix the beef into the vegetables to evenly combine and continue to cook until the beef is nearly cooked through, 2 to 3 minutes.

In a glass measuring cup, whisk together the water, black bean paste, hoisin, cornstarch, sugar, and salt. Pour the mixture into the pan and stir to combine. Bring the meat sauce to a simmer and allow it to thicken, about 1 minute. Simmer the sauce for 5 minutes more to allow the flavors to meld, then remove from the heat. Allow the sauce to cool for a few minutes before serving.

SERVE: Divide the noodles into individual bowls and pour the meat sauce on top. Top with cucumbers, party pickles, and green onions. Have your guests mix everything into the noodles and enjoy!

Wispy Mushroom Chow Mein

Serves 4 to 6

12 ounces (340 g) parcooked or steamed chow mein noodles

4 tablespoons (60 ml) neutral oil, such as grapeseed

12 ounces (340 g) wild mushrooms (like oyster or trumpet), pulled apart into thin strands

1 teaspoon kosher salt

⅓ cup (80 ml) soy sauce

2 tablespoons dark soy sauce

1 tablespoon toasted sesame oil

2 teaspoons sugar

½ teaspoon ground white pepper

4 green onions, thinly sliced on a bias

1 tablespoon sesame seeds

Excellent chow mein has a lightness and simplicity to it. The foundations of the dish are good noodles, soy sauce, and a pinch of sugar. The noodles must be thin and crispy, almost toasted, so they're sturdy enough to retain some space between themselves when they're piled high on a plate, rather than falling flat and compacting. Additional ingredients should be minimal in order to not weigh down the dish. Green onions are an absolute must, for their color and aromatic qualities. Instead of meat, this chow mein is made with hand-torn strands of wild mushrooms to keep the vegetarians in your life very happy.

BLANCH THE NOODLES: Bring a large pot of water to a boil over medium-high heat. Add the noodles and briefly blanch them, 1 to 2 minutes (or refer to the package directions for cooking times). Drain the noodles and rinse under cold water. Toss the noodles with a little bit of the neutral oil to prevent them from sticking.

SEAR THE MUSHROOMS: In a large cast-iron pan, heat 2 tablespoons of the neutral oil over medium-high heat. Working in batches, add the mushrooms in a single layer. Sear until the bottoms are deeply golden brown, 4 to 5 minutes, making sure to press down on the mushrooms with the back of the spatula every so often. Flip the mushrooms and cook until deeply browned on the other side, 4 to 5 minutes. Transfer the mushrooms to a plate and repeat with the remaining mushrooms. Return all the mushrooms to the pan and season with the salt. Toss and stir-fry the mushrooms until extra crisp, 3 to 5 minutes. Return the mushrooms to the plate.

STIR-FRY THE NOODLES: Add the remaining neutral oil to the pan, then add the noodles and toss to coat in the oil. Add the soy sauces, sesame oil, sugar, and white pepper and toss to combine. Cook, tossing every few minutes, to crisp up the noodles, 8 to 10 minutes. Add the mushrooms and green onions. Toss to combine and cook the noodles for a final few minutes to warm up the mushrooms. Transfer the noodles to a platter, sprinkle with the sesame seeds, and serve immediately.

Chow Mein Pancake

Serves 4 to 6

12 ounces (340 g) parcooked or steamed chow mein noodles

4 green onions, thinly sliced

⅓ cup (80 ml) neutral oil, such as grapeseed (or allium oil, pages 310–311, for extra flavor), plus more if needed

Hoisin

Kewpie mayo

This crispy disc of noodles, toasted in a pan until golden brown, is a true Cantonese delicacy. A chow mein pancake is often served topped with a saucy stir-fry that soaks into the noodles and softens them. But this recipe focuses on just the pancake and is intended to be served alongside other dishes like Chrysanthemum Salad with Lap Cheong Vinaigrette (page 116) or Hot-and-Sour Soup (page 298) for a textural crunch. For a slightly saucier variation, top the chow mein pancake with Triple Pepper Beef (page 57) or Basil Lime Eggplant (page 131).

BLANCH THE NOODLES: Bring a large pot of water to a boil over medium-high heat. Add the noodles and briefly blanch them, 1 to 2 minutes (or refer to the package directions for cooking times). Drain the noodles and rinse under cold water. Toss the noodles with a little bit of the oil to prevent them from sticking. Add the green onions (reserving some for topping later) and toss.

FRY THE PANCAKE: In a large cast-iron skillet, heat the oil over medium-high heat. Set a wire rack over a rimmed baking sheet. When the oil is hot, carefully add the noodles to the pan, forming them into an even disc. Fry the noodles until crisp and golden brown on the bottom, rotating the disc of noodles occasionally with a pair of chopsticks, 6 to 7 minutes. Flip the noodles (a wide fish spatula is perfect for this) and fry until crisp and golden brown on the other side, 6 to 7 minutes. Add another tablespoon or two of oil if needed to fry the other side. Transfer the noodles to the wire rack to cool.

SERVE: Transfer the noodles to a cutting board and cut into wedges. Slide the wedges onto a platter (keeping them together in disc form) and drizzle with hoisin and mayo. Top with the reserved green onions and serve.

Extra-Special XO Nian Gao

Serves 4 to 6

1 pound (454 g) sliced rice cakes

4 lap cheong (Chinese sausages), sliced on a bias

2 tablespoons extra-virgin olive oil

¾ pound (340 g) carrots (about 4 medium), sliced on a bias

4 green onions, whites and greens separated and sliced on a bias

3 tablespoons XO Sauce (page 303)

1 tablespoon soy sauce

½ teaspoon kosher salt

¼ teaspoon ground white pepper

There are sweet rice cakes, and there are savory rice cakes. Sweet rice cakes, like the Pistachio Pear Baked Nian Gao (page 340), are a dessert served during Lunar New Year. Savory rice cakes are sliced oval noodles of pounded rice that have a dense, chewy texture. It's good luck to make stir-fried nian gao for Lunar New Year because the dish's name sounds like the phrase for "higher year," promising a year better than the last. But it's also smart to keep a bag of rice cakes in the freezer so they're on hand whenever you want a quick stir-fry. A few spoonfuls of XO sauce make this dish extra special for Lunar New Year but easy enough for a regular Tuesday night.

SOAK THE RICE CAKES: In a medium bowl, cover the rice cakes in cool water and soak for 15 minutes, then drain. They will still be on the firm side.

RENDER THE LAP CHEONG: Place the lap cheong in a cold skillet. Cook over medium heat until the fat has rendered and the lap cheong is crispy on the underside, 3 to 4 minutes, then flip it over and cook until crispy on the other side, 1 to 2 minutes. Transfer the lap cheong to a plate.

STIR-FRY THE RICE CAKES: Increase the heat to medium-high and add the olive oil. Add the carrots and green onion whites. Sear until the bottoms of the carrots are crisp and golden, 3 to 5 minutes. With a wide spatula, flip the carrots and sear until crisp and golden on the other side, 3 to 5 minutes. Add the drained rice cakes, lap cheong, XO sauce, soy sauce, salt, and white pepper. Toss to combine and stir-fry, tossing frequently, until the rice cakes are crisp and browned around the edges, 7 to 10 minutes. Add the green onion greens and give everything one last toss.

SERVE: Transfer the rice cakes to a platter and allow to cool for a few minutes before serving.

Spam and Mac Soup

Serves 4 to 6

8 ounces (227 g) elbow macaroni

8 cups (1.92 L) Scrappy Chicken Stock (page 300), or 8 cups (1.92 L) water and 2 tablespoons chicken bouillon powder

1 cup (120 g) fresh or frozen corn kernels

1 cup (120 g) fresh or frozen peas

½ teaspoon kosher salt, plus more if needed

1 tablespoon extra-virgin olive oil

4 baby bok choy, cut in half

1 (12-ounce/340 g) can Spam, cut into thin strips

Chili Crunch (page 302, or store-bought; optional)

Spam can be quite divisive, but for lots of Asian kids, it's a special treat. The combination of Spam and macaroni in a soup is a Hong Kong–diner classic. I can't speak to the health benefits of Spam, but with the warm chicken broth, chewy macaroni, and floating bits of vegetables, this soup sure is comforting. The Spam in this recipe is cut into thin strips and fried until extra crispy—I think of them as "Spam fries." They're meant to lend some texture to the soup, but you'll be tempted to snack on a few before your bowl is ready.

COOK THE MACARONI: Bring a large pot of water to a boil. Add the macaroni and cook until al dente according to the package directions. Drain and rinse under cold water.

SIMMER THE SOUP: In a large pot, bring the stock to a simmer over medium-high heat. Reduce the heat to medium and stir in the corn, peas, and salt. Simmer until the broth is slightly sweet from the vegetables, 5 to 7 minutes. Stir in the macaroni and simmer for another minute to warm the noodles. Taste and add more salt if needed. Turn off the heat and let cool for a few minutes.

MEANWHILE, SEAR THE BOK CHOY: In a large skillet, heat the olive oil over medium-high heat. Add the bok choy, cut-side down, and sear, pressing on the bok choy with a spatula occasionally so it gets good contact with the pan, until deeply brown, 5 to 6 minutes. Flip the bok choy and cook until tender, 3 to 4 minutes. Transfer the bok choy to a plate.

FRY THE SPAM: In the same pan, spread the Spam into an even layer. Fry, tossing frequently, until crispy and browned around the edges, 6 to 8 minutes. Transfer the Spam to a plate lined with a paper towel and allow it to cool for a few minutes.

SERVE: Divide the soup into individual bowls and top with the seared bok choy and crispy Spam. Serve with a drizzle of chili crunch, if desired.

Reconnecting with Hong Kong

As young children, my parents lived in the same apartment complex in the So Uk area of Kowloon in Hong Kong. My dad remembers my mom's family because they had one of the first color televisions in the building. My mom and her family moved to the United States when she was a young girl in late 1960s, while my dad and his family stayed behind. They reconnected about twenty years later, when my mom traveled back to Hong Kong for the first time since moving to America. They got married soon thereafter, and then my dad moved with my mom to Cleveland, leaving his entire family and life half a world away.

When my brother and I were growing up, my dad made sure we had a connection to our Hong Kong roots by cooking Cantonese food and taking us on trips back to his home city so we could get a taste of proper dim sum and know what a good bowl of wonton mein (noodle soup) should look like. Most importantly, he wanted to ensure that we had a relationship with his side of the family. My earliest memories in Hong Kong include learning to use chopsticks for the first time (and accidentally breaking them), sitting for portraits at my yei yei's (paternal grandpa's) photography studio in Sham Shui Po, and constantly asking when we were going to get egg tarts again.

Whether it was due to school schedules or the fact that life was just too busy, I didn't visit Hong Kong for the long stretch between ages eight and nineteen. When I finally returned as a young adult, I was a completely different person. When I was very young, I spoke only Cantonese (at a typical child's level), but as I went to elementary school and spent less time in my grandparents' care, my Cantonese became broken. Losing the ability to speak a language is a strange phenomenon; later I learned that many other people who are also first-generation American share this experience. When I landed in Hong Kong at nineteen, my lack of fluency caused me to feel disconnected from my family there, and from the city I had loved from afar.

Your family's home country holds so much history and significance in the formation of your identity, but if you weren't born there, you can feel simultaneously connected and detached, as if you're a complete outsider. Not being able to communicate in the way you want to is frustrating, and I felt guilty about losing this seemingly essential part of my Asian-ness. Despite the language barrier, my ma ma (paternal grandma) taught me how to play mah-jongg (she's a shark), and I learned how to order an egg waffle from a street vendor on my own. Language doesn't stop you from forming memories, like hiking one of the prettiest peaks in the city with your grandpa and taking in the view with chocolate ice cream.

These days, I make an effort to travel back to Hong Kong more frequently. I don't ever want to let an entire decade pass by before I see my dad's side of the family again. My most recent trip back was with just my dad, after my yei yei passed away during the COVID-19 pandemic. I was terribly nervous about what my Hong Kong family would think of me. The years since my previous visit had been some of the most transformative periods of my life—I had changed careers and gotten married—and I hadn't quite relearned as much Cantonese as I had wanted to. Would they be disappointed that I still couldn't fully converse with them? Would they find it difficult to relate to me?

All that nervousness melted away when I hugged my ma ma on our first morning in Hong Kong. I was able to have unexpectedly meaningful bilingual conversations with my aunt about the loss of her dad (my yei

yei) and felt the heaviness in her words. My family and I met up for dim sum nearly every morning, a routine that felt so much like the weekend dim sum feasts I had with my family in Ohio. The opportunity to simply experience life in Hong Kong with my family reinforced my belief that there are ways to connect with people that don't involve words. Food is very much a universal love language, and family will always be family.

I promised that I would visit again much sooner, with more confidence in my Cantonese. Truth be told, the fifteen-hour flight to Hong Kong is brutal, but the approach into the city more than makes up for it. Through the plane window, you see a modern metropolis, glittering and buzzing, surrounded by water and lush mountains (not unlike San Francisco, actually). The view is breathtaking, and for me, it feels like coming home.

Shrimp Noodle Soup for the Soul

Serves 4

1½ pounds (681 g) head-on large shrimp (or 1 pound/454 g without heads), deveined

8 cups (1.92 L) Tomato Kombu Broth (page 301)

1 tablespoon kosher salt

1 tablespoon shrimp paste

1 teaspoon whole black peppercorns

3 big chunks fresh ginger, smashed

3 garlic cloves, smashed and peeled

1 pound (454 g) thin rice noodles

½ pound (227 g) shrimp balls or fish tofu, cut in half

1 tablespoon fish sauce

Fried Garlic (page 310)

Green onions, thinly sliced on a bias

If you're feeling sick or a little low, eating a steamy bowl of noodles makes everything feel better. The process of preparing a noodle soup is almost as healing. A fully developed noodle soup (one that doesn't start with a seasoning packet) takes patience and mindfulness. Here you'll enhance tomato kombu broth with shrimp shells and aromatics so it tastes salty like the ocean with a little kick from ginger and black pepper. Load up the steamy broth with shrimp balls or fish tofu (both can be found in the frozen section of an Asian grocery store) and enjoy the many treasures floating around in this warming noodle soup.

SIMMER THE BROTH: Peel the shrimp and save the shells and the heads (if using head-on shrimp). Place the peeled shrimp in the fridge while you make the broth. In a large pot, combine the tomato kombu broth, salt, shrimp paste, black peppercorns, ginger, garlic, shrimp shells, and shrimp heads (if using) and bring to a boil. Reduce the heat to maintain a simmer and cover. Simmer, stirring occasionally, for 30 to 35 minutes. (If you don't have tomato kombu broth already made, just prepare it with the rest of these ingredients and simmer for 60 minutes.)

MEANWHILE, PREPARE THE NOODLES: If using Three Ladies brand thin rice noodles, place the noodles in a large heatproof bowl, cover with warm water, and soak until pliable, about 45 minutes. Drain the noodles. Bring a large pot of water to a boil. Add the noodles and cook until tender with a chewy texture, 3 to 4 minutes. (If using another brand, prepare the noodles according to the package directions.) Drain the noodles and rinse under cold water. Divide the noodles into individual bowls and set aside.

COOK THE SHRIMP: Scoop all the solids out of the broth with a spider and discard. Add the shrimp, shrimp balls, and fish sauce to the pot and simmer in the broth until the shrimp are cooked through, 5 to 7 minutes. Turn off the heat and allow the soup to cool for a few minutes.

SERVE: Top each bowl of noodles with some shrimp and shrimp balls. Pour in the broth and top with fried garlic and green onions. Serve immediately.

Caramelized Onion and Beef Noodle Soup

Serves 4 to 6

3 tablespoons extra-virgin olive oil, plus more as needed

1½ pounds (681 g) yellow onions, thinly sliced

1 tablespoon granulated sugar

3½ teaspoons kosher salt, plus more as needed

2 pounds (908 g) boneless beef short ribs (or 3 pounds/1.36 kg bone-in), cut into 3-inch (7.5 cm) cubes

½ cup (120 ml) Shaoxing wine

10 cups (2.4 L) water

2 tablespoons soy sauce

1½ tablespoons doubanjiang

1 (1-inch/2.5 cm) piece rock sugar, or 1 tablespoon brown sugar

1 bay leaf

3 star anise pods

1 cinnamon stick

1 teaspoon whole white peppercorns

1 teaspoon whole cloves

1 pound (454 g) thin egg noodles

Green onions, thinly sliced on a bias, for garnish

My family didn't eat out much when I was young, but when we did, going to a steak house felt like the ultimate American luxury; the loaded salad bar and free bread were mind-blowing to us. This noodle soup channels the indulgence of an American steak house with flavors of Chinese beef noodle soup. The sweetness from the onions balances the earthy spices and richness from the beef. Short ribs are a spendier cut, but they have the perfect level of fattiness to break down in the broth. This recipe makes a lot of soup, but if you have leftovers, the flavor continues to deepen, making it even more flavorful the next day.

CARAMELIZE THE ONIONS: In a large pot, combine 2 tablespoons of the olive oil and the onions. Stir to coat and gently cook over medium-low heat, stirring occasionally, until the onions are a light caramel color, 30 to 40 minutes. Stir in the granulated sugar and 1½ teaspoons of the salt and cook, stirring occasionally, until the onions are deeply caramelized, 20 to 30 minutes. Transfer the onions to a bowl.

MEANWHILE, SALT THE BEEF: Place the short ribs on a cutting board or plate, sprinkle salt all over the beef, and allow it to sit on the counter for 30 minutes to bring it to room temperature. In the pot you used for the onions, heat the remaining 1 tablespoon olive oil over medium heat. Add the beef and sear until deeply browned on all sides, 3 to 4 minutes. Transfer the beef to a plate or bowl (this can be the same bowl as the onions).

SIMMER THE SOUP: Pour the Shaoxing wine into the pot and stir with a wooden spoon, making sure to scrape any browned bits from the bottom. Add the water, soy sauce, doubanjiang, rock sugar, and 2 teaspoons salt and bring to a simmer over medium-high heat.

Meanwhile, fill a spice bag (or make a bundle out of a piece of cheesecloth) with the bay leaf, star anise, cinnamon stick, white peppercorns, and cloves. When the water is at a simmer, add the spice bag, onions, and beef to the pot. Reduce the heat to medium-low, cover with a lid, and simmer until the beef is very tender, 2 to

3 hours (the longer the better). Periodically check the soup and skim off any fat that comes to the surface.

BOIL THE NOODLES: Bring a large pot of water to a boil over medium-high heat. Add the noodles and cook until al dente, 2 to 3 minutes (refer to the package directions for cooking times). Drain the noodles and rinse under cold water. Toss the noodles with some olive oil to prevent them from sticking together.

SERVE: Divide the noodles into individual bowls and spoon the broth over the noodles. Top with the caramelized onions, short ribs, and green onions and serve immediately.

Vegetables—whether from the garden, the farmers' market, or the produce aisle at the grocery store—are among my biggest kitchen inspirations. Homestyle Chinese cooking generally gives less priority to big chunks of meat, which is often seen as a luxury, and instead fills out meals with hearty leafy greens like gai lan (Chinese broccoli) and ong choy (Chinese spinach).

Not every vegetable in this chapter is specifically a Chinese variety; many can be found at your local grocery store or seasonal farmers' market. When I call for potentially new-to-you vegetables, I share what to look for when shopping for them and how to prep them. Paying special attention to washing and trimming vegetables helps them taste their best, so knowing how to prep your vegetables is as important as knowing how to cook them. Use these recipes to harness the full potential of every leaf, stalk, root, and bean. The recipes are organized by general cooking method, from no-cook to roasted, for easy selection based on what sort of cooking mode you're in.

Kohlrabi and Radish Salad with Chili Crunch

Serves 4

2 small kohlrabi (250 g), trimmed and peeled

2 medium watermelon radishes (275 g), trimmed

2 tablespoons Chili Crunch (page 302, or store-bought)

2 tablespoons Chinkiang vinegar

3 garlic cloves, grated

½ teaspoon kosher salt

This refreshing non–leafy green salad gets better as it sits in the fridge for a few days. Kohlrabi is an excellent vegetable to eat raw; it has the texture of a really firm apple or broccoli stem, with hints of sweetness and garlic. It pairs perfectly with colorful slices of peppery watermelon radish, but feel free to use plump red radishes or French Breakfast radishes instead. Malty, not-too-acidic black vinegar and hot, savory chili crunch make an iconic Chinese flavor pairing that brings out the best in nearly any vegetable.

PREP THE VEGETABLES: Fill a large bowl with ice and cold water. Thinly slice the kohlrabi and radishes with a mandoline (or a very sharp knife) and transfer to the bowl. Allow the vegetables to soak and get extra crunchy for at least 20 minutes and up to a few hours. Drain, shake off any excess water, and return them to the bowl.

MIX AND CHILL: Add the chili crunch, vinegar, garlic, and salt, tossing to combine evenly. Cover and chill the salad in the fridge for at least 20 minutes before serving to let the flavors meld. It will keep in the fridge for up to 5 days.

Wood Ear Mushroom Salad

Serves 4

6 ounces (170 g) fresh wood ear mushrooms (see Note), thinly sliced

1 Fresno chili, thinly sliced

1 tablespoon Chinkiang vinegar

1 tablespoon rice vinegar

1 tablespoon Chili Crunch (page 302, or store-bought)

1 tablespoon toasted sesame oil

½ teaspoon kosher salt

½ teaspoon sugar

1 teaspoon sesame seeds

⅓ cup (28 g) chopped fresh cilantro, leaves and tender stems

I knew I was marrying into the right family when I learned that my husband and his family love wood ear mushrooms. We served wood ear mushroom salad at our wedding welcome dinner, and it ended up being a favorite part of the meal for many of our guests. This recipe is modeled after the salad that everyone adored so much.

The flavor of wood ears is not very strong; the mushroom is prized mostly for its wonderfully springy and crunchy texture (and its health benefits). Some grocery stores stock fresh ones, but you can always find dehydrated wood ear mushrooms at any Chinese market. They are best eaten cooked (raw ones may contain a bacteria that could make you sick), so if you're using fresh wood ears, blanch them as directed in this recipe before using them in salads, soups, braises, and stir-fries.

BLANCH THE MUSHROOMS: Bring a medium pot of water to a boil. Fill a medium bowl with ice and water. Drop the mushrooms into the boiling water and blanch for 1 minute. Using a slotted spoon or spider, immediately transfer them to the ice bath to chill. Drain the mushrooms, shake off any excess water, and transfer to a medium bowl.

MIX AND CHILL: Add the chili, Chinkiang vinegar, rice vinegar, chili crunch, sesame oil, salt, and sugar to the mushrooms and toss to combine. Cover and chill in the fridge for at least 1 hour and up to 3 days before serving. Top with the sesame seeds and cilantro and serve.

NOTE: *If using dried wood ear mushrooms, place 2 ounces (57 g) in a medium heatproof bowl. Pour just-boiled water over the mushrooms and soak until pliable, 30 to 60 minutes. Drain and shake off any excess water before proceeding as directed.*

Smashed Ranch Cucumbers

Serves 4

1 pound (454 g) Persian cucumbers, roll cut (see page 27) into 2-inch (5 cm) pieces

4 green onions, thinly sliced

1½ tablespoons ranch seasoning mix

1 tablespoon rice vinegar

2 garlic cloves, grated

½ teaspoon kosher salt

Like any good Midwesterner, I can't resist ranch dressing. You will always find a bottle of it in my fridge and packets of Hidden Valley ranch seasoning mix in my pantry. I use the dried mix like a savory version of Fun Dip for carrot sticks, and I love sprinkling it on popcorn. Ranch seasoning on smashed cucumber salad makes it taste simultaneously Midwestern and Chinese. The juices released from the cucumbers mix with the herby seasoning and rice vinegar to make a light and refreshing vinaigrette. In the hot summer months, make a double batch, because sometimes a crunchy, hydrating cucumber salad is all you need to keep from overheating.

PREP THE CUCUMBERS: On a cutting board, carefully smash the cucumbers by pressing down on them with the side of a wide knife (a cleaver works well)—you want to keep the juices from splattering everywhere.

MIX AND CHILL: Transfer the cucumbers to a large bowl and add the green onions, ranch seasoning, vinegar, garlic, and salt. Toss to combine. Cover and chill in the fridge for at least 15 minutes before serving. It will keep in the fridge for up to 5 days.

Chrysanthemum Salad with Lap Cheong Vinaigrette

Serves 4

2 lap cheong (Chinese sausages), thinly sliced on a bias

2 tablespoons rice vinegar

1 tablespoon maple syrup

1½ teaspoons toasted sesame oil

½ teaspoon kosher salt

¾ pound (340 g) chrysanthemum greens, roughly chopped

½ cup (20 g) fresh basil leaves, torn or roughly chopped

½ Granny Smith apple, cored and cut into matchsticks

Chrysanthemum greens (tong ho), with the perfect balance of tender, frilly leaves and slightly crunchy stems, are lovely for salads. They are typically cooked with garlic or wilted in a soup or hot pot, but in their raw state, their flavor is light and delicate—a little grassy and peppery. When buying chrysanthemum greens, look for leaves that are dark green and still full of life (not wilted or yellow). Fresh basil amplifies the herbiness of the greens, and crispy bits of lap cheong act as the slightly indulgent element every salad needs. Use the rendered fat from the sausage to make a perfectly balanced vinaigrette.

COOK THE LAP CHEONG: Place the lap cheong in a cold skillet and set the pan over medium heat. Cook, allowing the fat to render, until the underside is crispy, 3 to 4 minutes. Flip and cook until crispy on the other side, 1 to 2 minutes more. With a slotted spoon, transfer the lap cheong to a plate and let cool.

MAKE THE DRESSING: Turn off the heat and allow the pan to cool for a few minutes, then add the vinegar, maple syrup, sesame oil, and salt. Whisk until the mixture is emulsified.

TOSS AND SERVE THE SALAD: Place the greens, basil, apple, and lap cheong in a large bowl. Pour over the dressing, toss until everything is combined, and serve.

Tried-and-True Gai Lan with Oyster Sauce

Serves 4

1 pound (454 g) gai lan

¼ cup (60 ml) water

1½ tablespoons oyster sauce

1 tablespoon extra-virgin olive oil

1 teaspoon toasted sesame oil

½ teaspoon kosher salt

½ teaspoon ground white pepper

Gai lan, also known as Chinese broccoli, is a member of the brassica family. It looks like broccoli rabe but is far less bitter (actually, it's not bitter at all); the stems are tender and sweet and the leaves have a nicely earthy, faintly mustardy flavor. Gai lan comes in a range of sizes from thin to thick and hearty; the thicker stalks can be more fibrous, so make sure to trim and peel the ends. There are so many applications for gai lan. You can blanch it as a topping for noodle soups, thinly slice it to stir-fry with beef (the OG beef and broccoli), or simply cook it with oyster sauce, which brings out its natural sweetness. This recipe is called tried-and-true gai lan because it's how you'll most likely find it prepared at Chinese restaurants and in many Chinese home kitchens.

PREP THE GAI LAN: Trim and discard the very ends of the gai lan stems. For larger stalks (with stems thicker than ½ inch/1 cm), use a paring knife or vegetable peeler to remove the tough, fibrous outer layer.

STEAM THE GAI LAN: In a large skillet, combine the gai lan and water. Bring to a simmer over medium-high heat, then cover. Steam the gai lan until the greens are tender and the stems are bright green but still have a snap, 4 to 5 minutes. Remove the lid and allow any excess moisture to evaporate.

STIR-FRY AND SERVE: Add the oyster sauce, olive oil, sesame oil, salt, and white pepper and toss to combine. Cook until the gai lan leaves start to sizzle, 3 to 5 minutes. Transfer to a serving platter, pour any sauce remaining in the pan over the gai lan, and serve.

VARIATION

You can use this preparation for other Asian hearty greens like yu choy and bok choy.

Black Bean and Garlic Ong Choy

Serves 4

1 pound (454 g) ong choy

2 tablespoons extra-virgin olive oil

2 tablespoons Black Bean and Garlic Paste (page 304, or store-bought)

2 teaspoons soy sauce

1 teaspoon toasted sesame oil

½ teaspoon sugar

½ teaspoon ground white pepper

¼ teaspoon kosher salt

Ong choy is also known as Chinese spinach, but it is not actually related to conventional spinach (and unlike conventional spinach, a pound of ong choy doesn't wilt down into a single serving). It has a blend of delicate, tender leaves and long, sturdy, hollow-cored stems that maintain some of their structural integrity when cooked. It pairs nicely with all kinds of sauces, but more often than not I reach for pungent, deeply savory black bean and garlic sauce. You can substitute conventional mature spinach, with big leaves and thicker stems, for ong choy, but avoid bagged baby spinach.

PREP THE ONG CHOY: Thoroughly wash the ong choy. Its growing environment can be quite sandy, so you may need to rinse it a few times. Trim off the bottom 1 inch (2.5 cm) of the stems, which can be fibrous, and cut the ong choy into 4-inch (10 cm) pieces.

STIR-FRY THE ONG CHOY: In a large skillet, heat the olive oil over medium heat. Add the black bean and garlic paste and cook until the garlic is browning and fragrant, about 2 minutes. Increase the heat to medium-high and add the ong choy, tossing to combine. Add the soy sauce, sesame oil, sugar, white pepper, and salt. Toss to combine and cook until the greens are tender and the sauce has reduced, 4 to 5 minutes.

SERVE: Transfer the greens to a serving platter. Pour the sauce from the pan over the top and serve.

Saucy Sesame Long Beans

Serves 4 to 6

½ cup (120 g) sesame paste or tahini, plus more if needed

⅓ cup (80 ml) water, plus more if needed

3 tablespoons rice vinegar

2 tablespoons maple syrup or honey

1 tablespoon soy sauce

1 teaspoon kosher salt

2 tablespoons extra-virgin olive oil

½ medium white onion, thinly sliced

1 pound (454 g) Chinese long beans, trimmed and cut into 6-inch-long (15 cm) pieces

Toasted sesame seeds

Chinese long beans can reach up to 3 feet (91 cm) in length; their flavor is similar to that of conventional green beans, but their texture is slightly less snappy. Quickly stir-frying long beans with onions until crispy and blistered and then laying them on a bed of nutty, sweet, and savory sesame sauce is my favorite way to prepare them. This recipe is heavy on the sauce because that's how I like it; the beans are great with rice or noodles, with the extra sauce draped over the top.

MAKE THE SESAME SAUCE: In a medium bowl, whisk together the sesame paste, water, vinegar, maple syrup, soy sauce, and salt until smooth. Add another tablespoon of water to thin the sauce or another tablespoon of sesame paste to thicken it, if necessary. Pour the sauce onto a shallow serving platter, reserving a little to drizzle over the beans.

STIR-FRY THE BEANS: In a large skillet, heat the olive oil over medium-high heat. Add the onion and cook, stirring occasionally, until just starting to brown around the edges, 4 to 5 minutes. Add the beans and cook, tossing occasionally, until just tender (they should retain a little snap), 6 to 7 minutes.

PLATE AND SERVE: Arrange the beans over the bed of sauce. Drizzle the remaining sauce over the beans and top with sesame seeds. Serve warm or at room temperature. You can also chill the beans in the fridge and serve as a cold side dish.

Pau Pau, the Urban Gardener

My pau pau was an early adopter of the urban gardening movement, even though she has zero clue what an urban gardener is. When my grandparents bought their house in downtown Cleveland in the 1970s, there was no yard, no grass, only asphalt. Pau Pau, coming from a long line of farmers, was determined to start a vegetable garden, so she tore up a big patch of pavement and forced my mom and her siblings to steal bricks from a local construction site, which she used to line the garden and build the beds. She used pipes and fencing material to build trellises for growing long beans and bitter melon. Over the years, the garden expanded to include beds made from recycled materials that ran down the walkway along the side of the house, and she eventually rigged up a system to collect rainwater for watering her vegetables. As a kid, I would wander through the garden, tugging on the Chinese long beans and smacking the winter melon because I'd seen my pau pau do it once. I counted the seeds that were drying out in the sun on the steps to the back door, and always hoped the neighborhood feral cat, which we affectionately named General Tso, would stop by for a pet.

Now in her nineties, Pau Pau is still gardening, though not on the level she used to. I aspire to reach her level of gardening prowess. My own garden in California is a place of peace and solace, and I find myself trying to be as resourceful as my grandmother. The yard that abuts mine is cared for by an Asian granny—I can tell by the makeshift trellis for the beans and the vibrant bitter melon that pop up each year. I mimic my neighbor's vegetable-growing schedule and make an effort to grow gai lan, tatsoi, and other Asian vegetables as a way to understand them even more and hopefully taste their most delicious versions. The Chinese long bean and winter melon seeds my pau pau gave me are so special because they originated from seeds she brought with her from Hong Kong (and from her village in China before that). I've had relative success with the beans, and watching the long strands grow, keeping a piece of her gardening tradition, is beyond rewarding.

Braised Celtuce

Serves 4

1 pound (454 g) celtuce
(3 or 4 stalks)

½ cup (120 ml) Scrappy
Chicken Stock (page 300;
see Note)

2 tablespoons Shaoxing
wine

½ teaspoon kosher salt,
plus more if needed

¼ teaspoon sugar

2 tablespoons extra-virgin
olive oil

The name might make you think this vegetable would taste like a combination of celery and lettuce, but celtuce is actually one of the most uniquely flavored vegetables. It has a robust nuttiness that you don't often get from a crisp, green vegetable and a texture most similar to thick asparagus. When picking out celtuce at your local Asian market, look for firm stalks and avoid ones with overly wilted leaves. Celtuce is delicious raw, but braising it releases the stalks' natural sweetness and transforms the texture from crunchy to melt-in-your-mouth tender. The braise is gentle in technique and in flavor to not overshadow the lovely qualities of the celtuce.

PREP THE CELTUCE: Trim the very ends of the celtuce stalks and remove any leaves. Peel away the tough fibrous outer layer with a vegetable peeler until the smooth, jade-like flesh is exposed. Cut the celtuce into 1½-inch (4 cm) pieces.

MIX THE BRAISING LIQUID: If using cold stock, warm it in the microwave until it's no longer jiggly, 1 to 2 minutes. In a medium bowl, combine the stock, Shaoxing wine, salt, and sugar and mix. Give it a taste and add more salt if needed (this will depend on the stock).

SEAR THE CELTUCE: In a large skillet, heat the olive oil over medium-high heat. Add the celtuce in a single layer, cut-side up, and sear until deeply browned around the bottom edges, 3 to 4 minutes. Flip and sear until deeply browned around the edges on the other side, 2 to 3 minutes. This gives the celtuce a very elegant appearance, but feel free to just give the pan a shake if you don't want to flip over every individual piece.

BRAISE AND SERVE: Reduce the heat to medium-low. Hover the lid over the pan (to protect yourself from splatter) and pour in the braising liquid. Place the lid on the pan and braise until the celtuce is very tender and most of the liquid has cooked off, 12 to 15 minutes. Transfer the celtuce to a platter and serve.

NOTE: *You can substitute ½ cup (120 ml) water and 1 teaspoon chicken bouillon powder for the stock.*

Fiery Garlic Chives and Summer Squash

Serves 4 to 6

2 tablespoons extra-virgin olive oil

1½ pounds (681 g) summer squash, roll cut (see page 27) into 1½-inch (4 cm) pieces

3 cups (200 g) Chinese garlic chives (2-inch/5 cm pieces)

2 tablespoons doubanjiang

2 tablespoons water

1 tablespoon honey

1 tablespoon soy sauce

1 teaspoon toasted sesame oil

¼ teaspoon kosher salt

¼ teaspoon ground white pepper

Garlic chive flowers (optional)

Chinese garlic chives are more robust than the conventional chives you might sprinkle over a baked potato. They have a slight crunch and a mild onion flavor, with a more intense, garlicky bite; flowering garlic chives are even crunchier because they've had more time to mature. I compare garlic chives to ramps, but they're less elusive and far more affordable. They are commonly treated as both an aromatic and a vegetable, but since not everyone might be ready to commit to eating a whole plate of garlic chives, I've paired them here with summer squash for balance. The sweetness of the squash complements the garlicky nature of the chives and helps mellow out the fiery spice of the doubanjiang. This is one of those vegetable dishes that tastes great hot from the pan, but is also excellent chilled.

SEAR THE ZUCCHINI: In a large skillet, heat the olive oil over medium-high heat. Add the squash, cut-side down, and cook until deep golden brown on the underside, 4 to 5 minutes, then flip and cook until both sides are evenly brown, 4 to 5 minutes.

STIR-FRY WITH CHIVES: Add the garlic chives, tossing to combine. Cook until the chives are aromatic and just starting to soften, about 1 minute. Reduce the heat to medium and add the doubanjiang, water, honey, soy sauce, sesame oil, salt, and white pepper. Toss everything to combine and cook until the sauce has reduced, 3 to 4 minutes.

PLATE AND SERVE: Transfer the squash to a serving platter and top with chive flowers, if you have some!

VARIATION

When you're ready to commit to a whole plate of garlic chives, omit the squash, triple the amount of chives (flowering chives are better in this application), and cut them into 4-inch-long (10 cm) pieces instead.

Basil Lime Eggplant

Serves 4 to 6

1 pound (454 g) Chinese eggplant, cut into 1 by 4-inch (2.5 by 10 cm) pieces

2 tablespoons rice vinegar

1 teaspoon kosher salt

3 tablespoons extra-virgin olive oil

Juice of 2 limes

1 tablespoon fish sauce

1 tablespoon oyster sauce

1 teaspoon sugar

½ teaspoon crushed red chili flakes

½ cup (20 g) fresh basil leaves, thinly sliced, plus whole leaves for garnish

There are eggplant haters in the world because they haven't yet eaten the right eggplant! To become a convert, try the slender Chinese or Japanese varieties, preferably in a vivacious shade of purple. These varieties have fewer seeds, thinner skin, sweeter flavor, and a slightly firmer texture than the more commonly available globe eggplant. When cooked properly, eggplant should be creamy and custard-like, never spongy. During peak eggplant season, I crave eggplant dishes that are vibrant and not at all heavy (like the eggplant Parm I love when the weather is cool). The key to keeping things light is acid. In this case, lime juice and vinegar brighten the flavor and keep the eggplant nice and purple, not a dull brown. Those acids also cut through the saltiness of the fish sauce and oyster sauce. Serve the dish while it's still steaming hot, draped over a bowl of rice (though it's also delightfully refreshing chilled).

SALT THE EGGPLANT: In a large bowl, combine the eggplant, vinegar, and salt. Allow the eggplant to sit at room temperature for about 15 minutes to drain excess water. Drain and pat dry with paper towels.

SEAR THE EGGPLANT: In a large skillet, heat the olive oil over medium-high heat. Add the eggplant in an even layer, cut-side down, and sear until golden brown on the bottom, 4 to 5 minutes. Flip and sear until golden brown on the other side, 4 to 5 minutes.

MEANWHILE, MIX THE SAUCE: In a small bowl, whisk together the lime juice, fish sauce, oyster sauce, sugar, and chili flakes.

Reduce the heat to medium, pour the lime juice sauce over the eggplant, and stir to combine. Cook until the sauce has reduced, 2 to 3 minutes. Remove the pan from the heat and add the sliced basil. Toss to combine (the heat from the pan will wilt the basil).

PLATE AND SERVE: Arrange the eggplant on a serving platter. Garnish with whole basil leaves and serve.

Stir-Fried Lotus Root

Serves 4 to 6

1 pound (454 g) lotus root

2 tablespoons extra-virgin olive oil

½ cup (82 g) skin-on raw peanuts

¼ cup (8 g) dried whole chilis

¼ cup (60 ml) water

2 tablespoons Shaoxing wine

1 tablespoon dark soy sauce

1 tablespoon brown sugar

1½ teaspoons Chinese five spice powder

1 teaspoon kosher salt

½ teaspoon ground white pepper

I was a little intimidated by lotus root when I first started cooking with it. How do you know which lotus root looks best at the market, for example? Do you have to peel the skin? The more I cooked with it, however, the more I realized that lotus root is just like potato, but with holes. They're both starchy vegetables, but lotus root maintains its crunchy texture even after a long braise. A few pointers: Look for lotus roots that are medium in size (2 to 3 inches/5 to 7.5 cm in diameter), firm, and not too lumpy, which will be easier to handle and easier to eat. I peel the skin, but that's a matter of personal preference. Soaking sliced lotus root in water will prevent it from oxidizing and remove some of its natural stickiness, which comes from sap in the root.

This stir-fry, in which spiced lotus root is tossed with dried chilis and crunchy peanuts, takes flavor inspiration from Chinese dry pot cooking, which has the flavors of traditional Chinese hot pot minus the soup aspect. It is earthy and spicy, but not overly so. Take this as a reminder that no vegetable is too intimidating to learn how to cook.

SOAK THE LOTUS ROOT: Fill a medium bowl halfway with water. Peel the lotus root, then slice it crosswise into ⅛-inch-thick (3 mm) rounds and immediately place the slices in the water to prevent discoloration. Let the lotus root soak for at least 15 minutes, or until you're ready to cook.

TOAST THE PEANUTS AND CHILIS: In a large skillet, heat the olive oil over medium heat. Add the peanuts and chilis. Cook, stirring and tossing continuously, until crisp and browned, 4 to 5 minutes. With a slotted spoon, transfer the peanuts and chilis to a small bowl.

STIR-FRY THE LOTUS ROOT: Drain the lotus root and pat dry. Place the lotus root in the hot pan (be careful, as the oil may splatter), stirring with a spatula. Increase the heat to medium-high and cook, tossing occasionally, until browned around the edges, 6 to 8 minutes. Add the wine, soy sauce, brown sugar, five spice, salt, and white pepper and stir to combine. Cook, tossing frequently, until the sugar caramelizes on the edges of the lotus root slices, 3 to 4 minutes. Add the peanuts and chilis and toss to combine. Cook for another minute, then transfer to a serving platter and serve.

Steamed Bitter Melon Stuffed with Black Bean and Garlic Pork

Serves 4 to 6

1 pound (454 g) green or white bitter melons (about 2 medium)

½ pound (227 g) ground pork

2 green onions, thinly sliced

2 tablespoons Black Bean and Garlic Paste, (page 304, or store-bought)

1 teaspoon sugar

1 teaspoon toasted sesame oil

1 teaspoon crushed red chili flakes

½ teaspoon kosher salt

¼ teaspoon ground white pepper

Bitter melon, as its name implies, is incredibly bitter. And astringent. My parents love it and are forever praising its endless health benefits. As nature would have it, one of the healthiest vegetables for you is also one of the toughest on your palate. I finally outgrew my distaste for bitter melon because of this recipe. Bitter melon benefits from fat to help coat the palate, a slightly heavier hand with salt, and just a touch of sweetness. This version of my family's steamed bitter melon is stuffed with black bean and garlic pork; it's homey and comforting, and the astringent flavor is refreshing. Embracing the bitterness can sometimes be a good thing.

PREP THE BITTER MELON: Bring a medium pot of water to a boil over medium heat. Trim the stems from the bitter melons. Slice the melons into 1½-inch-thick (4 cm) rings and scrape out the seeds with a spoon. Add the bitter melons to the boiling water and cook just until bright green and slightly softened, about 5 minutes. Scoop out the bitter melon with a spider, shaking off excess water, and transfer to a plate to cool. (If you really love bitter melon, you can use the boiling water to make Everyday Tong, page 294, and take advantage of all those added health benefits. Otherwise, discard it.)

MIX THE PORK FILLING: In a medium bowl, combine the pork, green onions, black bean and garlic paste, sugar, sesame oil, chili flakes, salt, and white pepper with clean hands or with a flexible spatula.

STUFF AND STEAM: Set up a bamboo steamer (see page 25). Stuff the bitter melon rings with the pork filling and arrange on a heatproof plate or tray (you might need to use two or steam in batches, depending on the size of your steamer). Place the plate of bitter melon in the steamer, cover, and set the steamer over the simmering water. Steam until the pork is cooked through, about 10 minutes. Allow the stuffed melon to cool slightly before serving.

Crispy Brussels Sprouts with Sriracha Mayo

Serves 4 to 6

1 pound (454 g) Brussels sprouts, patted dry and halved (or quartered if very large)

3 tablespoons extra-virgin olive oil

½ teaspoon kosher salt

2 tablespoons mayo, preferably Kewpie

1 tablespoon sriracha

2 teaspoons rice vinegar

1 tablespoon furikake

Place these Brussels sprouts on the table and your guests will make them disappear in a matter of seconds. The shatteringly crisp leaves are at their best with the tangy sriracha mayo and furikake. The trick for getting the sprouts extra crispy is to peel back the leaves, almost unfurling them. This creates more surface area for the oil to seep into the leaves and help the sprouts get extra crunchy in the oven. If your sprouts are on the larger side, pluck off some of the outer leaves and toss them into the mix to crisp up individually. This step adds a few minutes of prep work, but you'll be rewarded for your efforts with potato-chip-level crunch without having to break out the deep fryer.

WARM UP: Preheat the oven to 450°F (232°C).

ROAST THE BRUSSELS SPROUTS: Peel back the layers of the Brussels sprouts, unfurling the leaves, and place the Brussels sprouts on a large rimmed baking sheet. Add the olive oil and salt and toss to combine. Arrange all the sprouts cut-side down. Bake until very crispy, 15 to 18 minutes (no need to toss them).

MEANWHILE, MAKE THE SAUCE: In a small bowl, whisk together the mayo, sriracha, and vinegar. Using an offset spatula or the back of a spoon, spread the sauce on a serving platter.

PLATE AND SERVE: Place the crispy Brussels sprouts over the mayo mixture on the platter. Sprinkle the furikake over the top and serve.

Numbing Smashed Potatoes, or Tingly Taters

Serves 4 to 6

1½ pounds (681 g) small yellow potatoes

¼ cup (60 ml) extra-virgin olive oil

2 teaspoons ground Sichuan peppercorns

2 teaspoons cumin seeds

2 teaspoons crushed red chili flakes

1 teaspoon kosher salt

½ teaspoon ground white pepper

Sizzle Sauce (page 305), for serving

These smashed potatoes are inspired by my favorite stir-fried mala potatoes I get from the Sichuan restaurant near my house. Their version is crinkle-cut, but the seasoning here is the same and the shape is just as playful. *Mala* refers to a blend of primarily Sichuan peppercorns and spicy chilis, and lends its name to that buzzing, almost tingly sensation you get from eating Sichuan food. This spice mix also includes cumin seeds and white pepper to round out the heat with a little earthiness, turning these smashed potatoes into tingly taters.

BOIL THE POTATOES: Fill a large pot halfway with water and bring to a boil over medium-high heat. Add the potatoes and cook until tender (a paring knife should be able to easily pierce them), 20 to 25 minutes. Drain the potatoes and allow to cool for a few minutes.

WARM UP: Meanwhile, preheat the oven to 425°F (218°C). Drizzle 2 tablespoons of the olive oil over a large rimmed baking sheet.

MIX THE SPICE BLEND: In a large bowl or the pot the potatoes were cooked in, mix the potatoes with the remaining 2 tablespoons oil, the Sichuan peppercorns, cumin, chili flakes, salt, and white pepper. Arrange the potatoes in a single layer on the prepared baking sheet. Use the bottom of a heavy glass or measuring cup to smash each of the potatoes to a little less than ½ inch (1 cm) thick. Drizzle any oil left in the bowl over the potatoes.

ROAST AND SERVE: Roast the potatoes until crispy and golden brown, 25 to 28 minutes. Allow the potatoes to cool for a few minutes before serving with a bowl of sizzle sauce alongside for dipping.

Sweet-and-Sour Cauliflower

Serves 4 to 6

Neutral oil, such as canola, for frying

¾ cup (105 g) all-purpose flour

½ cup (85 g) rice flour

1 teaspoon kosher salt, plus more for seasoning

½ teaspoon ground white pepper

1¼ cups (300 ml) ice water

1 large head cauliflower (600 g), preferably Chinese cauliflower, cut into small florets

½ cup (120 ml) Pineapple Sweet-and-Sour Sauce (page 307)

Green onions, thinly sliced on a bias

This is not a cauliflower recipe that wants to trick you into thinking it's chicken. Let's just let cauliflower be its hearty, starchy, mild-flavored self. Chinese cauliflower grows less dense and has longer stems and smaller florets that are ideal for battering and frying. There are more nooks and crannies for the delicate batter to coat, which means the cauliflower gets extra crunchy! This fried cauliflower is irresistible straight out of the oil, but a toss in sweet-and-sour sauce transforms it into a dynamic dish that makes a great party appetizer or a meal with a side of rice and a tasty protein like Roasted Salmon with Sambal Vinaigrette (page 51).

HEAT THE OIL: In a large heavy-bottomed pot, warm 3 inches (7.5 cm) of oil over medium heat to 380°F (193°C). Set a wire rack over a rimmed baking sheet.

MEANWHILE, MAKE THE BATTER: In a large bowl, whisk together the all-purpose flour, rice flour, salt, and white pepper. When the oil is at or close to temperature, add the ice water to the flour mixture and mix until the batter is runny yet slightly thick.

DREDGE AND FRY THE CAULIFLOWER: Working in batches of 5 or 6 florets at a time, dip the cauliflower in the batter, shake off the excess, and carefully lower the florets into the oil. Move the cauliflower around with a pair of chopsticks so the florets don't stick together. Fry until crispy and golden brown, 3 to 4 minutes. Transfer the cauliflower to the wire rack with a spider, sprinkle with a bit of salt, and repeat with the remaining cauliflower.

SAUCE AND SERVE: While the fried cauliflower is still hot, transfer it to a large bowl, add the sweet-and-sour sauce, and toss to lightly coat. Transfer to a platter, top with green onions, and serve. Alternatively, instead of coating the cauliflower, serve the sweet-and-sour sauce in a dish on the side for dipping.

Salted Egg Yolk Squash Rings

Serves 4 to 6

Neutral oil, such as grapeseed, for frying

1 pound (454 g) delicata squash (about 2 medium)

¾ cup (113 g) all-purpose flour

2 tablespoons cornstarch

½ teaspoon kosher salt, plus more for seasoning

3 salted egg yolks, homemade (opposite page) or store-bought

1 cup (240 ml) ice water

Salted egg yolks are not actually overly salty. Rather, they are buttery and rich. Salt curing is a way of preserving egg yolks, and transforms their texture to something similar to Parmesan cheese. Salted egg yolk fried chicken and vegetables, especially pumpkins, are a delicacy at Chinese restaurants. Sometimes the fried ingredient is tossed in a creamy salted egg yolk sauce, and sometimes the yolks are incorporated right into the batter. I'm a fan of the latter option and always gravitate toward fried squashes when they're available because I love their starchy texture and how it contrasts with the light crunch of the batter. Delicata squash have thin, edible skins and are much easier to slice and break down than a chunky kabocha or kuri squash. Cutting them into rings not only is playful but allows you to eat them as quickly as possible with one hand while your other is holding a cold beer (a perfect pairing). If you have any leftover batter, slice an onion and make some salted egg yolk onion rings.

HEAT THE OIL: In a large heavy-bottomed pot, warm 3 inches (7.5 cm) of oil over medium heat to 380°F (193°C). Set a wire rack over a rimmed baking sheet.

MEANWHILE, PREP THE SQUASH: Trim the stems off the squash and cut the squash in half crosswise. Scoop out the seeds with a spoon. Slice the squash into thin (⅛-inch-thick/3 mm) rings.

MIX THE BATTER: In a medium bowl, whisk together the flour and cornstarch. Add the salt and grate in 2½ salted egg yolks, reserving the remaining ½ yolk for later. Add the ice water and whisk until just combined; avoid overmixing.

FRY THE SQUASH RINGS: Working in batches, dip the squash rings into the batter, shaking off any excess, and then carefully drop them into the hot oil. Avoid overcrowding the pot, which will reduce the oil temperature. Stir the squash rings with a pair of chopsticks or tongs to prevent sticking and fry until the squash is tender and the batter is golden brown and crisp, 2 to 3 minutes. Transfer to the wire rack with a spider, sprinkle with a little salt, and repeat with the rest of the squash.

SERVE: Arrange the squash rings on a platter and grate the remaining ½ egg yolk over the top. Serve immediately.

Salted Egg Yolks

You can purchase salted egg yolks at Chinese grocery stores, but if you find yourself with an excess of egg yolks (maybe you were making meringue, or you're really into egg white omelets), salt the yolks yourself!

Makes 6 egg yolks

A lot of kosher salt

6 large egg yolks

SALT THE YOLKS: Fill a loaf pan or shallow resealable container with ½ inch (1 cm) of kosher salt. Make 6 indentations in the salt with a spoon or the bottom of an eggshell. Place an egg yolk in each of the indentations and cover with a thin layer of salt. Cover with plastic wrap or a lid and refrigerate for at least 3 days and up to 7 days (the longer they cure, the saltier they will be).

RINSE THE YOLKS: Remove the egg yolks from the fridge and wash the salt away under cold running water or by dunking in a bowl of cold water. Gently pat the yolks dry with a paper towel and place them on a plate. At this point, they are ready to use in recipes like Joong (page 279).

DRY THE YOLKS: To preserve the yolks, or for a texture that you can grate, preheat the oven to its lowest temperature, 200°F (93°C) at the most. Line a quarter sheet pan with parchment paper and arrange the salted yolks on the pan. Bake until dull and dry, about 2 hours. Allow the yolks to fully cool and then store in a resealable container in the fridge for up to 1 month.

Everything tastes better under the warmth of the sun. I'm grateful that living in California means I can host friends and family in our backyard most months of the year. Growing up in Ohio, I could not wait for the snow to finally melt and looked forward to the warmer months, even if it meant a humid Midwestern summer. June through early September meant riding roller coasters at Cedar Point, waiting in line at Apple Cart for ice cream cones, the yearly "Chinese Picnic" at Lake Erie, and my birthday backyard cookout!

I love the lack of constraints when hosting outside. You're not stuck in a hot kitchen, you can invite more people than you have folding chairs for, and not everything needs to be served at the same time. Most of the recipes in this chapter don't require you to actually cook outside. There are raw bites, craveable dips, mayo-y salads, my mom's famous fried chicken, and a reason or two to fire up the grill. These recipes could easily be served indoors year-round, but on a gloriously sunny day, take these dishes outside.

Oysters with Mandarin Mala Mignonette

Serves 4 to 6

½ cup (120 ml) freshly squeezed mandarin orange juice (from about 2 oranges)

¼ cup (30 g) minced shallot (about 1 small)

¼ cup (60 ml) rice vinegar

1½ teaspoons ground Sichuan peppercorns

¼ teaspoon kosher salt

2 dozen small oysters (Kumamotos or your favorite variety)

Sriracha or Crystal hot sauce

It's difficult not to fall in love with oysters when you live in San Francisco, thanks to the city's proximity to Tomales Bay (a nearby inlet, home to some of the best oysters) and its countless quality seafood markets. You can hardly go to a backyard gathering without seeing someone shucking oysters for a crowd. That someone is often my husband, who pops them open effortlessly. I'll occasionally step in to give his wrists a break, but my attempts are not nearly as graceful. My favorite oysters are small and have a clean ocean taste: a little sweet, briny, and not too buttery. As for accompaniments, I like this twist on the classic French mignonette, made of shallots, vinegar, and pepper.

The peppercorns add citrusy, piney notes, and fresh Mandarin orange juice helps tame the acidity of the rice vinegar. What's most striking is how beautiful the oysters look against the muted orange color of the mignonette.

MAKE THE MIGNONETTE: Place the orange juice, shallot, vinegar, Sichuan peppercorns, and salt in a clear jar with a lid. Twist on the lid and shake to combine, then let sit at room temperature for about 15 minutes to allow the shallot to pickle slightly, or refrigerate for up to a week.

SHUCK AND SERVE: Shuck the oysters, taking care to reserve their brine, and arrange on a serving platter (with ice, if you're fancy). Top each oyster with a spoonful of the mignonette and a dab of hot sauce and serve immediately.

Tomato and Hamachi Crudo

Serves 4 to 6

1 pound (454 g) sushi-grade hamachi (see Note)

½ pound (227 g) tomatoes (including some green ones if you can find them), cut into small wedges

1 Fresno chili or jalapeño, thinly sliced

1 or 2 green onions, thinly sliced on a bias

¼ cup (60 ml) soy sauce

3 tablespoons rice vinegar

Crudo is one of my favorite things to make if I'm contributing to someone else's gathering because it's a low-effort, high-impact kind of dish. You can easily slice the fish and mix the soy sauce and vinegar in advance, transport the fish on ice packs, and then assemble the crudo on-site. When you announce that it's ready, the fish will disappear in a matter of moments, so you don't need to worry about keeping it chilled much longer.

Here a few fresh ingredients—tomatoes, green onions, and hot chili—add some tart-sweet-hot character to the dish. But I encourage you to make the crudo uniquely your own. Change up the fish (salmon, tuna, or scallops are great swaps for hamachi) and replace the tomatoes for juicy oranges or extra-tart golden gooseberries. If you're craving more heat, add a drizzle of the spicy oil from Chili Crunch (page 302). If you enjoy plating food or styling charcuterie boards, you will love arranging crudo.

PLATE THE CRUDO: With a very sharp knife, thinly slice the fish against the grain at a steep angle (about 60 degrees) to create more surface area. Arrange the slices neatly on a platter. Scatter the tomatoes, chili, and green onions over the top.

SAUCE AND SERVE: In a small bowl, whisk together the soy sauce and vinegar. Pour the mixture over the fish and serve immediately.

NOTE: *To pick the best fish: When choosing fish for crudo, look for sushi-grade fish, meaning it has been commercially frozen and is meant to be served raw, and use it the same day. You could use salmon, tuna, or even scallops, but I gravitate toward hamachi for its light and delicate texture and flavor; just make sure you trim off any dark red flesh (this is the bloodline, which can taste like iron), or ask the fishmonger to do it.*

Poached Prawns with Ginger Cocktail Sauce

Serves 4 to 6

8 cups (1.92 L) water

1 (3-inch/7.5 cm) piece fresh ginger, cut into 1-inch (2.5 cm) chunks and smashed

2 bay leaves

1 tablespoon kosher salt

2 pounds (908 g) shell-on large prawns (or shrimp), preferably with heads on

For the cocktail sauce

½ cup (120 ml) ketchup

2 tablespoons grated fresh ginger

2 teaspoons Chinkiang vinegar

2 teaspoons soy sauce

This riff on cocktail shrimp, featuring big prawns or shrimp, brings me back to warm days spent with my dad's family in Hong Kong, when we would take the ferry to Lamma Island or Cheung Chau and stop for lunch at one of the many waterfront restaurants. There's an element of instant gratification because after you point to whatever tasty crustaceans look good to you in the fish tanks, the cooks prepare them on the spot, however you want.

Here thick slices of ginger and bay leaves infuse the poaching liquid with subtle spice that accentuates the natural salinity and sweetness of the prawns. Cooking them with the shells on will protect their texture and help them taste their best and most prawny selves. Don't be afraid of sucking on the heads, either; they carry so much delightful flavor. For a twist on conventional cocktail sauce, try grated fresh ginger mixed with a splash of black vinegar and soy sauce.

SET UP THE POACHING LIQUID AND ICE BATH: In a large pot, combine the water, ginger, bay leaves, and salt and bring to a boil over medium-high heat. Reduce the heat to medium-low and simmer for 30 minutes. Meanwhile, fill a large bowl with ice and fresh water.

POACH THE SHRIMP: Add the prawns to the water (in batches, if needed) and cook until they turn bright pink, about 5 minutes. With a spider or slotted spoon, transfer the prawns to the ice bath to stop the cooking; let chill for 10 minutes. Drain the shrimp, shaking off any excess moisture.

MAKE THE COCKTAIL SAUCE: In a medium bowl, whisk together the ketchup, ginger, vinegar, and soy sauce.

SERVE: Arrange the prawns on a serving platter (over ice, if you want to keep them extra chilled) and serve with the cocktail sauce on the side.

Typhoon Deviled Eggs

Serves 4 to 6

For the deviled eggs

6 large eggs

2 tablespoons mayo, preferably Kewpie

2 teaspoons rice vinegar

2 teaspoons sriracha

½ teaspoon kosher salt

¼ teaspoon ground black pepper

For the typhoon breadcrumbs

1 tablespoon extra-virgin olive oil

1 (1-inch/2.5 cm) piece fresh ginger, peeled and minced

2 garlic cloves, minced

1 green onion, thinly sliced

¼ cup (20 g) panko breadcrumbs

2 tablespoons pork floss

These deviled eggs get an update in the form of savory pork floss and a heavy shower of typhoon breadcrumbs. A blend of panko, garlic, and ginger, typhoon breadcrumbs are popular in Hong Kong sprinkled over seafood. The name is inspired by the debris left behind after a typhoon (Hong Kong has a serious rainy season). For porky goodness, use Chinese pork floss—fluffy strands of dehydrated pork beloved for jook, breads, and now deviled eggs, too.

COOK THE EGGS: Bring a medium pot of water to a boil over high heat. Fill a large bowl with equal parts cold water and ice. Using a spider or slotted spoon, gently lower the eggs into the boiling water and cook until hard-boiled, 10 to 11 minutes. Immediately transfer the eggs to the ice bath to chill for at least 15 minutes, then drain.

MAKE THE FILLING: Peel the eggs and cut each one in half lengthwise. Scoop out the yolks and transfer them to a medium bowl. Place the egg whites on a platter. With a fork, break up the yolks into fine crumbles. Add the mayo, vinegar, sriracha, salt, and black pepper to the same bowl. Mix until smooth.

PIPE THE DEVILED EGGS: Transfer the yolk mixture to a piping bag or a zip-top bag with one corner snipped off to act as the piping tip. Press the filling toward the tip and pipe it into the hollow of each egg white half. Cover and chill the eggs in the fridge until ready to serve, up to 3 days.

MAKE THE TYPHOON BREADCRUMBS: In a small pan, heat the olive oil over medium heat. Add the ginger, garlic, and green onion and stir to coat in the oil. Cook the aromatics, stirring occasionally, until just starting to lightly brown, 1 to 5 minutes. Add the breadcrumbs and stir to combine. Cook, stirring occasionally, until the breadcrumbs are golden brown, 3 to 4 minutes. Transfer to a small bowl to cool. Crumble in the pork floss and stir to combine.

TOP THE EGGS AND SERVE: Right before serving, sprinkle the typhoon breadcrumbs all over the deviled eggs.

White and Black Bean Dip

Serves 4 to 6

1 (15-ounce/425 g) can cannellini beans, drained and rinsed

3 tablespoons rice vinegar

1 teaspoon kosher salt

½ teaspoon ground white pepper

½ teaspoon crushed red chili flakes

¼ cup (60 ml) extra-virgin olive oil

2 tablespoons Black Bean and Garlic Paste (page 304, or store-bought)

Potato chips, crackers, or snappy vegetables, for serving

If you're looking for me at a party, I'll be stationed right next to the chips and dip. That's the ideal location, because you can consistently graze while chatting with everyone who stops by for a bite. I support all varieties of dips, but a truly great bean dip speaks to me loudest. Beans can handle a lot of seasonings without losing any of their, for lack of a better word, beany flavor or their hearty creaminess. Here velvety-smooth pureed cannellini beans are topped with sizzling fermented black bean and garlic oil. Double the beans, double the fun.

BLEND THE BEANS: Place the cannellini beans, vinegar, salt, white pepper, chili flakes, and 1 tablespoon of the olive oil in a food processor. Puree until very smooth. Transfer to a shallow serving bowl, swirling the puree to reach the edges of the bowl.

MAKE THE BLACK BEAN AND GARLIC SIZZLE OIL: In a small skillet, heat the remaining 3 tablespoons olive oil over medium-low heat. Add the black bean and garlic paste and cook, stirring constantly with a flexible spatula, until fragrant and starting to break down, about 3 minutes.

SERVE: Pour the hot oil over the beans and serve with potato chips, crackers, or vegetables.

Garlicky Whipped Tofu Dip

Serves 4 to 6

1 pound (454 g) silken tofu, drained

Zest and juice of 1 lemon

3 garlic cloves, peeled

1 teaspoon apple cider vinegar

1 teaspoon kosher salt

½ teaspoon ground black pepper

2 tablespoons extra-virgin olive oil

2 tablespoons toasted pistachios, finely chopped (see page 340, or store-bought)

1 teaspoon toasted sesame seeds

Potato chips, crackers, or snappy vegetables, for serving

Serve this dip to people without prefacing that the creamy white stuff is tofu; I bet your guests will have no idea the dip is lacking in the dairy department. Would this dip taste great with a base of crème fraîche or yogurt? Of course. But silken tofu is so versatile and will make any vegan or dairy-free friends in your life very happy. In a matter of seconds in a food processor, the tofu blends into a luscious and punchy dip that's then topped with good olive oil and crunchy nuts and seeds.

WHIP THE TOFU: Place the tofu, lemon zest, lemon juice, garlic, vinegar, salt, and black pepper in a food processor. Blend until silky smooth. Transfer the whipped tofu to a serving bowl and swirl to the edges with a spoon, creating deep valleys for the oil.

ADD THE TOPPINGS AND SERVE: Drizzle the olive oil over the whipped tofu. Top with the pistachios and sesame seeds. Serve with potato chips, crackers, or vegetables.

Curried Surimi Salad
with Buttery Crackers

1 pound (454 g) surimi
(imitation crab), roughly
chopped

¼ cup (60 g) mayo,
preferably Kewpie

3 green onions, finely
chopped

1½ teaspoons sambal oelek

1 teaspoon oyster sauce

½ teaspoon curry powder

¼ teaspoon kosher salt

¼ teaspoon ground white
pepper

Buttery crackers,
preferably Club, for
serving

You might know surimi as imitation crab and may have only
encountered it in a California roll, but a surimi salad on a buttery
cracker is a peak nostalgic comfort snack. This Kewpie-coated
salad feels like a blast from the 1990s, but I think it should make
a resurgence. A touch of curry powder and sambal elevates the
salad to a summer staple that's fresh, exciting, and satisfying.

In a medium bowl, mix the surimi, mayo, green onions, sambal,
oyster sauce, curry powder, salt, and white pepper with a flexible
spatula until well combined. Cover the bowl and chill in the fridge
for at least 2 hours and up to 5 days before serving with the crackers.

Banh Mi Pasta Salad

Serves 6 to 8

1 pound (454 g) fusilli

2 cups (300 g) Party Pickles (page 309), roughly chopped

⅓ cup (80 g) minced red onion

½ cup (30 g) chopped fresh cilantro

1 jalapeño, minced

½ cup (120 g) mayo, preferably Kewpie

2 tablespoons fish sauce

2 tablespoons oyster sauce

2 tablespoons sriracha

½ teaspoon kosher salt

½ teaspoon ground white pepper

The credit for this genius pasta salad concept goes to my husband. One day, while devouring a banh mi at our favorite local shop, he said, "If you replace the bread with pasta, this would make a really great pasta salad." I knew I married that man for a reason. Just like the sandwich, this dish is creamy, spicy, tart, and refreshing all at once, in perfect measure. It's reminiscent of Hawaiian mac salad, but just a little more vibrant.

Like many pasta salads, this one tastes better the longer it chills in the fridge, so make it in advance of your next party. And if you want to be everyone's favorite friend, consider making a double batch so guests can take a container home.

COOK THE PASTA: Bring a large pot of water to a boil over high heat. Add the pasta and cook until al dente according to the package directions. Drain the pasta and rinse under cold water.

MIX AND CHILL: In a large bowl, combine the pasta, pickles, onion, cilantro, jalapeño, mayo, fish sauce, oyster sauce, sriracha, salt, and white pepper. Cover the salad and chill in the fridge for at least 2 hours and up to 5 days before serving.

Garden Veggie Potato Salad

Serves 6 to 8

4 large eggs

2 pounds (908 g) russet potatoes, peeled and cubed

6 green onions, cut on a bias

2 celery stalks, thinly cut on a bias

1 large kohlrabi (180 g), peeled and finely diced

½ cup (75 g) fresh or frozen corn kernels

½ cup (120 g) mayo, preferably Kewpie

3 tablespoons rice vinegar

1 tablespoon oyster sauce

1½ teaspoons kosher salt

1 teaspoon ground black pepper

1 teaspoon sugar

What makes a great potato salad is everything *but* the potato. It's really about the perfect amount of creamy binder (in my world, that is mayo) and the tasty bits that add interest and dimension. This recipe is modeled after the two great potato salad loves of my life: my mom's eggy, very Midwestern-leaning version, and the tiny scoop of banchan flecked with crisp vegetables from my go-to Korean restaurant. A scattering of eggs and vibrant vegetables deliver a balance of textures and make for quite a light, refreshing side dish. A scoop of this potato salad is the ideal plate neighbor for a few grilled ribs (page 182) and teriyaki beef skewers (page 177).

COOK THE EGGS: Bring a medium pot of water to a boil over high heat. Fill a large bowl with equal parts cold water and ice. Using a spider or slotted spoon, gently lower the eggs into the boiling water. Cook until hard-boiled, 9 to 10 minutes. Immediately transfer the eggs to the ice bath, but keep the water boiling (you'll use it to cook the potatoes). Chill the eggs in the ice bath for at least 15 minutes, then drain.

COOK THE POTATOES: Using a spider or slotted spoon, gently lower the potatoes into the boiling water. Cook until tender, 18 to 24 minutes. Drain the potatoes and transfer to a bowl. Let cool completely.

MIX AND CHILL: Peel and quarter the eggs (they will break down more as you mix the salad). Place them in a large bowl and add the green onions, celery, kohlrabi, corn, mayo, vinegar, oyster sauce, salt, black pepper, and sugar. Mix with a flexible spatula until evenly combined. Cover the bowl and chill in the fridge for the best flavor, at least 2 hours and up to 5 days.

Coconut Crunch Coleslaw

Serves 4 to 6

¾ cup (180 ml) full-fat canned coconut milk, preferably Aroy-D or Chaokoh

2 green onions

Juice of 2 limes

1 tablespoon rice vinegar

1 tablespoon extra-virgin olive oil

1½ teaspoons kosher salt

½ teaspoon ground black pepper

6 cups (400 g) finely shredded green cabbage (cut by hand or on a mandoline)

Chili Crunch (page 302, or store-bought)

⅓ cup (23 g) Fried Shallots (page 311)

A coconut milk slaw is a nice creamy vegan alternative to mayo-based slaws. Here the slightly sweet flavor of the coconut milk is a cooling foil to the fiery chili crunch that gets drizzled on top. Full-fat coconut milk from a can, preferably Aroy-D or Chaokoh, will ensure the dressing is thick and creamy so you don't end up with a watery slaw. For an added layer of crunch, use sturdy tortilla chips to dig into this slaw (but if you can get your hands on some big shrimp chips instead, you won't be sorry). To make this more of a complete meal, top the slaw with Orange Pepper Popcorn Chicken (page 44).

MAKE THE DRESSING: Place the coconut milk, green onions, lime juice, vinegar, olive oil, salt, and black pepper in a bullet blender or other small blender. Blend until mostly smooth, with some flecks of green onion remaining, about 30 seconds.

TOSS THE SLAW: In a large bowl, toss the cabbage with the dressing until fully coated. Cover the bowl and chill in the fridge for at least 20 minutes and up to 4 days before serving.

ADD TOPPINGS AND SERVE: When ready to serve, top the salad with a generous drizzle of chili crunch and pile on the fried shallots.

Little Shrimp Patties

Serves 4 to 6

1 pound (454 g) large (16/20 count) shrimp, peeled and deveined

¼ cup (15 g) fresh Thai basil, plus more leaves for topping

1 jalapeño, stemmed

2 tablespoons cornstarch

1½ tablespoons oyster sauce

1 tablespoon fish sauce

½ teaspoon sugar

½ teaspoon kosher salt

½ teaspoon ground white pepper

½ teaspoon baking powder

2 tablespoons extra-virgin olive oil

Fresh mint leaves, for topping

Patties are another party and cookout staple. Serving them as a small bite at a barbecue is a good idea because they're incredibly delicious whether they're freshly fried, at room temp, or chilled. They tend to get demolished quickly. The key to fish patties with a cloudlike interior is a quick boil before frying. The patties are a great make-ahead option, and they travel well, too. For a heftier bite, load one into a Little Gem leaf and top with Party Pickles.

SET UP: Bring a large pot of water to a boil over high heat. Set a wire rack over a rimmed baking sheet.

MAKE THE SHRIMP MIXTURE: In a food processor, combine the shrimp, basil, jalapeño, cornstarch, oyster sauce, fish sauce, sugar, salt, white pepper, and baking powder. Process until very smooth and airy, about 1 minute.

BOIL THE SHRIMP PATTIES: Working in batches, scoop 1½ tablespoons of the shrimp mixture (I use a 1½-tablespoon/ ¾-ounce cookie scoop) and gently lower each patty into the boiling water. Boil until the patties expand and float to the top, about 2 minutes. With a slotted spoon or spider, transfer the patties to the wire rack. Repeat with the remaining shrimp mixture.

PAN-FRY THE SHRIMP PATTIES: When all the patties are cooked, heat the olive oil in a large skillet over medium-high heat. Working in batches, fry the patties until crispy and golden brown on the bottom, 1 to 2 minutes. Flip and fry until crispy and golden brown on the other side, 1 to 2 minutes.

PLATE AND SERVE: Arrange the patties on a serving platter and scatter with torn mint and basil leaves. The patties can also be chilled in the fridge for a few hours before serving.

Char Siu Mushrooms

Serves 4 to 6

Neutral oil, such as grapeseed, for grilling

2 pounds (908 g) extra-large portobello or shiitake mushrooms

½ cup (120 ml) honey

¼ cup (60 ml) ketchup

¼ cup (60 ml) hoisin

¼ cup (60 ml) oyster sauce

2 tablespoons extra-virgin olive oil

1 teaspoon Chinese five spice powder

1 teaspoon kosher salt

1 teaspoon crushed red chili flakes

½ teaspoon ground white pepper

How do you turn a mushroom skeptic into a mushroom fanatic? Give the mushrooms the char siu pork treatment. Start with the biggest mushroom caps you can get—extra-large shiitakes are great, but portobellos may be easier to find. Slather the caps in homemade char siu sauce, then grill until nicely charred yet still super juicy and serve them in thick slices to share. If you're a big mushroom lover, an entire cap would be glorious on a toasted fluffy bun; you may never miss meat at a cookout again.

FIRE UP THE GRILL: Preheat the grill to medium-high (between 450° and 500°F/232° and 260°C) for at least 30 minutes. Pour some neutral oil onto a bundle of paper towels and, holding them with tongs, rub them over the grill grates to lightly coat with oil.

PREP THE MUSHROOMS: While the grill is preheating, clean the mushrooms by dabbing them with a damp paper towel to take away any dirt. Remove and discard the stems.

MAKE THE GLAZE: In a medium bowl, mix the honey, ketchup, hoisin, oyster sauce, olive oil, five spice, salt, chili flakes, and white pepper to combine.

GRILL THE MUSHROOMS: Brush both sides of each mushroom cap with the glaze (you will have some left over; reserve it for brushing). Place the mushrooms on the grill over direct heat, gill-side up, and cover the grill. Grill for about 5 minutes, brush on some more glaze, and flip. Cover and grill for 5 minutes more, then brush with glaze again and flip. Cover and grill for 5 minutes more, or until the mushrooms are deeply charred.

SERVE: Transfer the mushrooms to a cutting board and let cool for 5 minutes. Cut into thick slices and serve.

Momma Cho's Fried Chicken

Serves 6 to 8

3 pounds (1.36 kg) chicken wings (flats and drumettes)

5 tablespoons (38 g) cornstarch

2 tablespoons oyster sauce

1½ tablespoons extra-virgin olive oil

1½ teaspoons kosher salt

½ teaspoon ground white pepper

½ teaspoon sugar

1 large egg

½ cup (65 g) rice flour

2 tablespoons water

Neutral oil, such as canola, for frying

NOTE: If it's difficult to regulate the oil temperature and the fried chicken skin is not as crisp as you like, you can double-fry the chicken: When all the wings have been fried, bring the oil temperature back to 380°F (193°C) and, working in batches, drop each wing back into the oil. Fry for just 1 minute before transferring to the wire rack.

This recipe has helped bridge the gap for many relationships in my life, from childhood friends who were eager to have dinner at my house in hopes of eating my mom's fried chicken to my in-laws when they met my parents for the first time prior to our wedding. Everyone's always in a happier and chattier mood with some fried chicken in their belly.

Two key elements in the marinade make my mom's recipe so craveable: cornstarch tenderizes the chicken and keeps it juicy, and oyster sauce gives the wings a sweet-salty foundation of flavor. Rice flour in the batter helps it fry up into the most delicate, crunchiest coating you've ever tasted. The chicken is superb moments after frying—don't be surprised if people start to flock toward the fryer as soon as the wings come out of the oil. I always make sure to save a few wings in the fridge as a chef's snack, because cold fried chicken is an absolute treat.

MARINATE THE WINGS: In a large bowl, combine the chicken, 3 tablespoons of the cornstarch, the oyster sauce, olive oil, salt, white pepper, and sugar and toss to coat evenly. Cover the bowl and allow the chicken to marinate at room temperature for 20 to 30 minutes.

WARM UP THE OIL: Meanwhile, in a heavy-bottomed pot or wok, heat 3 inches (7.5 cm) of neutral oil over medium-high heat to 380°F (193°C). Set a wire rack over a baking sheet lined with paper towels.

BATTER AND FRY THE WINGS: Add the egg, the remaining 2 tablespoons cornstarch, the rice flour, and the water to the bowl with the chicken and toss until the chicken is evenly coated. The batter should be the consistency of buttermilk (runny but not too thin). Add a little more water if it's too thick.

Working in batches of 6 to 8 wings, lift each wing from the bowl, shaking it to let excess batter drip off, then carefully drop it into the hot oil. With a pair of chopsticks or tongs, gently move the wings around to keep them from sticking together. Cook until the chicken is golden brown and cooked through, 6 to 7 minutes, stirring the wings occasionally. Transfer the fried chicken to the rack. Repeat with the remaining chicken, allowing the oil to return to 380°F (193°C) between batches.

DIG IN: Let the wings cool for a few minutes before serving.

Grilled Teriyaki Beef Skewers

Serves 4 to 6

2 pounds (908 g) flank steak

⅓ cup (80 ml) hoisin

⅓ cup (80 ml) soy sauce

¼ cup packed (50 g) brown sugar

1 teaspoon crushed red chili flakes

1 teaspoon toasted sesame oil

½ teaspoon ground white pepper

½ teaspoon Chinese five spice powder

½ teaspoon curry powder

4 garlic cloves, grated

Neutral oil, such as grapeseed, for grilling

At our family restaurant, beef skewers were often arranged on a pupu platter with an assortment of other snackable bites like crab rangoon and egg rolls. That visual alone feels like a blast from the 1980s-and-'90s-dining-trends past. When the restaurant closed its doors and my goong goong retired, the only person he entrusted the recipe to was my dad, who took it upon himself to keep the delicious stick meat tradition going at our family barbecues. Teriyaki sauce can often be cloyingly sweet, but here the soy-sugar mixture is grounded with five spice and curry powder, which give the beef an earthy complexity.

NOTE: *If you don't have a grill, the beef skewers can be seared in a cast-iron pan over medium high-heat until browned and charred around the edges, 2 to 3 minutes each side.*

MARINATE THE STEAK: Thinly slice the steak against the grain (about ¼ inch/6 mm thick) and transfer it to a resealable container or a large bowl. Add the hoisin, soy sauce, brown sugar, chili flakes, sesame oil, white pepper, five spice, curry powder, and garlic. Toss to combine. Transfer to the fridge to marinate for at least 1 hour and up to 1 day.

FIRE UP THE GRILL: Soak 10 to 12 bamboo skewers in water for at least 1 hour before grilling to prevent burning. At least 30 minutes before you're ready to cook, preheat the grill to medium-high (between 450° and 500°F/232° and 260°C). Pour some neutral oil onto a bundle of paper towels and, holding them with tongs, rub them over the grill grates to lightly coat with oil.

SKEWER THE BEEF: While the grill is preheating, remove the beef from the fridge and let it come to room temperature. Drain the skewers. Thread each slice of beef onto a skewer and transfer to a platter or rimmed baking sheet.

GRILL THE SKEWERS AND SERVE: Lay the skewers on the grill grates over direct heat and cook (with the grill lid open) until lightly charred on the underside, about 3 minutes. Flip and cook on the other side for another minute. Transfer the skewers to a platter and serve.

Grilled Fish Balls

Serves 6

Neutral oil, such as grapeseed, for grilling

2 tablespoons ketchup

2 tablespoons hoisin

2 teaspoons toasted sesame oil

1 teaspoon curry powder

1 teaspoon crushed red chili flakes

2 (20-ounce/557 g) packages fish balls, defrosted if frozen

You could make your own fish balls (it's a similar process to making the Little Shrimp Patties on page 171), but Asian grocery stores are always stocked with premade fish balls. I grab a package as often as I can, because they're great additions to noodle soups and hot pots. If it's grilling season, throwing a few fish balls on a skewer and charring them on the grates is always a good idea. This recipe is inspired by the fish ball skewers that are sold practically everywhere in Hong Kong, a popular street snack sold deep-fried, grilled, or (most commonly) draped in a savory curry sauce. Grilling the fish balls makes them extra crispy and blistered.

FIRE UP THE GRILL: Soak six bamboo skewers in water for at least 1 hour before grilling to prevent burning. At least 30 minutes before you're ready to cook, preheat the grill to medium-high (between 450° and 500°F/232° and 260°C). Pour some neutral oil onto a bundle of paper towels and, holding them with tongs, rub them over the grill grates to lightly coat with oil.

MAKE THE BARBECUE SAUCE: In a medium bowl, whisk together the ketchup, hoisin, sesame oil, curry powder, and chili flakes.

ASSEMBLE THE SKEWERS: Skewer the fish balls, sliding 4 or 5 onto each skewer. Transfer to a platter and brush the barbecue sauce all over the fish balls.

GRILL THE SKEWERS AND SERVE: Lay the skewers on the grill grates over direct heat and cook (with the grill lid open) until lightly charred on both sides, 2 to 3 minutes per side. Transfer the skewers to a platter and serve.

Lemon Togarashi Grilled Chicken

Serves 4 to 6

2 pounds (908 g) chicken breasts (2 or 3)

Finely grated zest and juice of 1 lemon

2 tablespoons extra-virgin olive oil

2 teaspoons togarashi

1 teaspoon ground Sichuan peppercorns

1 tablespoon sugar

1 teaspoon garlic powder

1½ teaspoons kosher salt

½ teaspoon ground white pepper

½ teaspoon ground turmeric

Neutral oil, such as grapeseed, for grilling

Grilled chicken doesn't tend to generate much excitement, and grilled chicken breast maybe even less. But when you add some citrus and spice, magical things happen ("magical" meaning juicy, flavorful chicken). Togarashi, a citrusy Japanese spice blend, pairs nicely with Sichuan peppercorns, creating a cross-cultural version of mala spice. While the chicken is on the grill, the spices form a magnificent charred crust. If you have extra lemons, grill a few cut halves beside the chicken to squeeze over the top, too.

MARINATE THE CHICKEN: Pat the chicken dry and place in a resealable container (a zip-top bag works great). Add the lemon zest, lemon juice, olive oil, togarashi, Sichuan peppercorns, sugar, garlic powder, salt, white pepper, and turmeric. Mix until the chicken is evenly coated. Transfer to the fridge to marinate for at least 2 hours and up to 24 hours.

FIRE UP THE GRILL: About an hour before you're ready to grill, take the chicken out of the fridge and let it come to room temperature. Preheat the grill to medium-high (between 450° and 500°F/232° and 260°C) for at least 30 minutes. Pour some neutral oil onto a bundle of paper towels and, holding them with tongs, rub them over the grill grates to lightly coat with oil.

GRILL THE CHICKEN: Place the chicken breasts on the hot grill over direct heat and close the lid. Grill until the underside of the chicken has dark char marks, 6 to 7 minutes. Flip and grill until the internal temperature of the chicken reaches 165°F (74°C) and there are dark char marks on the other side, 6 to 7 minutes.

SERVE: Transfer the chicken to a cutting board and allow it to cool for 15 minutes before slicing and serving.

Chili Cumin Spiced Pork Ribs

Serves 4 to 6

3 pounds (1.36 kg) pork ribs, back membrane removed

3 tablespoons cumin seeds

2 tablespoons crushed red chili flakes

2 tablespoons kosher salt

1 tablespoon garlic powder

1 tablespoon sugar

2 teaspoons ground white pepper

Olive oil, if charring in the oven

Neutral oil, such as grapeseed, if charring on the grill

When I was an architectural intern in Beijing, I went to the grilled meat vendor in the alley near my office every Friday after work. It was a perfect place to pull up to with coworkers or newly made friends for a snack and a cold beer. The quickly fired meat skewers were heavily encrusted in cumin and ground chilis and kissed by the flames of the charcoal grill. The memory of those skewers inspired the fiery, earthy spice rub on these pork ribs (if you can get your hands on some lamb ribs, it would be amazing on those, too).

When cooking ribs, don't rush the process. Their connective tissue needs plenty of time to break down in order to get to the falling-off-the-bone stage. Cook the ribs low and slow in the oven, or cook them on the grill, as long as you maintain a consistently low temperature. At the very end, you finish the ribs on the grill (or under the broiler) to give them a charred crust. Whichever way you cook them, get some napkins ready, because eating these ribs will get your hands dirty.

SET UP: Preheat the oven to 300°F (149°C). Lay a big piece of foil over a large rimmed baking sheet. Place the ribs in the center of the foil.

MAKE THE SPICE RUB: In a medium bowl, stir together the cumin, chili flakes, salt, garlic powder, sugar, and white pepper. Sprinkle half the spice mixture over the ribs and then firmly it press it into the meat. Flip the ribs and sprinkle the remaining spice mixture over the other side, firmly pressing it into the meat. Wrap the ribs tightly in the foil.

BAKE THE RIBS: Bake the ribs, bone-side down, until very tender, 2½ to 3 hours. Carefully unwrap the ribs and discard the foil. Allow the ribs to cool for a few minutes before handling again.

To char the ribs in the oven: Increase the oven temperature to 450°F (232°C). Set the ribs on a wire rack over the baking sheet. Brush the ribs lightly with olive oil and bake until crisp and lightly charred around the edges, 15 to 18 minutes.

To char the ribs on the grill: Preheat the grill to medium-high (between 450° and 500°F/232° and 260°C) for at least 30 minutes. Pour some neutral oil onto a bundle of paper towels and, holding them with tongs, rub them over the grill grates to lightly coat with oil. Transfer the ribs to the grill, placing them bone-side down over direct heat. If the ribs are so tender that they start to break apart if you attempt to transfer the whole rack, cut the rack into 5- or 6-rib sections to make it easier to grill. Close the grill lid and cook until the bottoms of the ribs are lightly charred, about 4 minutes. Flip the ribs, cover again, and cook until the other side is lightly charred, about 4 minutes.

REST AND SERVE: Transfer the rack of ribs to a cutting board and let cool for 15 minutes before slicing the ribs for serving.

Make Your Own Luck

Lunar New Year is the most festive and widely celebrated holiday for Chinese people. It is traditionally a time of rest and reunion among families. Lunar New Year is also filled with superstitions that certain foods or acts could bring bad luck to you for the entire year to follow. The significance of this holiday can result in enormous pressure to make sure you celebrate the right way.

My husband and I host a celebratory Lunar New Year dinner at home every year, and I don't strictly adhere to every tradition. Many years I've "messed up" by cutting my hair at the wrong time or making jook for dinner before I realized it was bad luck. Traditions serve to remind us of the past and keep us rooted there, but I think it's perfectly fine to create traditions that help define our own notions of good fortune.

What follows is not a comprehensive, be-all-and-end-all guide to everything that you should and shouldn't do for Lunar New Year.

Rather, I've included a few simple acts of good luck, unlucky things I've done but lived to tell the tale, and a few of my very own favorite annual traditions.

Good Luck Traditions

Cleaning the house before the first day of the lunar new year: Sweeping away dust is like sweeping away any bad luck from the year before, so you can start fresh.

Hanging couplets (strips of red paper with Chinese characters written on them): These are said to have the power to repel bad luck and bad spirits and welcome good luck instead.

Wearing red: The luckiest of colors!

Eating lucky foods: Have all the oranges, dumplings, spring rolls, and gold-wrapped candies you want!

Unlucky Things I've Done but Lived to Tell the Tale

Cutting or washing your hair: Tradition says your hair can hold good fortune, so cutting it during the celebration of the new year is like throwing all your luck away. Not washing your hair for fifteen days is a hard ask, but you're not supposed to wash it for the same reasons you're not supposed to cut it—all that good fortune seemingly goes down the drain.

Eating jook: This rice porridge is considered a poor man's food, so the theory is that eating it during Lunar New Year doesn't propel you in the best direction financially. To counteract this, I tend to load mine up with fancier, more luxurious ingredients so it doesn't feel quite so meager, like in my XO Scallop Jook (page 210).

My Own Traditions

Decorating with citrus: Oranges represent joy in Chinese culture, and these little pops of brightness around the house bring lots of it.

Arranging a vase of budding branches: I use cherry blossom branches or any variety of fruiting tree; the blossoms symbolize vitality (and look gorgeous, too).

Making paper lanterns: I lean into my crafty side with this one; homemade lanterns strung around the house look so much cuter and more homey than store-bought ones, and the act of making them by hand helps me get into the spirit of the holiday.

Creating a new dumpling: I develop a new dumpling flavor that incorporates elements I wish for in the new year (like health, wealth, or peace). You can do the same by following the suggestions for Your Own Family Dumplings (page 236).

Joyous moments in life—the big ones, of course, but the small ones, too—are worthy of a banquet. I've spent so many birthdays, graduations, and other celebrations huddled around a big table with a group of extended family and friends. You're all happily elbow to elbow with each other, trying your best to reach for the juiciest slice of duck breast and hoping there's a piece of honey walnut shrimp left by the time the platter makes its way to you. A Chinese restaurant banquet often consists of eight courses (a very lucky number), starting with soup, then an onslaught of braised meats, steaming platters of seafood, piles of noodles, and possibly a vegetable or two, all exiting the kitchen in quick succession.

At home, you don't need to cook eight dishes to host a grand meal (unless you're feeding a lot of people). Think of a banquet as more of a mindset. You could make a special meal for a date night in, just you and your partner, or for a reunion of friends because your college besties just rolled into town. Many of these dishes are meant to be shared and served alongside one another or recipes from other chapters. Steamed rice (see pages 286–291) is a natural accompaniment, but when it's a bigger dinner, you might want to skip the rice to make room for more braised lamb or pork belly.

Shacha Roast Chicken

Serves 4 to 6

1 (4-pound/1.8 kg) chicken

1 tablespoon kosher salt

For the shacha sauce

2 tablespoons shrimp paste

4 garlic cloves, finely grated

1 (2-inch/5 cm) piece fresh ginger, peeled and grated

1 teaspoon sugar

½ teaspoon ground white pepper

4 tablespoons (½ stick/57 g) unsalted butter, cut into cubes and chilled

A good roast chicken is a sign that whoever is in the kitchen knows what they're doing, which is also a sign that they might make a great life partner. This is evident in the countless recipes for "engagement chicken," a recipe with life-changing promise if ever there was one. So you can see why I felt a lot of pressure developing a standout roast chicken recipe. Over the years, I have spatchcocked, marinated, brined, and basted so many chickens for the sake of research, but it wasn't until I took a trip to Hong Kong with my dad that I realized what my roast chicken was missing.

Shacha sauce is a popular Chinese dipping sauce that's often incorporated into stir-fries. While shacha relies heavily on dried shrimp and fish, it doesn't have an especially strong seafood or fishy flavor. Instead, what you get is the natural sweetness and salinity (or umami) of seafood. My homemade shacha sauce is not quite as salty as the store-bought version, leaning more on the shrimp paste and pungent bite of freshly grated garlic and ginger. Here the shacha melds with chicken fat and rich butter to create an irresistible sauce to spoon over the chicken. You'll want to mop up every last bit of it with some bread. I wouldn't be surprised if one happy couple out there gets engaged after enjoying this chicken.

SPATCHCOCK THE CHICKEN: Place the chicken breast-side down on a cutting board and remove the backbone with kitchen shears, cutting clean through the ribs about ½ inch (1 cm) from the backbone on either side. Discard the backbone (or reserve it for making stock; see page 300). Flip the chicken over and firmly press down on the breastbone to break it and flatten the chicken. Transfer the chicken, skin-side up, to a large cast-iron skillet.

WARM UP: Preheat the oven to 425°F (218°C).

SALT THE CHICKEN: Pat the chicken dry with paper towels, then rub the salt over the skin and underside. Allow the chicken to sit at room temperature for 30 minutes (you'll start to see moisture appear on the skin).

(recipe continues)

MEANWHILE, MAKE THE SHACHA SAUCE: In a medium bowl, combine the shrimp paste, garlic, ginger, sugar, and white pepper.

ROAST THE CHICKEN: Pat the chicken dry again with paper towels. Rub the shacha sauce over the skin and underside of the chicken. Tuck in the wings and surround the chicken with the cubes of butter. Roast the chicken, basting it with the butter and pan drippings every 15 minutes, until it registers 160°F (71°C) at the thickest part of the breast and the skin is crisp and deeply browned, 60 to 75 minutes.

REST AND SERVE: Allow the chicken to rest in the pan for at least 20 minutes before transferring it to a cutting board. Carve the chicken and transfer the pieces to a platter. Spoon the buttery chicken drippings over the chicken and serve.

Chop Shop Pork Belly

Serves 6 to 8

1 tablespoon sugar

2 teaspoons kosher salt

1 teaspoon Chinese five spice powder

1 teaspoon garlic powder

½ teaspoon ground ginger

½ teaspoon ground white pepper

2½ to 3 pounds (1.13 to 1.36 kg) pork belly

1 tablespoon rice vinegar

I find the window displays at Chinatown chop shops as captivating as any department store holiday window. After all, Chinese barbecue is an entire art form. The hanging roast ducks, soy sauce chickens, and slabs of blistered pork belly gleam and shimmer, showing off their best angles and enticing anyone with hungry eyes to stop and take them home. At our neighborhood chop shop in Cleveland (which was really just a stand at the back of a Chinese grocery store), my mom taught me how to pick out a good piece of pork belly: a relatively flat piece, with a close to 2:1 ratio of meat to fat (a little more meat to fat is better for eating).

Making chop shop–caliber pork belly at home starts with finding a cut of pork belly that will set you up for success. My mom's advice still holds true, especially the flatness part. Because the heat is one-directional in a home oven, a flat piece of pork belly will render and eventually blister more evenly. Next, you need ample time to dry out the pork skin twice—first before baking and then while it's in the oven. Before the pork belly goes into the oven, a brush of vinegar and a sprinkle of salt will draw out initial moisture, and then it needs to air-dry in the fridge, ideally for 24 hours. When it's done cooking in the oven, the skin will look dehydrated. At the very end, you blast the broiler and watch as the pork skin bubbles and crackles. The whole process is mesmerizing to watch, and the pork that results is incredibly satisfying to cut into and enjoy.

SEASON THE PORK BELLY: In a small bowl, stir together the sugar, ½ teaspoon of the salt, the five spice, garlic powder, ginger, and white pepper to combine. Pat the pork belly dry with paper towels. Score the underside of the pork belly (the meaty side), making shallow parallel cuts 1 inch (2.5 cm) apart. Sprinkle the spice mixture evenly over the scored meat and rub it into the cuts. Wrap the bottom and sides of the pork belly with foil, leaving the skin exposed.

SALT THE PORK BELLY SKIN: Flip the pork belly skin-side up. Brush the skin with the vinegar and sprinkle evenly with the remaining 1½ teaspoons salt. Place the pork on a rimmed baking sheet or plate and transfer to the fridge for 2 hours to allow the salt to pull some of the moisture out of the skin.

Remove the pork from the fridge and wipe the salt and moisture off with paper towels; the skin should be completely dry at this point. Take a bundle of bamboo or metal skewers (a fork or the tip of a paring knife works, too) and poke the skin all over, making sure to not poke deep enough to penetrate the meat. Return the pork to the fridge and let it air-dry, uncovered, for at least 18 hours and up to 36 hours.

ROAST THE PORK BELLY: Preheat the oven to 350°F (177°C) with a rack in the lower third. Pat the pork skin dry again if you see any moisture. Transfer the pork, skin-side up, to a rimmed baking sheet. Bake on the lower rack until the pork skin looks evenly dehydrated, 90 to 100 minutes. Transfer the pork to a rack about 10 inches (25 cm) away from the broiler. Turn on the broiler (on a low setting, or 450°F/232°C, if possible) and broil until the skin is puffy and crispy, 7 to 9 minutes. Watch it closely during this stage (it's okay to open the oven door for a peek), because the puffy pork belly skin can go from beautifully golden brown to burnt quickly. If you get any very dark brown spots while the rest of the pork skin is still waiting to puff up, cover those areas with foil.

SLICE AND SERVE: Allow the pork to cool for at least 30 minutes, then transfer it to a cutting board. For the cleanest cuts, use a sharp serrated knife to cut the pork into 1½-inch (4 cm) pieces and serve alongside the other dishes in your meal. Store leftovers in an airtight container in the fridge for up to 4 days and reheat in the oven at 350°F (177°C) until hot and crispy, 10 to 12 minutes.

Tea-Brined Duck Breast

Serves 4 to 6

For the tea brine

2 cups (480 ml) water

¼ cup (22 g) loose black tea leaves

¼ cup (50 g) sugar

3 tablespoons kosher salt

2 teaspoons dark soy sauce

3 star anise pods

1 cinnamon stick

1 (1-inch/2.5 cm) piece fresh ginger, smashed

1 teaspoon whole cloves

1 teaspoon Chinese five spice powder

1 teaspoon whole black peppercorns, or ½ teaspoon freshly ground black pepper

1½ pounds (681 g) duck breasts (about 4 medium)

1 tablespoon extra-virgin olive oil

Green onions, thinly sliced on a bias, for garnish

Dark soy sauce or hoisin, for serving

Chili House in the Inner Richmond District of San Francisco makes one of the best ducks I've ever had. While most people call in advance orders for the restaurant's Peking duck, I opt for their tea-smoked duck instead. It's equally succulent, with crispy skin and an earthy, complex flavor. Making a similar version at home is surprisingly simple when you use duck breasts, which are much more manageable than an entire bird. Instead of smoking, a potent brine of black tea steeped with spices permeates the duck and keeps the meat incredibly juicy as it cooks. The key to cooking duck breast properly at home is to not rush the process.

MAKE THE TEA BRINE: In a medium saucepan, combine the water, tea leaves, sugar, salt, dark soy sauce, star anise, cinnamon stick, ginger, cloves, five spice, and black peppercorns. Bring to a simmer over medium heat. Simmer, uncovered, for 5 minutes, then turn off the heat and allow the brine to cool completely. Strain the tea brine through a fine-mesh sieve into a glass measuring cup.

BRINE THE DUCK: Pat the duck breasts dry with paper towels and place in a resealable container or zip-top bag. Pour in the tea brine and cover with a lid or seal the bag. Refrigerate for at least 8 hours and up to overnight.

COOK THE DUCK: Thirty minutes before cooking, transfer the duck to a cutting board or plate (discard the brine) and pat the skin dry with paper towels. Allow the duck breasts to come to room temperature.

Drizzle the olive oil into a large cast-iron pan; do not heat the oil. Place the duck in the pan, skin-side down, and set the pan over medium-low heat. Cook the duck breasts until the skin is deeply browned and crispy, 12 to 15 minutes (it will look dark from the dark soy sauce, but that doesn't mean it's burnt!). Flip the duck and cook until it has reached your desired doneness, 3 to 4 minutes more for medium.

SLICE AND SERVE: Transfer the duck to a cutting board and allow it to rest for at least 15 minutes. Cut the duck into ½-inch-thick (1 cm) slices at a slight angle and transfer to a platter. Garnish with green onions and serve with a small dish of dark soy sauce or hoisin for dipping.

Sparerib Clay Pot Rice

Serves 4 to 6

1 pound (454 g) spareribs, cut into individual ribs

2 tablespoons Black Bean and Garlic Paste, (page 304, or store-bought)

1 tablespoon Shaoxing wine

2 tablespoons plus 2 teaspoons extra-virgin olive oil

2 teaspoons cornstarch

1 teaspoon kosher salt

½ teaspoon ground white pepper

1¾ cups plus 2 tablespoons (450 ml) water

1½ cups (315 g) jasmine rice

4 green onions, thinly sliced

2 lap cheong (Chinese sausages), thinly sliced

2 carrots, thinly sliced

Dark soy sauce

Clay pot cooking is coveted for its minimalist approach and, of course, for the layer of toasted rice at the bottom. In Hong Kong, clay pot stalls are especially popular in winter, when nothing is as comforting as a warm pot of rice flavored by the rendered fat of pork ribs, Chinese sausage, or eel. Every ingredient, from the fragrant jasmine rice to the final drizzle of dark soy sauce when you lift the lid, works in harmony. You don't need a clay pot to make this at home, though I recommend it. Traditional Chinese clay pots can withstand high heat and retain heat evenly for a very long time, but a medium Dutch oven produces similar results. These ribs, coated in black bean and garlic paste, are my hands-down favorite, but you can make endless variations of clay pot rice. Try topping the rice with Steamed Pork Cake with Chives and Cilantro (page 61) and cracking an egg on top for the last few minutes of steaming. For vegetarian options, use sliced egg tofu or spiced pressed tofu.

MARINATE THE SPARERIBS: In a medium bowl, combine the spareribs, black bean and garlic paste, Shaoxing wine, 2 teaspoons of the olive oil, the cornstarch, salt, and white pepper and toss until the ribs are evenly coated. Cover the bowl and transfer to the fridge to marinate for at least 1 hour and up to 1 day.

ARRANGE THE CLAY POT: In a large clay pot (or a 4-quart/3.75 L Dutch oven), rinse the rice under cold water to remove the starch. Drain the rice and return it to the pot along with the 1¾ cups plus 2 tablespoons (450 ml) fresh water. Add the green onions and stir to combine. Arrange the ribs, lap cheong, and carrots over the rice. Set the clay pot over medium-high heat and bring the water to a boil. Reduce the heat to medium-low, cover, and simmer until the rice and spareribs are cooked through, 15 to 18 minutes.

CRISP THE RICE: Uncover the clay pot to allow the steam to escape. Increase the heat to medium-high and slowly drizzle the remaining 2 tablespoons olive oil around the perimeter of the clay pot. You should hear the oil start to sizzle after a few moments. Carefully lift the clay pot just off the burner and rotate it consistently so the edges of the rice get crispy, 3 to 4 minutes.

SERVE: Drizzle dark soy sauce over the pot and serve.

Red-Braised Lamb

Serves 4 to 6

1½ pounds (681 g) lamb shanks (2 or 3)

1 teaspoon kosher salt

½ teaspoon ground white pepper

2 tablespoons extra-virgin olive oil

¼ cup (60 ml) Shaoxing wine

4 cups (960 ml) water

2 tablespoons rock sugar (about a 1½-inch/4 cm chunk) or brown sugar

2 tablespoons soy sauce

2 tablespoons dark soy sauce

Red-cooking or red-braising is a Shanghai style of slow-cooking meat with dark soy sauce and sugar until the meat is fall-apart tender and lacquered in a glossy red sauce. Red-braised pork belly, or hong shao rou, is the most popular option, but any meat with lots of connective tissue that benefits from long, undisrupted time in a steamy pot can be prepared this way (as can firm tofu and tofu knots). Lamb shanks, which are typically a tough cut, are incredible when red-braised, with the gaminess of the meat actually complementing the sweetness of the sauce.

SEAR THE LAMB: Season the lamb shanks all over with the salt and white pepper. In a large Dutch oven, heat the olive oil over medium-high heat. Add the shanks and sear, turning, until deeply browned on all sides, 3 to 5 minutes on each side. Transfer the shanks to a plate.

BRAISE THE LAMB: Reduce the heat to medium and pour in the wine, stirring and scraping the bottom of the pot with a spatula or wooden spoon. Add the water, sugar, and both soy sauces. Bring to a simmer, stirring to dissolve the sugar, then return the lamb to the pot. Reduce the heat to maintain a gentle simmer, cover, and braise the lamb until the meat is falling-off-the-bone tender and nearly all the liquid has reduced, 2 to 3 hours, turning the shanks every 30 minutes so they cook evenly. Uncover the pot and simmer until the braising liquid has reduced to a thick, glossy sauce, 5 to 15 minutes.

SERVE: Transfer the lamb shanks to a serving platter. Spoon the sauce over the lamb and serve.

Oxtail and Daikon Stew

Serves 4 to 6

1 tablespoon neutral oil, such as grapeseed

2 pounds (908 g) oxtails

5 cups (1.2 L) water

¾ pound (340 g) daikon radish, cut into large chunks

1 (2-inch/5 cm) piece fresh ginger, peeled and thinly sliced

4 star anise pods

¼ cup (60 ml) Shaoxing wine

¼ cup (60 ml) soy sauce

2 tablespoons rock sugar (about a 1½-inch/4 cm chunk) or brown sugar

1½ teaspoons kosher salt

1 teaspoon ground black pepper

This dish just smells like Lunar New Year to me. The aroma of oxtail and daikon stew simmering away on the stove, with its delicious wafts of meat and spices, instantly conjures memories of walking into my grandparents' house, leaving the frigid winter air behind and being greeted by the warmth of the kitchen and my extended family. The daikon in the stew is key, adding lightness and sweetness to an otherwise heavy dish; it also absorbs the flavor of the stew without turning to mush. Eating the meat off the oxtails leaves your lips feeling slightly fatty and sticky (which is considered a good thing) from all the collagen. So as my pau pau would say, "Have more and you'll have beautiful skin!"

SEAR THE OXTAILS: In a large Dutch oven, heat the oil over medium-high heat. When the oil is hot, add the oxtails and sear, turning, until deeply browned all over, 3 to 5 minutes on each side.

BRAISE THE OXTAILS: Add the water, daikon, ginger, star anise, Shaoxing wine, soy sauce, sugar, salt, and black pepper. Stir to combine and bring the mixture to a simmer. Reduce the heat to maintain a gentle simmer, cover, and simmer until the oxtails are very tender, 2 to 3 hours.

SERVE: Remove the lid and allow the oxtails to cool for about 15 minutes before serving.

VARIATION

If you want to turn this into more of a soup than a stew, increase the water to 10 cups (2.4 L) and serve in a bowl with a bundle of rice noodles.

Coconut Short Ribs with Creamy Butternut Squash

Serves 4 to 6

2 pounds (908 g) boneless short ribs (or 3 pounds/1.36 kg bone-in short ribs), cut into 2-inch (5 cm) pieces

2 teaspoons kosher salt

2 tablespoons extra-virgin olive oil

2 pounds (908 g) butternut squash, peeled and cut into 3-inch (7.5 cm) cubes

1 (13.5-ounce/ 400 ml) can full-fat coconut milk

1½ cups (360 ml) water

1 (2-inch/5 cm) piece fresh ginger, sliced

4 garlic cloves, smashed and peeled

½ large white onion, sliced into crescents

2 tablespoons rock sugar (about a 1½-inch/4 cm chunk) or brown sugar

2 tablespoons dark soy sauce

1 teaspoon ground black pepper

Gingery Brown Rice (page 290), for serving

Green onions, thinly sliced on a bias, for garnish

When in doubt, braise it in coconut milk. This recipe is one of the many reasons I keep a supply of full-fat coconut milk in my pantry. In this braise, the coconut milk melds with the fat from the short ribs and the starch from the butternut squash, and over the course of a couple of hours at a constant simmer, the coconut milk will gradually caramelize (thanks to its own natural sugars) and reduce to a velvety sauce. The active time in this recipe is very low, which is the beauty of a braise. You just throw everything into a pot, set a timer, and walk away (but not *too* far!). A few hours later, you have a perfect fall-through-winter meal, a hearty, magnificently aromatic main course.

SEASON THE SHORT RIBS: Arrange the short ribs on a large plate or cutting board and season on all sides with the salt. Let stand for 30 minutes to come to room temperature.

BRAISE: In a large Dutch oven, heat the olive oil over medium-high heat. Add the short ribs and sear, turning, until deeply browned on both sides, 3 to 4 minutes per side. Add the squash, coconut milk, water, ginger, garlic, onion, sugar, soy sauce, and black pepper. Give everything a good stir and bring to a simmer. Reduce the heat to medium-low to low and cover. Simmer until the liquid has reduced by half and the short ribs are very tender, 2 to 3 hours.

SERVE: Uncover the pot and allow the short ribs to cool for 15 minutes before serving with rice, garnished with green onions.

Hot Honey Mayo Shrimp

Serves 4

¼ cup (60 g) mayo, preferably Kewpie, plus a little more if needed

1½ tablespoons hot honey

1 teaspoon rice vinegar

½ teaspoon crushed red chili flakes

½ teaspoon kosher salt

½ teaspoon ground white pepper

Neutral oil, such as grapeseed, for frying

¼ cup (30 g) rice flour

¼ cup (30 g) cornstarch

1 large egg white

1 pound (454 g) large (16-count) shrimp, peeled and patted dry

Green onions, thinly sliced on a bias

At any proper Chinese American banquet dinner, ordering a plate of honey walnut shrimp is nonnegotiable. Everyone goes wild when the crispy shrimp tossed with sweet, creamy sauce in a nest of brightly blanched broccoli and sprinkled with candied walnuts appears on the table. The sauce is typically a blend of sweetened condensed milk and mayo, with or without honey. This version utilizes hot honey instead, which delivers on the sweetness of the original version while also balancing the creaminess with some much-needed heat. It also creates a beautiful glaze so the shrimp can shine bright on their own.

PREPARE THE SAUCE: In a large bowl, whisk together the mayo, hot honey, vinegar, chili flakes, salt, and white pepper. If it's a little thin, add another teaspoon of mayo; it should have a thick and creamy consistency.

HEAT THE OIL: In a large cast-iron pan, heat 1 inch (2.5 cm) of oil over medium-high heat until it just starts to shimmer. Reduce the heat if needed to maintain a fry temperature of 375°F (191°C). Line a baking sheet with paper towels and set a wire rack on top.

FRY THE SHRIMP: In a medium bowl, combine the rice flour and cornstarch. In a separate medium bowl, whip the egg white by hand until frothy (chopsticks or a whisk work great for this), about 2 minutes. Add the shrimp to the egg white and toss to coat completely. Working in batches of 6 to 8, toss the shrimp in the rice flour mixture and then carefully lower them into the hot oil by hand. Fry until the shrimp are lightly golden brown and crisp, 60 to 90 seconds on each side. Using a spider or chopsticks, transfer the shrimp to the rack. Repeat with the remaining shrimp.

TOSS THE SHRIMP AND SERVE: While the shrimp are still hot, add them to the bowl of sauce and toss to coat completely. Transfer to a platter, top with green onions, and serve.

XO Scallop Jook

Serves 4 to 6

10 cups (2.4 L) water

¼ cup (20 g) dried shrimp, roughly chopped

1 (1½-inch/4 cm) piece fresh ginger, peeled and grated

1 tablespoon plus 1 teaspoon coarse salt

½ teaspoon ground white pepper

1 cup (215 g) jasmine rice

12 large scallops

2 tablespoons extra-virgin olive oil

4 green onions, thinly sliced

2 tablespoons XO Sauce (page 303)

Fried Shallots (page 311)

Jook is a slow-cooked rice porridge that most Chinese people have been eating since they were babies; it's the humblest of dishes, requiring only the bare minimum of rice, water, and salt. Its simplicity and ability to stretch a cup of rice into a dinner for four does not necessarily make it a celebration food. But I made jook for one of my first Lunar New Years away from home. This unintentionally went against tradition, because jook is considered a poor man's food (I didn't know any better). To turn it into a banquet-worthy meal, top it with scallops and drizzle on some XO sauce, to make it feel and taste far more indulgent than your everyday jook. Just because a dish starts off humble doesn't mean it needs to stay that way.

SIMMER THE JOOK: In a large pot, combine the water, dried shrimp, ginger, 1 tablespoon of the salt, and the white pepper and bring to a boil over medium-high heat. Add the rice and stir continuously for about 1 minute to prevent it from sticking to the bottom, then reduce the heat to medium-low. Set the lid on top, but leave a gap for steam to escape, then simmer, stirring every 10 minutes, until the jook thickens and gets creamy, about 1 hour. You may have to gradually lower the heat as the jook reduces because as the water cooks out, the jook will start to bubble and splatter more rapidly.

MEANWHILE, SEAR THE SCALLOPS: Pat the scallops dry with paper towels and season both sides with the remaining 1 teaspoon salt. In a large cast-iron skillet, heat the olive oil until shimmery and very hot. Add the scallops to the pan and sear, undisturbed, until the bottoms are deeply golden brown, 2 to 3 minutes. Flip the scallops and sear until deeply golden brown on the other side, about 2 minutes.

SERVE: When the jook is thick, stir in the green onions and turn off the heat. Allow the jook to cool for a few minutes, then transfer it to a deep serving platter for sharing or into individual bowls. Top with the seared scallops, a drizzle of XO sauce, and fried shallots, then serve.

Salt and Pepper Squid

Serves 4 to 6

1 pound (454 g) squid heads and tentacles, cleaned, beaks removed

⅓ cup (40 g) cornstarch

1½ teaspoons kosher salt

1 teaspoon ground white pepper

1 large egg white

2 teaspoons toasted sesame oil

1 teaspoon sugar

½ teaspoon ground Sichuan peppercorns

Neutral oil, such as canola, for frying

⅓ cup (40 g) rice flour

Basil leaves (optional)

Pineapple Sweet-and-Sour Sauce (page 307), for serving

"Salt and pepper" is more than *just* salt and pepper when you're referring to Chinese food. The term defines a particular Chinese dish. You can "salt and pepper" just about anything; the technique involves breading and frying and is most commonly applied to tofu or shrimp. The ideal salt-and-pepper batter is light, to produce the crispest coating, and the seasoning is heavy on white pepper, which has a spicier, funkier flavor than black pepper. Giving squid the salt-and-pepper treatment is a no-brainer.

MARINATE THE SQUID: Cut the squid heads into ½-inch-thick (1 cm) rings and slice off the tentacles, but keep them intact. In a medium bowl, combine the squid, 1 tablespoon of the cornstarch, ½ teaspoon of the salt, ½ teaspoon of the white pepper, the egg white, and the sesame oil. Allow the squid to marinate at room temperature for 15 minutes.

MAKE THE SEASONING BLEND: In a large bowl, combine the remaining 1 teaspoon salt, remaining ½ teaspoon white pepper, the sugar, and the Sichuan pepper.

FRY THE SQUID AND BASIL: In a large heavy-bottomed pot, heat 2 to 3 inches (5 to 7.5 cm) of neutral oil until it reaches 375°F (191°C). Line a large plate with paper towels.

In a medium bowl, whisk together the rice flour and the remaining cornstarch. Working in batches, remove the squid from the marinade, shaking off any excess, then dip it into the rice flour mixture. Toss to coat, then shake off any excess and carefully lower the squid into the hot oil. Fry the squid, stirring occasionally with chopsticks to prevent the pieces from sticking together, until light golden brown and crisp, 3 to 4 minutes. With a spider, transfer the squid to the paper towel–lined plate. Repeat with the remaining squid, bringing the temperature back up to 375°F (191°C) between batches. If using the basil leaves, make sure they are completely dry before frying to avoid splatter. Fry the leaves until crispy and translucent, about 30 seconds, and transfer to the plate.

SEASON AND SERVE: While each batch of squid is still hot, toss it in the seasoning blend until evenly coated. Let the squid cool briefly before topping with the fried basil, if using, and serving with the sweet-and-sour sauce for dipping.

Steamed Sea Bass with Miso Leeks

Serves 4

2 large (750 g) leeks

1 pound (454 g) Chilean sea bass, cut into 4 square fillets

1 teaspoon kosher salt

½ teaspoon ground white pepper

2 tablespoons extra-virgin olive oil

1 cup (240 ml) water

1 tablespoon mirin

1 tablespoon soy sauce

1 tablespoon white miso paste

1 teaspoon sugar

¼ teaspoon crushed red chili flakes

Dark soy sauce

Perfect Steamed Jasmine Rice (page 286), for serving

A whole steamed fish is traditionally served at Lunar New Year because the Chinese word for "fish," *yu*, sounds a lot like the word for "abundance." But if you want to break from tradition every once in a while and you're not interested in cooking an entire fish, you can get meaty fillets of Chilean sea bass already trimmed and cleaned for you at the fish counter. With fillets, there's no stress about removing scales or pin bones. Chilean sea bass is a good choice for a special-occasion splurge because it has a silky yet hearty texture with a nice fattiness to it and cooks like a dream. (Black cod and red snapper make good, less pricey substitutes.) Here leeks braise beneath the fish, nearly melting into the flavorful broth while perfuming the fish as it cooks.

SLICE THE LEEKS: Trim off the root ends of the leeks and thinly slice the white and green parts. Transfer to a bowl and thoroughly rinse to remove any grit, then drain the leeks.

SEASON THE FISH: Pat the fish dry and season with ½ teaspoon of the salt and ¼ teaspoon of the white pepper.

STIR-FRY THE LEEKS: In a large skillet with a lid, heat the olive oil over medium-high heat. Add the leeks and stir-fry until golden brown around the edges, 5 to 6 minutes.

BRAISE: In a small bowl, whisk together the water, mirin, soy sauce, miso, sugar, chili flakes, remaining ½ teaspoon salt, and remaining ¼ teaspoon white pepper. Pour the miso mixture into the pan and bring to a simmer. Reduce the heat to medium-low or low, cover, and gently simmer the leeks until just tender, 10 minutes. Place the fish fillets on top of the leeks and cover the pan again. Simmer until the leeks are very tender and the fish is cooked through, 14 to 16 minutes.

SERVE: Transfer the fish to a serving platter and spoon the reduced sauce and braised leeks over the top. Serve with a drizzle of dark soy sauce over rice.

Steamed Dungeness Crabs with Tomato Butter

Serves 4 to 6

4 live Dungeness crabs (2½ to 3 pounds/1.13 to 1.36 kg each)

2 tablespoons extra-virgin olive oil

1 shallot, minced

1 (2-inch/5 cm) piece fresh ginger, peeled and minced

4 garlic cloves, minced

1 jalapeño, minced

1 large tomato (150 g), roughly chopped

1 tablespoon ketchup

1 teaspoon kosher salt

1 teaspoon sugar

1 teaspoon fish sauce

4 tablespoons (½ stick/57 g) unsalted butter, cut into cubes

As soon as Dungeness crab season rolls around, people in the Bay Area perk up. The season typically runs from early January to April. I patiently wait for my fishermen friends to call me up and ask if I'm interested in a few crabs. Neighbors I rarely see will even knock on my door to offer up a crab because somehow they have extra. The answer is always yes!

The meat of a freshly steamed crab is pure and delicious on its own. But a spoonful of slightly spicy tomato butter with some rice and flakes of crabmeat is truly otherworldly. Put any extra steamed crabs in the fridge and stir-fry them the next day with loads of green onions and ginger (see opposite page). Keep in mind that cracking the shells before stir-frying means that when it's time to eat, all you have to do is pull the shells off and lick all the flavor off your fingers.

If you don't have access to Dungeness crabs, smaller varieties of crab, lobster, and jumbo prawns would make great substitutes in this recipe.

STEAM THE CRABS: Fill a lidded large pot with water to a depth of 2 inches (5 cm) and bring to a boil. Depending on the size of the crabs and your pot, add 1 or 2 crabs to the boiling water and cover. Steam the crabs for 15 minutes (or 18 minutes, if they're on the larger side). Using tongs, transfer the crabs to a large rimmed baking sheet. Repeat with the remaining crabs, adding more water to the pot as needed.

CLEAN THE CRABS: When the crabs are cool enough to handle, remove the "apron" on the underside of each and open the body by grabbing the back end of the shell. The orange and creamy-looking "crab butter" in the top shell is delicious mixed with cooked rice or used as a dip for the crabmeat. Remove the gills, which are inedible, by scraping them from the main body with a spoon. Next, cut the legs and attached chambers apart.

MAKE THE TOMATO BUTTER: In a large pan, heat the olive oil over medium-high heat. Add the shallot, ginger, garlic, and jalapeño, tossing to combine. Cook until the aromatics are just starting to soften, 3 to 4 minutes. Stir in the tomato, ketchup, salt, sugar, and fish sauce and cook until the tomato is jammy and broken down, 5 to 7 minutes. Add the butter and stir until it has melted and everything is combined. Transfer the tomato butter to a small bowl.

CRACK THE SHELLS AND SERVE: Pick the meat from the chambers of the crab and remove the shells from the legs using a shell cracker. Serve the crabmeat with the tomato butter for dipping.

VARIATION

Steamed Crabs Stir-Fried with Chili Crunch and Ginger

Serves 4

In a large skillet, heat 2 tablespoons Chili Crunch (page 302, or store-bought) and 1 tablespoon olive oil over medium-high heat. Stir in the shredded whites of 4 green onions and 1 (2-inch/5 cm) piece fresh ginger, peeled and cut into matchsticks. Allow the aromatics to sizzle until just starting to soften, 3 to 4 minutes. Add 2 broken-down steamed crabs, 1 teaspoon curry powder, ½ teaspoon kosher salt, and ¼ teaspoon ground white pepper and toss until everything is evenly coated. Stir-fry until the crabs are warmed through, 4 to 5 minutes. Transfer to a platter, top with the shredded greens of the 4 green onions, and serve.

Vermicelli and Clams

Serves 4

2 pounds (908 g) Manila clams

2 tablespoons extra-virgin olive oil

8 garlic cloves, minced

2 cups (480 ml) water

2 tablespoons soy sauce

½ teaspoon sugar

¼ teaspoon ground white pepper

2 bundles (4 ounces/120 g) fun see (thin bean thread noodles)

2 green onions, thinly sliced

XO Sauce (page 303; optional)

Much like Italian linguine and clams, this dish is best enjoyed along the water, with the sun shining and a glass of wine in hand. But it's also delicious eaten in your kitchen, straight out of the pot. This is a popular menu offering in Hong Kong, especially among the restaurants on the smaller islands. Starch-based noodles like glass vermicelli have the superpower of soaking up liquid while maintaining their bouncy texture. As the clams steam, the noodles absorb the extra broth, and by the time the shells fully open, they're infused with intense garlicky flavor. If you're craving a little heat, a drizzle of XO sauce complements the briny seafood flavor and puts this right over the top.

CLEAN THE CLAMS: Rinse the clams to remove any grit. Discard any clams that are cracked or already open.

STEAM THE CLAMS: In a large braiser or heavy-bottomed pot with a lid, heat the olive oil over medium heat. Stir the garlic into the oil and let it gently sizzle until softened and just starting to brown, 4 to 7 minutes. Stir in the water, soy sauce, sugar, and white pepper and bring to a simmer. Add the fun see and clams. Reduce the heat to maintain a simmer, cover, and steam until the clams open, 7 to 8 minutes.

SERVE: Remove the lid and, using tongs, discard any unopened clams, then toss the noodles with the clams. Top with the green onions and serve, drizzled with XO sauce, if you like.

Beer Mussels with Sambal and Lime

Serves 4 to 6

2 pounds (908 g) mussels

1 tablespoon extra-virgin olive oil

4 garlic cloves, smashed and peeled

1 (1-inch/2.5 cm) piece fresh ginger, smashed

⅔ cup (160 ml) beer (wit, saison, or sour)

¼ cup (60 ml) fresh lime juice (from 2 to 3 large limes)

2 tablespoons sambal oelek

1 tablespoon fish sauce

2 teaspoons brown sugar

¼ teaspoon kosher salt

Roughly chopped fresh cilantro

Mussels are a "treat yourself, but don't work too hard" meal. This is a dinner that feels special and impressive, but takes only 15 minutes to prepare. When I think of mussels, two images come to mind: the cart that gets pushed around at dim sum that brings freshly stir-fried mussels to the table, and a heaping pot of beer-steamed mussels and french fries in a very dimly lit beer bar. You could say this dish is a combination of the two. A Belgian witbier is a reliable option for this recipe because it lacks bitterness and is generally crisp in flavor. A saison also works well, but the acidity from a fruity sour beer is a stunning flavor pairing with the tart lime and spicy sambal oelek. While you're enjoying the mussels, don't waste a drop of the broth. Dunk sourdough bread in it or spoon it over San Francisco Garlic Noodles (page 90) for a truly satisfying meal.

CLEAN THE MUSSELS: Rinse the mussels to remove any grit and remove their beards, if they have any. Discard any mussels that are cracked or already open.

STEAM: In a large heavy-bottomed pot, heat the olive oil over medium heat. Stir in the garlic and ginger. Sizzle until the aromatics are softened and starting to brown, 4 to 6 minutes. Add the beer, lime juice, sambal, fish sauce, brown sugar, and salt. Stir and bring to a simmer. Immediately add the mussels, reduce the heat to maintain a simmer, and cover. Steam the mussels until they open, 7 to 8 minutes; discard any that don't fully open.

SERVE: Top the mussels with the cilantro and serve.

Buddha's Delight

Serves 4 to 6

8 medium dried shiitake mushrooms (2 ounces/65 g)

Neutral oil, such as grapeseed, for frying

4 dried bean sticks (2.5 ounces/75 g), broken into 2-inch (5 cm) pieces

2 tablespoons extra-virgin olive oil

1 (2-inch/5 cm) piece fresh ginger, peeled and thinly sliced

4 garlic cloves, thinly sliced

4 green onions, whites and greens separated and sliced on a bias

2 cups (480 ml) water

2 tablespoons soy sauce

2 tablespoons doubanjiang

½ teaspoon kosher salt

½ teaspoon ground white pepper

2 bundles (4 ounces/120 g) bean thread noodles

4 medium bok choy, halved or quartered

8 ounces (227 g) spiced pressed tofu, cut into strips

A dish made popular by monks, Buddha's delight is traditionally eaten on Lunar New Year's Day, when it's customary to stick to a strictly vegetarian diet for the day to welcome good luck. This version features four different bean-centric ingredients: bean stick, doubanjiang (spicy broad bean paste), bean thread noodles, and pressed tofu (made from soybeans). I learned from my mom to lightly fry the bean stick first, which causes it to blister and puff up like a chicharron (fried pork rind), the better to soak up all the flavors of the braise. You don't have to wait for Lunar New Year to experience this dish—it's delicious all year round.

SOAK THE MUSHROOMS: In a heatproof medium bowl, cover the mushrooms with hot water and weight them down with a heavy plate or bowl to keep them submerged. Soak the mushrooms until they are plump and hydrated, 30 to 45 minutes. Drain and squeeze out any excess water. Trim off and discard the stems and cut the caps in half.

FRY THE BEAN STICKS: Line a plate with paper towels. In a medium skillet, heat about 1 inch (2.5 cm) of neutral oil over medium-high heat. Test the temperature by dipping a wooden chopstick in the oil: if tiny bubbles appear around the chopstick, the oil is hot enough. When the oil is hot, carefully add the bean sticks and fry until blistered, 30 to 60 seconds. Use tongs or chopsticks to transfer the bean sticks to the paper towel–lined plate.

PREPARE THE BRAISE: In a large heavy-bottomed pot with a lid, heat the olive oil over medium heat. Stir in the ginger, garlic, and green onion whites and allow the aromatics to gently sizzle until they're just starting to soften and brown around the edges, 4 to 6 minutes. Add the water, soy sauce, doubanjiang, salt, and white pepper. Stir to combine and bring the mixture to a simmer. Tuck the noodles into the braising liquid and arrange the bean sticks, mushrooms, bok choy, and tofu in the pot. Reduce the heat to maintain a simmer, cover, and simmer until the noodles are tender and most of the liquid has been absorbed by the noodles or evaporated, about 10 minutes.

SERVE: Remove the lid and toss the noodles with a pair of tongs. Top with the green onion greens and serve.

Cooking for people is one of the most generous acts of service, but cooking *with* people is way more fun! Most people are more than eager to lend a hand in the kitchen, especially if it's an opportunity to learn a new dish or if you're making something they may be intimidated to try on their own. This chapter is filled with recipes that benefit from assembly-line-style production—think golden spring rolls and a bounty of wontons. Clear the table, turn on some tunes, pour a few drinks (which might affect quality control over time, so be warned), assign your stations, and make it a party. With a few extra hands on deck, you'll have a mountain of crispy-bottomed dumplings in no time. Cooking together is the perfect opportunity to catch up on gossip, start a little friendly competition, or just teach a new kitchen skill to friends and family.

Cho Family Dumplings

Makes 48 dumplings

For the dough

4 cups (500 g) all-purpose flour, plus more as needed

½ teaspoon kosher salt

1 cup plus 2 tablespoons (270 ml) just-boiled water, plus more if needed

For the filling

1 pound (454 g) ground pork

1 pound (454 g) shrimp, peeled, deveined, and minced

4 cups (240 g) finely shredded cabbage

6 green onions, chopped

2 tablespoons oyster sauce

2 teaspoons toasted sesame oil

1 teaspoon kosher salt

1 teaspoon sugar

½ teaspoon ground white pepper

Olive oil

Chili Crunch (page 302, or store-bought), for serving

Dumpling Dip (page 306), for serving

XO Sauce (page 303), for serving

My family's dumplings are as classic as they come. They might even look a lot like your family's dumplings. The filling is a succulent combination of pork and shrimp. A juicy dumpling relies on vegetables with a high water content, such as cabbage, which adds lightness and moisture to the mix here, balancing the fatty meat. Homemade dumpling dough is what sets an extraordinary dumpling apart from an average one. Store-bought wrappers never give you the toothsome chew of a dough you knead yourself. In my family, we prefer a slightly higher ratio of dough to filling, and my dad is the master at rolling out dumpling wrappers with thin edges and a plump center (see page 233).

If it's your first time making homemade dumpling dough, measure the ingredients with a digital scale to ensure the right consistency. If you covet a crunchy, blistered dumpling bottom, you can pan-fry the dumplings, but they're equally delicious steamed or boiled.

MAKE THE DOUGH: In a large bowl, whisk together the flour and salt, then pour in the hot water. With a flexible spatula, mix to form a shaggy dough, less than a minute. In the bowl or on the counter, knead until you have a smoothish dough (it should be tacky but not stick to your hands), 5 to 6 minutes. If the dough feels too dry, add a tablespoon of hot water (or a little more if needed); if it's too sticky, add a tablespoon of flour (or a little more if needed). Form the dough into a ball and wrap tightly in plastic wrap. Let the dough rest at room temperature for at least 30 minutes and up to 2 hours, or in the fridge overnight.

MAKE THE FILLING: In a large bowl, mix the pork, shrimp, cabbage, green onions, oyster sauce, sesame oil, salt, sugar, and white pepper with a flexible spatula. Cover the bowl and refrigerate until you're ready to assemble the dumplings.

WRAP THE DUMPLINGS: Line a large rimmed baking sheet with parchment paper. Unwrap the dough and divide it in half; rewrap one half and set aside. Form the other half into a 1-inch-thick (2.5 cm) log. With a bench scraper or knife, divide the log into 24 equal pieces. (The easiest way to do this is to divide the log into eighths by repeatedly cutting the dough portions in half, and then divide each eighth into thirds. Math is useful after all!)

Working with one piece of dough at a time (keep the remaining pieces covered with a clean towel), pinch the dough into a round resembling a thick coin. On a work surface lightly dusted with flour, flatten the dough with your palm, then use a dowel rolling pin to roll it into a 4-inch (10 cm) round. Lift the dough round off the work surface (use the bench scraper to help, if needed) and hold it in the palm of your nondominant hand. Place a heaping tablespoon of the filling in the center. Carefully bring the edges of the dough together and pleat to enclose the filling (to choose a pleat style, see page 234), then place the dumpling on the prepared baking sheet. Repeat with the remaining dough and filling.

To pan-fry the dumplings: In a large nonstick pan or well-seasoned cast-iron pan, heat 2 tablespoons olive oil over medium heat. Working in batches, arrange the dumplings in the pan. You should hear a gentle sizzle when they hit the pan; if the oil is crackling too loudly, reduce the heat slightly. Fry the dumplings until the bottoms are lightly golden brown, 1 to 2 minutes. Hover a fitted lid over the pan (to protect yourself from splatter) and carefully pour in ¼ cup (60 ml) water. Cover the pan with the lid, reduce the heat to medium, and steam the dumplings for 7 minutes. If the water evaporates too quickly, add another tablespoon to the pan. Remove the lid and cook until any remaining moisture boils off and the bottoms of the dumplings are crisp again, 1 to 2 minutes. Transfer the dumplings to a platter, bottom-side up so they don't get soggy, and allow to cool for a few minutes. Repeat with the remaining dumplings, adding a little more oil to the pan between batches.

To steam the dumplings: Set up a bamboo steamer (see page 25). Brush the steamer with olive oil or line it with parchment paper so the dumplings won't stick. Working in batches, arrange the dumplings in the steamer; they can be close together but should not be touching. Cover with the lid and set the steamer over the simmering water. Steam for 7 to 8 minutes, then remove the steamer basket and set it on a wire rack. Remove the lid and transfer the dumplings to a platter to cool for a few minutes. Repeat with the remaining dumplings, adding more water to the pot as needed.

To boil the dumplings: Bring a large pot of water to a boil. Add a batch of dumplings to the water (the number depends on the size of your pot, but I normally do 8 to 10 at a time—try not to add too many, which will bring down the water temperature too much). Stir the pot so the dumplings don't stick to the bottom, and boil for 7 to 8 minutes. They will start to float before the filling is finished cooking. Scoop the dumplings out of the water with a spider, shake off any excess water, and transfer to a platter to cool for a few minutes. Repeat with the remaining dumplings, adding more water to the pot if needed.

SERVE: Serve the dumplings with the chili crunch, dumpling dip, and XO sauce for dipping.

NOTE: *If any of your dumplings have small tears or are not completely sealed, avoid boiling them because they will burst in the pot. Stick to pan-frying or steaming them instead!*

HOW TO FREEZE DUMPLINGS

Homemade dumplings freeze beautifully. Place a tray of raw dumplings in the freezer (no need to cover) and freeze until solid, about 2 hours. Transfer the dumplings to a zip-top bag and store in the freezer for up to 3 months. You can cook the frozen dumplings just as you would freshly made ones—*never* defrost frozen dumplings before cooking, unless you want a goopy mess. To boil or steam frozen dumplings, increase the cooking time to 12 to 15 minutes; to pan-fry, increase the water to ⅓ cup (80 ml) and steam with the lid on for 12 to 13 minutes.

Divide and Conquer: Dumplings

Some of my happiest memories with my family involve making dumplings. Everyone has a specific role in the assembly process. My mom prepares the filling and cooks the formed dumplings; my dad rolls out dumpling wrappers at lightning speed; I pleat them as uniformly as my fingers can manage; and my brother is there to provide comic relief with his attempts at pleating (but he's really there to eat the dumplings, and so is my husband). Making dumplings will always be my favorite group-bonding activity. If you're craving connection, invite people to your house to make dumplings, and you'll be surprised how much your community will grow.

Stations/Responsibilities

dough team   rolling team   filling team   pleating team   cooking team

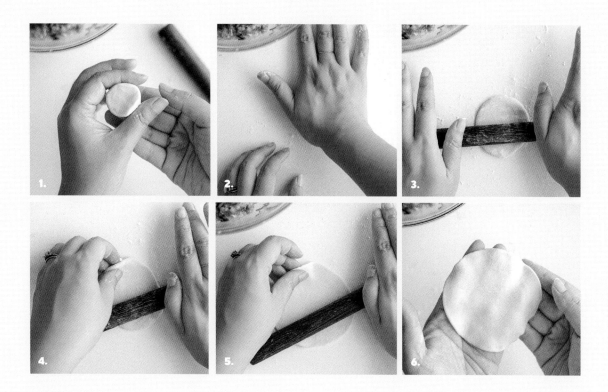

The Wrappers

1. Pinch the dough into a round resembling a thick coin.
2. Flatten the dough with your palm.
3. Place the rolling pin over the center of the dough. Apply pressure on the rolling pin with your hand and roll the pin outward toward the edge of the dough.
4. Rotate the dough counterclockwise about 30 degrees.
5. Place the rolling pin back over the center of the dough and repeat the rolling-and-rotating process again and again, until you have a dumpling wrapper that is about 4 inches (10 cm) in diameter. Focus on applying more pressure around the edge of the wrapper to make it thinner than the center.
6. Lift the wrapper off the counter and start pleating!

The Classic Pleat

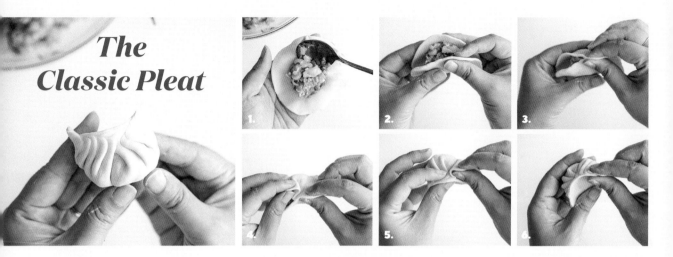

1. Place a heaping tablespoon of filling in the center of the wrapper.
2. Fold the wrapper in half like a mini taco.
3. Pinch the very top of the taco (the top edges of the wrapper) together until the dough sticks.
4. Bring the right edge of the dumpling wrapper over to the center (where you just pinched) and pinch it in place to create your first pleat. Repeat on the same side three or four times until the right side is fully pleated.
5. Do the same on the left side.
6. Pinch the edge of the dumpling so it is thin and fully sealed.

The Braid

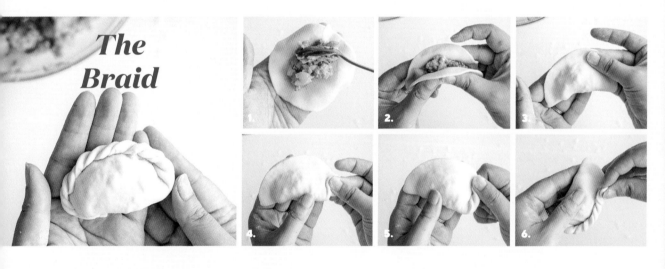

1. Place a heaping tablespoon of filling in the center of the wrapper.
2. Fold the wrapper in half to form a half-moon.
3. Pinch the edges closed to fully seal.
4. Hold the dumpling in your nondominant hand with the flat edge facing you.
5. With your dominant hand, fold the rounded edge of the wrapper onto itself, creating a twist.
6. Repeat this motion, following the curve of the dumpling, until the whole edge is twisted.

The Squiggle

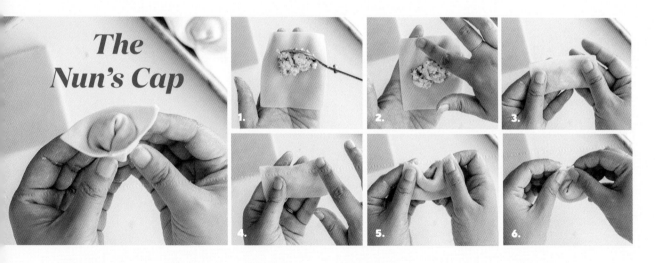

1. Place a heaping tablespoon of filling in the center of the wrapper.
2. Fold the wrapper in half to form a half-moon.
3. Pinch the edges closed to fully seal.
4. Bend the pinched edge of the dumpling wrapper into a wave or squiggle pattern, gently pinching it where the folds form to hold them in place.
5. Repeat the fold back and forth to form a squiggle.

The Nun's Cap

1. Place a heaping teaspoon of filling in the center of the wrapper.
2. Dab your finger in some water and wet the edges of the wrapper.
3. Fold the wrapper in half and pinch the edges closed to fully seal.
4. Hold the dumpling in your nondominant hand with the folded edge facing away from you.
5. Fold in your middle or index finger of the hand holding the dumpling and dent the belly of the dumpling.
6. Bring the two far corners of the dumpling together, overlapping them slightly, and pinch until the dough sticks.

Your Own Family Dumplings

I challenge you to create your own family dumplings. This nearly foolproof equation for dumpling filling will accommodate whatever ingredients you have: all work perfectly well. It could be ground pork one week and turkey the next; if cabbage isn't available, Tuscan kale or chrysanthemum greens could easily take its place. Beyond the availability of ingredients, this dumpling equation is flexible enough to accommodate a range of individual flavor and dietary preferences, too—just fill in the blanks with whichever protein, vegetables, aromatics, and so on you prefer.

The recipe is straightforward and forgiving, and the combinations are endless. How about duck and leek dumplings? Yes, please! Caramelized onion venison dumplings with charred cabbage? I'll take a dozen!

Make Your Own Dumplings Recipe Card

2 pounds (908 g) _____
(PROTEIN)

4 cups (about 300 g) _____
(HEARTY VEGETABLE)

1½ cups (129 g) _____
(AROMATICS)

2 tablespoons _____
(DARK BROWN ASIAN SAUCE)

1 tablespoon _____
(SOMETHING SPICY)

MUST-HAVE SEASONINGS:

2 teaspoons sesame oil   1 teaspoon coarse salt

1 teaspoon sugar   ½ teaspoon ground white pepper

Here are some ideas to get you started:

The Sweet and Spicy Bird
Ground turkey + grated sweet potato + leeks + hoisin + doubanjiang + must-have seasonings

Down-to-Earth Dumplings
Lamb + mushrooms + caramelized onions + dark soy sauce + chili crunch + must-have seasonings + 1 teaspoon ground cumin

The Fresh Catch
Salmon + bok choy + fresh basil + fish sauce + sriracha + must-have seasonings

Choose one from each list:

PROTEINS	ground chicken, ground turkey, ground lamb, ground plant-based meat, crumbled extra-firm tofu, finely chopped shrimp, finely chopped fish
HEARTY VEGETABLES	shredded kale, grated carrots, grated zucchini, minced mushrooms, finely chopped bok choy
AROMATICS	any onion, leeks, Chinese garlic chives (add a little minced garlic or ginger, if you like)
DARK BROWN ASIAN SAUCES	oyster sauce, hoisin, fish sauce, soy sauce, dark soy sauce
SOMETHING SPICY	sriracha, sambal oelek, Chili Crunch (page 302), XO Sauce (page 303), doubanjiang, 1 teaspoon crushed red chili flakes, minced fresh chilis
MUST-HAVE SEASONINGS	sesame oil, sugar, coarse salt, ground white pepper

Chicken, Corn, and Jalapeño Wontons with Miso Butter

Makes 48 wontons

For the wontons

1 pound (454 g) boneless, skinless chicken thighs

1½ cups (180 g) fresh, frozen, or canned corn kernels (drained, if canned)

1 jalapeño, minced

⅓ cup (15 g) fresh basil, thinly sliced

2 tablespoons oyster sauce

1 teaspoon sugar

1 teaspoon kosher salt

½ teaspoon ground white pepper

48 store-bought medium-thick wonton wrappers

For the miso butter

8 tablespoons (1 stick/113 g) unsalted butter

2 tablespoons white miso paste

1 tablespoon soy sauce

Green onions, thinly sliced on a bias

Toasted sesame seeds

If you could wrap up summer in a dumpling, it would taste like these sweet, spicy, and buttery wontons. The aromatic basil, sweet summer corn, and extra-spicy jalapeño will make you want to keep a stockpile of these in your freezer all year long. After they're cooked, the slippery, meaty wontons are tossed in a rich miso butter sauce that manages to heighten (rather than muddle) all the fresh flavors. On a cool night, serve these as a wonton soup with the Tomato Kombu Broth (page 301) or Scrappy Chicken Stock (page 300), and add a bundle of thin egg noodles to the bowl while you're at it.

MAKE THE FILLING: Place the chicken thighs in a food processor. Pulse a few times to break them down into a thick, chunky paste. Transfer the chicken to a large bowl. Add the corn, jalapeño, basil, oyster sauce, sugar, salt, and white pepper and mix with a flexible spatula until combined. Cover and refrigerate until you're ready to assemble the wontons, up to 1 day.

ASSEMBLE THE WONTONS: Line a large rimmed baking sheet with parchment paper and fill a small bowl with water. Working with one at a time, fill each wonton wrapper with a heaping teaspoon of the filling (avoid overfilling them, which will cause the wontons to burst). Dip your fingertip in the water and run it over the edges of the wrapper. Fold the wrapper in half, pushing out any air that may be trapped in the filling and pressing the edges to firmly seal. Bring the two folded corners of the wonton together to form a nun's cap dumpling (see page 235). Place the wonton on the prepared baking sheet and repeat with the remaining wrappers and filling.

COOK THE WONTONS: Bring a large pot of water to a boil. Add a batch of wontons to the water (the number will depend on the size of your pot; I normally cook 12 to 16 at a time—try not to add too many, which will bring down the water temperature too much). Stir so the wontons don't stick to the bottom, and boil for 7 to 8 minutes. They will start to float before the filling has finished cooking. Using a spider, scoop out the wontons, shake off excess water, and transfer to a platter to cool for a few minutes. Repeat with the remaining wontons.

MAKE THE MISO BUTTER: In a large pan, melt the butter over medium-low heat. Whisk in the miso until incorporated, then add the soy sauce and whisk until smooth.

SERVE: Pour the miso butter over the platter of just-cooked wontons and toss to combine. Top with green onions and sesame seeds and serve.

<u>VARIATION</u>

Chicken, Corn, and Jalapeño Wonton Soup

Serves 4

8 cups (1.92 L) Tomato Kombu Broth (page 301) or Scrappy Chicken Stock (page 300)

4 baby bok choy, halved lengthwise

48 Chicken, Corn, and Jalapeño Wontons (opposite page), cooked

Thinly sliced green onions, for topping

Fried Garlic (page 310), for topping

In a large pot, bring the kombu broth to a simmer over medium-high heat. Reduce the heat to medium-low and add the bok choy. Simmer until the bok choy is tender, 5 to 8 minutes. Turn off the heat and allow the soup to cool for a few minutes. Fill individual bowls with the cooked wontons and top with the bok choy. Pour the soup into the bowls and serve topped with green onions and fried garlic.

Mapo Tofu Wontons

Makes 48 wontons

For the filling

1 (16-ounce/454 g) block extra-firm tofu

1 (2-inch/5 cm) piece fresh ginger, peeled and grated

4 green onions, finely chopped, plus 1 thinly sliced on a bias

2 tablespoons cornstarch

1 tablespoon doubanjiang

1 tablespoon Chili Crunch (page 302, or store-bought)

1 teaspoon finely ground Sichuan peppercorns

1 teaspoon toasted sesame oil

1 teaspoon kosher salt

½ teaspoon ground white pepper

48 store-bought medium-thick wonton wrappers

For the sauce

2 tablespoons extra-virgin olive oil

¾ pound (340 g) mushrooms, such as oyster, maitake, or brown beech, torn apart

1 tablespoon doubanjiang

1 tablespoon Chili Crunch (page 302, or store-bought)

(ingredients continue)

Whether you eat meat or not, chances are you'll be fighting for the last of these vegan wontons. Mapo tofu is typically made with ground pork and silken tofu, but here meaty mushrooms take the place of the pork. These wontons are on the spicy side, but not overwhelmingly so. They're folded into a classic shape known as the nun's cap (see page 235), a little cup that captures the perfect amount of fiery mapo sauce in each bite.

For this recipe, use store-bought wonton wrappers. Make sure to buy thick or at least medium-thick wonton wrappers; the thin wrappers are much too delicate and tend to disintegrate when boiled.

MAKE THE FILLING: Drain the tofu by cutting slits in the packaging and pouring out the water. Wrap the tofu in paper towels and press by setting a cutting board with a heavy object on top, to remove excess moisture, about 15 minutes. Working over a large bowl, crumble the tofu into small pieces by hand (the pieces will continue to break down when you mix the filling). Add the ginger, chopped green onions, cornstarch, doubanjiang, chili crunch, Sichuan peppercorns, sesame oil, salt, and white pepper and mix until well combined.

ASSEMBLE THE WONTONS: Line a large rimmed baking sheet with parchment paper and fill a small bowl with water. Working with one at a time, fill each wonton wrapper with a heaping teaspoon of the filling (avoid overfilling them, which will cause the wontons to burst). Dip your fingertip in the water and run it over the edges of the wrapper. Fold the wrapper in half, pushing out any air that may be trapped in the filling and pressing the edges firmly to seal. Bring the two folded corners of the wonton together to form a nun's cap dumpling (see page 235). Place the wonton on the prepared baking sheet and repeat with the remaining wrappers and filling. If you have any filling left over, you can add that directly to the sauce if you like, or store it in the fridge for up to 3 days to use for more wontons later.

COOK THE WONTONS: Bring a large pot of water to a boil. Add a batch of wontons to the water (the number will depend on the size of your pot; I normally cook 12 to 16 at a time—try not to add too

1 teaspoon toasted sesame oil

1 teaspoon sugar

½ teaspoon kosher salt

½ teaspoon ground white pepper

2 cups (480 ml) water

2 teaspoons cornstarch

many, which will bring down the water temperature too much). Stir so the wontons don't stick to the bottom, and boil until they float to the top, 5 to 6 minutes. Using a spider, scoop the wontons out of the water, shake off excess water, and transfer to a platter to cool for a few minutes. Repeat with the remaining wontons.

MAKE THE SAUCE: In a large skillet or cast-iron pan, heat the olive oil over medium-high heat. Add the mushrooms in a single layer and sear, pressing down on the mushrooms with a spatula or setting a heavy pan on them as they cook, until the bottoms are crisp and deep golden brown, 5 to 7 minutes. Flip the mushrooms and sear until crisp and golden brown on the other side, 5 to 7 minutes. Reduce the heat to medium. If you have any extra filling, this is the time to add it to the sauce. Add the doubanjiang, chili crunch, sesame oil, sugar, salt, and white pepper and toss to combine.

In a glass measuring cup, whisk together the water and cornstarch to make a slurry. Pour the slurry over the mushrooms and gently stir the sauce as it simmers and starts to thicken. Reduce the heat to maintain a gentle simmer and cook for about 10 minutes to reduce.

SERVE: Pour the sauce over the wontons to cover. Top with the bias-cut green onion and serve immediately.

HOW TO FREEZE AND REHEAT WONTONS

Place the uncooked wontons on a parchment-lined baking sheet and freeze until solid, about 1 hour. Transfer the wontons to a resealable container and store in the freezer for up to 6 months. Pan-fry, boil, or steam the frozen wontons just as you would freshly made ones; just allow 3 to 5 minutes more cooking time to make sure the filling is fully cooked. Never defrost frozen wontons before cooking.

Fun Kor (Vegetable Crystal Dumplings)

Makes 48 dumplings

4 dried shiitake mushrooms

⅓ cup (55 g) skin-on Chinese peanuts

2 tablespoons extra-virgin olive oil

1½ cups (150 g) finely chopped celery (from about 3 stalks)

1 (8-ounce/226 g) can water chestnuts, drained and minced

4 green onions, finely chopped

1½ cups (360 ml) water

2 tablespoons cornstarch

2 tablespoons soy sauce

1 tablespoon Shaoxing wine

½ teaspoon kosher salt

½ teaspoon ground white pepper

2¼ cups (270 g) wheat starch, plus more as needed

⅔ cup (75 g) tapioca starch

⅔ cup (75 g) sweet potato starch

½ teaspoon ground turmeric (optional)

(ingredients continue)

There's an overwhelming number of dumplings to choose from when you go out for dim sum, but the array of crystal dumplings gleams the brightest. The most famous of these are har gow (crystal shrimp dumplings). They look like little gems, and through their translucent skin, you can catch a glimpse of the filling inside. The dough is made with a blend of starches that produces the dumplings' glassy appearance and bouncy chew. Each of the starches contributes a specific property to the dough: wheat starch provides structure, making the dough easier to handle; sweet potato starch creates a more translucent dough; and tapioca starch gives the dumplings a tender softness and slight stretch. A touch of turmeric transforms their appearance from diamond-like to amberish (you can leave it out, if you wish). Fun kor is a Teochew style of crystal dumpling; it is lesser known but no less delicious. The filling is a blend of vegetables and crunchy peanuts, all bound together in a luscious sauce that melts within the wrapper while it steams.

PREP THE MUSHROOMS: Place the shiitakes in a heatproof medium bowl and cover with just-boiled water. Weight down the mushrooms with a heavy plate or bowl and soak until pliable and rehydrated, 45 to 60 minutes. Drain the mushrooms, squeezing out any excess water, then trim off and discard the stems and mince the caps.

TOAST THE PEANUTS: Heat a large skillet over medium heat. Add the peanuts and toast, shaking the pan frequently, until fragrant and lightly toasted, 6 to 8 minutes. Transfer to a bowl and let the peanuts cool completely, then roughly chop them.

MAKE THE FILLING: In the same skillet, heat the olive oil over medium heat. Add the celery, water chestnuts, mushrooms, and green onions. Stir to combine and cook until the vegetables just start to soften, 3 to 5 minutes. In a glass measuring cup, stir together the water, cornstarch, soy sauce, Shaoxing wine, salt, and white pepper. Pour the mixture into the pan and cook, gently

½ teaspoon kosher salt

1¼ cups (300 ml) boiling water

3 tablespoons canola oil, plus more if needed

To serve
Chili Crunch (page 302, or store-bought)

Dumpling Dip (page 306)

XO Sauce (page 303)

stirring, until the sauce comes to a simmer and thickens, 1 to 2 minutes. Transfer to a heatproof bowl, then add the chopped peanuts and combine. Cover the bowl with plastic wrap and refrigerate until the filling is completely cool, about 1 hour; the chilled filling should be firm and scoopable.

MAKE THE DOUGH: In a large bowl, whisk together the wheat starch, tapioca starch, sweet potato starch, turmeric (if using), and salt. Pour the boiling water over the starches; do not mix. Immediately cover with plastic wrap and steam for 15 minutes. Uncover the bowl and add the canola oil, mixing with a flexible spatula to form a shaggy dough. Knead the dough in the bowl or on the counter until it is very smooth and not at all sticky (it should feel like Play-Doh), 1 to 2 minutes. Form the dough into a ball. It is now ready to use, but if you aren't assembling your dumplings right away, wrap the dough tightly in plastic wrap and let it rest at room temperature for up to 2 hours (any longer, and it may dry out).

ASSEMBLE THE DUMPLINGS: Line a large rimmed baking sheet with parchment paper. Unwrap the dough and divide it in half; rewrap one half and set aside. Form the other half into a 1-inch-thick (2.5 cm) log. With a bench scraper, divide the dough into 24 equal pieces. (The easiest way to do this is to divide the log into eighths by repeatedly cutting the dough portions in half, and then divide each eighth into thirds. Math is useful after all!)

Working with one piece of dough at a time (keep the remaining pieces covered with a clean towel), roll the dough into a smooth ball. On a work surface lightly dusted with wheat starch, flatten the dough with your palm, then use a dowel rolling pin to roll it into a 4-inch (10 cm) round. Lift the dough round off the work surface (use the bench scraper to help, if needed), hold it in the palm of your nondominant hand, and place a heaping tablespoon of the filling in the center. Carefully bring the edges of the dough together and pleat to enclose the filling (to choose a pleat style, see page 234), then place the dumpling on the prepared baking sheet. Repeat with the remaining dough and filling.

STEAM THE DUMPLINGS: Set up a bamboo steamer (see page 25). Brush the steamer with canola oil or line it with a round of parchment paper so the dumplings won't stick. Working in batches, arrange the dumplings in the steamer;

they can be close together but should not be touching. Cover with the lid and set the steamer over the simmering water. Steam for 7 to 8 minutes. Remove the steamer basket and set it on a wire rack. Remove the lid and allow the dumplings to cool for a few minutes before touching them (they will be very sticky at first), then transfer them to a platter. Repeat with the remaining dumplings, adding more water to the pot as needed. Serve with the dipping sauces.

Hom Chi
(Fried Glutinous Rice Potato Dumplings)

Makes 28 dumplings

For the filling

½ cup (40 g) dried shrimp

2 tablespoons extra-virgin olive oil

1 large kohlrabi (about 180 g), peeled and finely diced

4 green onions, thinly sliced

½ pound (227 g) ground pork

1 tablespoon olive vegetable paste

1 tablespoon oyster sauce

1½ teaspoons kosher salt

1 teaspoon sugar

½ teaspoon Chinese five spice powder

½ teaspoon ground white pepper

For the dough

2 medium russet potatoes (327 g), peeled and cut into large chunks

3 cups (400 g) glutinous rice flour, plus more if needed

2 tablespoons canola oil, plus more if needed

Sesame seeds, for topping

Neutral oil, for frying

The dough for these Toisan-style fried dumplings is made with potatoes and glutinous rice flour and stuffed with salty pork and dried shrimp. As a kid (and still today), I looked forward to the few times a year my pau pau would make a giant batch for the family.

Hom chi are similar to pierogi, but the process for forming them is unlike any other type of dumpling. You mold a piece of dough into a hollow bell shape, like a coin pouch, and then spoon the filling inside. My pau pau typically adds finely chopped pickled mustard greens to the filling, but I add a spoonful of olive vegetable paste. This Chinese condiment is also made with pickled mustard greens, but the addition of fermented olives lends a slightly intense savory flavor to the filling; you can buy olive vegetable paste at most Chinese grocery stores. Straight from the oil, these dumplings are delicately crispy, but if you let them cool the texture gets pleasantly chewy.

SOAK THE SHRIMP: Place the shrimp in a small heatproof bowl. Cover with hot water and let soak for 30 minutes. Drain and mince the shrimp.

MAKE THE FILLING: In a large skillet, heat the olive oil over medium-high heat. Add the shrimp, kohlrabi, and green onions. Stir-fry until the mixture is fragrant and the green onions start to lightly brown, 5 to 6 minutes. Add the pork and break it up with the edge of a spatula. Add the olive vegetable paste, oyster sauce, salt, sugar, five spice, and white pepper and stir to combine. Cook, stirring frequently, until the pork is browned and cooked through, 5 to 7 minutes. Transfer the filling to a bowl and let cool completely.

MAKE THE DOUGH: Bring a large pot of water to a boil. Add the potatoes and boil until very tender, about 20 minutes. With a spider, scoop out the potatoes, shake off any excess water, and transfer to a large bowl. Measure out and reserve 1½ cups (360 ml) of the starchy cooking water. Using a balloon whisk or masher (or a stand mixer fitted with the paddle attachment), mash the potatoes until very smooth. While the potatoes are still hot, add the rice flour, reserved potato cooking water, and canola oil and mix with a flexible spatula to form a shaggy dough, about 1 minute. Knead the dough in the bowl or on the counter until very smooth, 2 to 3 minutes. If the dough feels too dry, add another tablespoon of hot water (or a little more, if needed); if the dough feels too sticky, add another tablespoon of rice flour (or a little more, if needed). Transfer the dough to a clean bowl and lightly coat with oil to keep it from drying out.

FORM THE DUMPLINGS: Line a large rimmed baking sheet with parchment paper. Pinch off a golf ball–size piece of dough and roll it between your hands until smooth. Flatten the dough between your palms. Holding the flattened dough in the palm of your nondominant hand, press your other thumb into the dough while slowly rotating it around the thumb to create a tubular shape in your palm. Fill the tube of dough with a heaping tablespoon of the cooled pork mixture and pinch the open end closed, tearing off any excess dough (you can use it for the next dumpling). Gently roll the filled dough between your hands to form a football-shaped dumpling, then place it on the prepared baking sheet. Repeat with the remaining dough and filling. When all the dumplings have been formed, dab a little water on top of each and sprinkle with a few sesame seeds.

FRY THE DUMPLINGS: Set a wire rack over a rimmed baking sheet or large plate. In a large heavy-bottomed pot, heat 3 inches (7.5 cm) of canola oil to 360°F (182°C). Working in batches, carefully drop the dumplings into the hot oil one at a time, giving them a gentle nudge with chopsticks so they don't stick to the bottom of the pot or to each other. Fry until the dumplings are golden brown and float to the top, about 3 minutes. Using a spider, scoop the dumplings out of the oil and transfer to the rack. Repeat with the remaining dumplings.

SERVE: Enjoy the dumplings while they are fresh and crispy, or at room temperature (the texture gets chewier as they cool).

A Glimpse of the Past

Sitting around a big table, forming dumplings by hand for hours with your friends and family, allows unique opportunities for stories to be shared. The first time my pau pau taught me how to make her Hom Chi (page 251) was one of the only times I've ever heard her speak about her parents, my great-grandparents. My pau pau insisted I practice over and over again with a single piece of dough until I had shaped the wrapper just right, because that's the way she was taught. As I fiddled away with the dough, she shared that her mother, a cold woman who valued her sons more than her daughters, had never taught her to cook. Instead, my pau pau had relied on her village aunties to teach her their ways in the kitchen and how to navigate life. She also told me about her father, a gentle farmer who loved her dearly. His love for her made life more tolerable, especially at a time when simply being a young woman was hard enough.

A story like this is something my pau pau would never have shared with me if we were simply sitting in front of the television. Working side by side with her and hearing her stories gave me insight into who she was, beyond simply the stoic and strong woman I'd always known. These days, when I make old-world recipes like hom chi, I imagine how the dumplings I'm eating must taste similar to the dumplings my pau pau learned to make eighty years ago; maybe hers even looked imperfect like mine. There are moments when I cook with my pau pau that give me a glimpse of the childlike version of her. Like how she uses the little nub of extra dough to transform the last hom chi into a swan just for the fun of it. I try to picture her as a girl, bringing a batch of freshly fried hom chi, still crispy from the hot oil but perfectly chewy, to her dad, and how proud he must have been that she had helped make them.

Cheesy Chrysanthemum and Mushroom Pockets

Makes 12 pockets

For the dough

3 cups (375 g) all-purpose flour, plus more as needed

¼ teaspoon kosher salt

¾ cup plus 2 tablespoons (208 ml) just-boiled water

For the filling

2 tablespoons extra-virgin olive oil

1 pound (454 g) portobello mushrooms, roughly chopped

1 tablespoon sriracha or sambal oelek

1 tablespoon soy sauce

½ teaspoon kosher salt

2 cups (90 g) chopped chrysanthemum greens

2 cups (180 g) shredded mozzarella cheese

1 cup (108 g) finely chopped Chinese garlic chives

3 tablespoons extra-virgin olive oil, for frying

These oversize pan-fried dumplings are a spin on two of my favorite treats: Chinese chive pockets, a specialty of Northern China, and Hot Pockets, the microwave-ready frozen pastries that fueled my high school days in Ohio. Mine are filled with chrysanthemum greens, which are tender, very flavorful greens, but if you can't find them, baby spinach or kale are fine substitutes.

MAKE THE DOUGH: In a large bowl, whisk together the flour and salt, then pour in the hot water. With a flexible spatula, mix to form a shaggy dough, less than a minute. In the bowl or on the counter, knead until you have a smoothish dough (it should be tacky but not stick to your hands), 5 to 6 minutes. If the dough feels too dry, add a tablespoon of hot water (or a little more if needed); if it's too sticky, add a tablespoon of flour (or a little more if needed). Form the dough into a ball and wrap tightly in plastic wrap. Let the dough rest at room temperature for at least 30 minutes and up to 2 hours (any longer and it has a tendency to get sticky).

MAKE THE FILLING: In a large skillet, heat the olive oil over medium-high heat. Add the mushrooms and cook, stirring often, until reduced in volume and golden brown around the edges, 8 to 10 minutes. Add the sriracha, soy sauce, and salt and toss to combine. Cook to let the flavors meld, about 1 minute, then transfer the mixture to a large bowl. Let cool completely. Add the greens, mozzarella, and garlic chives and stir to evenly combine.

ASSEMBLE THE POCKETS: Line a large rimmed baking sheet with parchment paper. Unwrap the dough and divide it into 12 equal pieces. Form each portion of dough into a smooth ball and cover with a clean kitchen towel to prevent them from drying out. On a lightly floured surface, flatten one ball with your palm, then use a dowel rolling pin to roll it into a 6-inch (15 cm) round. Spoon about ¼ cup (70 g) of the filling into the center of the dough. Fold the dough over to form a half-moon shape, pressing out any air trapped inside, then pinch the edges to seal. Crimp the edge of the dough into a twist by folding the edge over and over again like an empanada (see "The Braid," page 234). Transfer

the dumpling to the prepared baking sheet and repeat with the remaining dough and filling.

COOK THE POCKETS: Set a wire rack over a baking sheet. In a large skillet, heat the olive oil over medium heat. Working in batches, carefully add the dumplings (as many as you can fit in an even layer in the pan) to the hot oil and fry, pressing down on them with a spatula periodically, until the bottoms are blistered and deep golden brown, 3 to 4 minutes. Flip and cook, pressing down on them with a spatula periodically, until blistered and deep golden brown on the other side, 3 to 4 minutes. Transfer the pockets to the rack and repeat with the remaining pockets.

SERVE: Enjoy immediately or keep warm in a 250°F (121°C) oven until ready to serve.

Whitefish Rangoon

Makes 32 wontons

6 ounces (170 g) smoked mackerel, skin and any large bones removed

1 (8-ounce/226 g) package cream cheese, at room temperature

4 green onions, finely chopped

½ teaspoon ground white pepper

32 store-bought medium-thick wonton wrappers

Neutral oil, such as canola, for frying

Pineapple Sweet-and-Sour Sauce (page 307), for serving

If you love classic crab rangoon, then you're going to be obsessed with whitefish rangoon. These crave-worthy fried triangles, a Chinese American takeout staple stuffed with a Jewish-deli-inspired whitefish salad filling, embody the blend of cultures between my husband and me. The smokiness of the mackerel and the tangy, creamy cream cheese enveloped by a crunchy fried wonton wrapper are what dreams are made of.

MAKE THE FILLING: In a medium bowl, break up the mackerel into small flakes with a fork. Add the cream cheese, green onions, and white pepper and mix with a flexible spatula until evenly combined.

ASSEMBLE THE RANGOON: Line a large rimmed baking sheet with parchment paper and fill a small bowl with water. Working with one at a time, fill each wonton wrapper with a scant tablespoon of the filling (avoid overfilling them, which will cause the wontons to burst). Dip your fingertip in the water and run it over the edges of the wrapper. Bring the center point of each edge of the wrapper together and firmly pinch until they stick, forming four petals. Gently pinch the wrapper around each petal to fully seal in the filling. Place the wonton on the prepared baking sheet and repeat with the remaining wrappers and filling.

FRY THE RANGOON: Set a wire rack over a rimmed baking sheet. In a large heavy-bottomed pot or wok, heat 3 inches (7.5 cm) of the oil over medium heat to 380°F (193°C). Carefully add 6 to 8 wontons to the hot oil and fry until blistered and golden brown, 60 to 90 seconds. Using a spider, transfer the fried wontons to the rack and repeat with the remaining wontons. Serve immediately with sweet-and-sour sauce for dipping.

The Next Generation of Dumplings

I like to joke that of course I ended up with a partner who shares a name with a sandwich, and my husband, Reuben, jokes that he's been eating Chinese food for longer than I've been alive (which is technically true). Reuben hails from New Jersey, is Jewish, and has an extremely high spice tolerance and an impressively open-minded palate. He was the one who introduced me to the best dim sum spot in San Francisco. I was skeptical at first, but I shouldn't have been. Good Luck Dim Sum has the best har gow (crystal shrimp dumplings) I've ever tasted, which was very much a green flag for our relationship. On one of our first dates, Reuben told me that in elementary school, he would trade his lunch of cold pizza for his classmate's sliced tongue sandwich (another very specific green flag). He loves to visit Cleveland with me because he gets to eat my family's food. His favorite dish is white fungus soup, which I think was a sign to my entire family that he was a keeper.

Reuben has been influential in my life and my cooking. When it comes to trying new foods, he is the most willing and respectful person I have ever met; it's inspiring. Just as I cook and study Chinese food as a way of honoring my family and its traditions, I make an effort to learn about his Jewish and Eastern European roots by following his mom's noodle kugel recipe and trying to perfect rebbetzin

coffee cake. In the decade we've been together, I've learned a few of the ways that Jewish and Chinese cultural traditions are similar, especially as they relate to food, like eating Chinese food on Christmas Day and an eagerness to celebrate any holiday with a multicourse meal.

My food often centers on the experience of growing up Chinese in Ohio and of building a life in the Bay Area, but also, of course, on my family, which now means something different. Family used to mean my parents, brother, and grandparents whom I grew up with, but now family also means my husband, his relatives, and the diverse group of friends we surround ourselves with. I think about our future children, too, how they will have to navigate the world as a blend of both of us. I anticipate their unique challenges, which will be quite different from those I encounter on my own identity journey, but I also imagine a rewarding and distinctly delicious life.

They will learn how to make Joong (page 279) just like their great–pau pau, while also perfecting their potato latke technique every Hanukkah. At some point, when we make Cho Family Dumplings (page 229), they will have to figure out which tasks in the group assembly line suit them best. At other times, like when I make Whitefish Rangoon (page 258) or a version of matzo ball soup with rice noodles, I'll

tell them that what they're eating is a unique and tasty way of representing our family. My hope is that through our food and the community that envelops our home, they will feel understood and also aware of where and who they come from, so they don't feel like they have to choose between being one thing or the other but are instead the next generation and evolution of our two worlds combined.

Chicken and Cabbage Spring Rolls

Makes 25 spring rolls

For the filling

1 pound (454 g) chicken breast tenderloins, thinly sliced

1 (1-inch/2.5 cm) piece fresh ginger, peeled and grated

4 tablespoons (60 ml) oyster sauce

1 tablespoon Shaoxing wine or bourbon

1 tablespoon cornstarch

2 teaspoons toasted sesame oil

1 teaspoon kosher salt

¾ teaspoon ground white pepper

2 bundles (4 ounces/120 g) glass noodles

3 tablespoons extra-virgin olive oil

6 cups (360 g) shredded cabbage

1 large carrot (160 g), cut into matchsticks

4 green onions, thinly sliced on a severe bias

1 tablespoon sriracha

To assemble and serve

¼ cup (60 g) all-purpose flour

¼ cup (60 ml) water

25 store-bought spring roll wrappers

(ingredients continue)

A towering presentation of neatly stacked spring rolls is a Lunar New Year staple, and the golden brown appetizers symbolize wealth in the new year because of their resemblance to gold bricks. In my family, spring rolls are also a popular edible gift because they freeze, travel, and reheat incredibly well. When my brother and I were in college, we always got a batch of foil-wrapped packets of spring rolls to take back to school after visits home because my parents feared we weren't eating enough. When your friends have a baby, try stocking their freezer with spring rolls. If you want to give your dinner guests a take-home treat, see them off with a personal pack of spring rolls.

Over the years, my mom developed an ingenious way to bake spring rolls, which renders them just as crisp and indulgent as the more common fried version without having to heat up a vat of oil. But if you're in the mood to deep-fry, those instructions are here, too. You can't go wrong with either method.

MARINATE THE CHICKEN: In a medium bowl, mix together the chicken, ginger, 2 tablespoons of the oyster sauce, the wine, cornstarch, sesame oil, ½ teaspoon of the salt, and ¼ teaspoon of the white pepper to combine. Cover and allow the chicken to marinate at room temperature for 15 minutes or in the refrigerator for up to 24 hours.

MEANWHILE, SOAK THE NOODLES: Place the glass noodles in a heatproof medium bowl and add hot water to cover. Cover the bowl and soak the noodles until hydrated, 8 to 10 minutes. Drain the noodles and transfer to a large rimmed baking sheet. Snip the noodles with kitchen shears a few times to break them up into slightly smaller pieces.

PREPARE THE FILLING: In a large skillet, heat 2 tablespoons of the olive oil over medium-high heat. Add the marinated chicken and stir-fry until browned on the edges and mostly cooked through, 5 to 6 minutes. Transfer the chicken to the baking sheet. Heat the remaining 1 tablespoon olive oil in the same pan over medium-high heat. Add the cabbage and toss to coat in the oil. When the cabbage starts to soften, after about 2 minutes, add the remaining ½ teaspoon salt and ½ teaspoon white pepper. Stir-fry the cabbage until golden on the edges, 6 to 8 minutes,

Olive oil, if baking the rolls

Neutral oil, such as canola, if frying the rolls

Pineapple Sweet-and-Sour Sauce (page 307), for serving

then transfer to the baking sheet. Add the carrot, green onions, sriracha, and remaining 2 tablespoons oyster sauce to the filling mixture and toss to combine. Let the filling cool completely.

ASSEMBLE THE SPRING ROLLS: In a small bowl, stir together the flour and water to make a paste (you will use this to seal the spring rolls). Peel the spring roll wrappers apart. Working with one at a time, position a wrapper on a work surface in front of you, orienting it like a diamond so one corner is facing you. Place about ⅓ cup (50 g) of the filling just below the center of the wrapper. Press the filling into a 1 by 4-inch (2.5 by 10 cm) log shape. Lift the bottom corner of the wrapper and fold it up and over the filling. With your finger, tuck the wrapper back toward you, tightening it around the filling. Fold the left and right corners of the wrapper tightly over the filling. Brush some of the flour paste over the top corner of the wrapper and then tightly roll up the spring roll and press the seam to seal. Place the assembled spring roll on a rimmed baking sheet and repeat with the remaining wrappers and filling.

To bake the spring rolls: Preheat the oven to 350°F (177°C) and line a large baking sheet with parchment paper. Arrange the spring rolls on the prepared baking sheet, spacing them 1 inch (2.5 cm) apart. Lightly brush each spring roll with olive oil, flipping them over to brush both sides. Bake for 20 minutes, then flip and bake for 20 minutes more, until crispy and golden brown. Let the spring rolls cool for a few minutes before serving.

To fry the spring rolls: Set a wire rack over a rimmed baking sheet. In a large heavy-bottomed pot or wok, heat 3 inches (7.5 cm) of neutral oil over medium heat to 380°F (193°C). Carefully add 3 or 4 spring rolls to the hot oil and fry, gently moving them around and rotating them with a pair of chopsticks or tongs, until golden brown, 3 to 4 minutes. Remove the spring rolls from the oil, shaking off any excess, and place them on the rack. (If you want to keep them warm and crispy longer, pop them in the oven at 250°F/121°C; just don't forget about them!) Repeat with the remaining spring rolls.

SERVE: Enjoy with sweet-and-sour sauce.

FREEZING AND REHEATING SPRING ROLLS

Spring rolls can be frozen either before they're cooked or after; the choice is yours. Arrange the spring rolls on a quarter sheet pan or plate and freeze until solid, then transfer them to a resealable container and store in the freezer for up to 3 months. To cook frozen raw spring rolls, bake or shallow-fry them following the directions on the opposite page, adding an extra 1 to 2 minutes of frying time; no need to defrost. Reheat frozen cooked spring rolls in the oven or a toaster oven at 350°F (177°C) until crisp and warmed through, about 10 minutes.

Divide and Conquer: Spring Rolls and Egg Rolls

Just like making dumplings, assembling spring rolls is a group effort. The wrappers are almost always store-bought, which cuts down on the overall time the process takes. All you need is a team to focus on crafting the filling, a person or two to wrap, and a dedicated person for manning the fryer or oven, if you're going the baked route. In no time you'll have a tower of crispy golden brown rolls to enjoy together!

Stations/Responsibilities

filling team   wrapping team   cooking team

Wrap the Perfect Roll

1. Position a wrapper like a diamond, with one corner facing you.
2. Place the filling just below the center of the wrapper and press it into a 1 by 4-inch (2.5 by 10 cm) log shape.
3. Lift the bottom corner of the wrapper and fold it up and over the filling.
4. With your finger, tuck the wrapper back toward you, tightening it around the filling.
5. Fold the left and right corners of the wrapper tightly over the filling.
6. Brush some flour paste over the top corner of the wrapper.
7. Tightly roll up the spring roll and press the seam to seal.

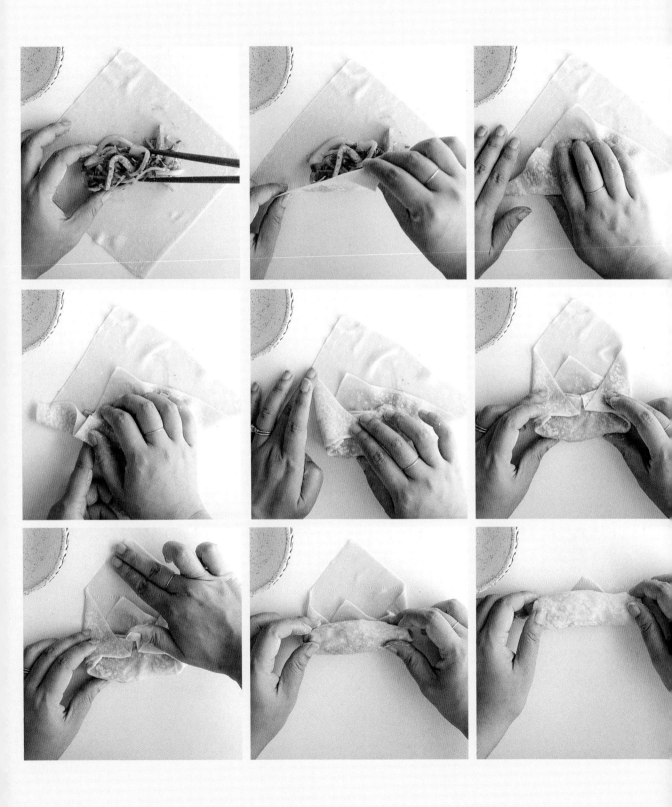

Daan Bing Egg Rolls

Makes 12 egg rolls

6 large eggs

2 teaspoons soy sauce

3 teaspoons extra-virgin olive oil

1 cup (60 g) chopped fresh cilantro

½ medium white onion, thinly sliced into crescents

2 tablespoons doubanjiang

2 tablespoons hoisin

1 tablespoon toasted sesame seeds

2 teaspoons toasted sesame oil

12 store-bought egg roll wrappers

Neutral oil, such as canola, for frying

These egg-filled rolls are a play on one of the most beloved Chinese breakfasts. Daan bing (or jian bing in Mandarin) is a Chinese crepe layered with eggs, leafy herbs, savory sauces like hoisin and doubanjiang, and typically something crispy like a fried cracker or youtiao (Chinese doughnut). Here a fried egg roll wrapper stands in for the crepe as well as the "something crispy." The interior is filled with a savory, spicy blend of eggs and cilantro. Like anything fried, these are heavenly when served fresh from the hot oil, but I've indulged in a few straight from the fridge for breakfast, and they were just as excellent. The chewiness of a cold wrapper is reminiscent of the texture of a green onion pancake.

MAKE THE FILLING: In a medium bowl, whisk together the eggs and soy sauce. Heat a large nonstick pan over medium heat. Add 1 teaspoon of the olive oil and swirl it around to coat the pan. Add about one-third of the egg mixture and swirl it around the pan to form a thin layer. Cook until the eggs are just set, 30 to 45 seconds. With a flexible spatula, loosen the edges around the pan, lift the crepe out, and transfer to a cutting board. Add another teaspoon of the oil to the pan and cook another third of the egg mixture the same way, stacking the second crepe on top of the first. Repeat with the remaining oil and egg mixture. Cut the stacked egg crepes into ¼-inch-wide (6 mm) strips and transfer to a medium bowl to cool. Add the cilantro, onion, doubanjiang, hoisin, toasted sesame seeds, and sesame oil to the bowl and gently toss to combine.

ASSEMBLE THE EGG ROLLS: Fill a small bowl with water. Peel the egg roll wrappers apart. Working with one at a time, position a wrapper on a work surface in front of you, orienting it like a diamond so one corner is facing you. Place about ⅓ cup (50 g) of the filling just below the center of the wrapper. Press the filling into a 1 by 4-inch (2.5 by 10 cm) log shape. Lift the bottom corner of the wrapper and fold it up and over the filling. With your finger, tuck the wrapper back toward you, tightening it around the filling. Fold the left and right corners of the wrapper tightly over the filling. Brush water over the top corner of the wrapper and then tightly roll up the wrapper and press the seam to seal. Place the assembled egg roll on a rimmed baking sheet and repeat with the remaining wrappers and filling.

FRY THE EGG ROLLS: Set a wire rack over a rimmed baking sheet. In a large heavy-bottomed pot or wok, heat 3 inches (7.5 cm) of neutral oil over medium heat to 380°F (193°C). Add 3 or 4 egg rolls to the hot oil and fry, gently moving them around and flipping them with a pair of chopsticks or tongs, until golden brown all over, 3 to 4 minutes. Remove the egg rolls from the oil, shaking off any excess, and transfer to the rack. Allow the egg rolls to cool for a few moments before serving. (If you want to keep them warm and crispy for a longer period, pop them in a 250°F/121°C oven—just don't forget about them!) Repeat with the remaining egg rolls.

Crispy Shrimp and Chive Bean Curd Rolls

Makes 8 bean curd rolls

6 bean curd sheets, about 7 by 9 inches (18 by 23 cm)

1 pound (454 g) large shrimp, peeled and deveined

1 cup (100 g) finely chopped Chinese garlic chives

3 tablespoons cornstarch

1 tablespoon soy sauce

1½ teaspoons kosher salt

1 teaspoon toasted sesame oil

½ teaspoon ground white pepper

Extra-virgin olive oil, for brushing

2 teaspoons water

Pineapple Sweet-and-Sour Sauce (page 307), for serving

Bean curd (also known as tofu skin) is greatly underrated. The skins are made by simmering soy milk, without stirring, until a thin layer of bean curd forms on the surface. This delicate layer is then swiftly lifted away from the pot with a pair of chopsticks and shaped into a flat sheet or gathered into wrinkled sticks known as bean stick. Available fresh or dried, bean curd is an amazing addition to soups and braises. The flat sheets in particular make a genius substitute for egg roll or spring roll wrappers. When the skins come in contact with hot oil, they go from soft and silky to shatteringly crisp.

Dried bean curd sheets are easily found at Chinese grocery stores. When selecting a pack, check to make sure the sheets aren't too banged up (watch out for broken sheets or cracked edges), which will make forming the rolls difficult. You could deep-fry the rolls, but it's much easier to bake them, and the baked rolls are just as crispy as fried. Also, the slippery texture of the skins makes it challenging to get a tight seal on the rolls, which can cause them to unravel in a pot of oil, but they keep neatly on a sheet pan in the oven with no problem.

SOAK THE BEAN CURD: Place the bean curd sheets in a rimmed shallow dish. Fill the dish with warm water and soak the sheets until pliable, 15 to 20 minutes. Drain the water and pat the sheets dry with paper towels.

MAKE THE FILLING: In a food processor, combine the shrimp, chives, 2 tablespoons of the cornstarch, the soy sauce, salt, sesame oil, and white pepper. Process until the mixture is very smooth and airy, about 1 minute.

WARM UP: Preheat the oven to 400°F (204°C) and line a rimmed baking sheet with parchment paper. Lightly brush the parchment paper with olive oil.

ASSEMBLE THE ROLLS: In a small bowl, whisk together the remaining 1 tablespoon cornstarch and the water to make a paste (you will use this to seal the rolls). Position one bean curd sheet on a cutting board, with a short edge of the sheet closest to you. Place about ¼ cup (70 g) of the filling just below the center of the sheet. Press the filling into a 1 by 4-inch (2.5 by 10 cm) log shape. Brush the edges of the sheet with the cornstarch paste. Lift the lower edge of the sheet and fold it up and over the filling. With your finger, tuck the wrapper back toward you, tightening it around the filling. Fold the left and right edges of the sheet tightly over the filling and then tightly roll up the sheet and press the seam to seal. Place the assembled bean curd roll on the prepared baking sheet, seam-side down, and repeat with the remaining bean curd sheets and filling, spacing the rolls 1 inch (2.5 cm) apart.

BAKE THE ROLLS: Lightly brush the surface of each spring roll with olive oil. Bake until the rolls are lightly browned and very crisp (no need to flip them), 15 to 20 minutes. Let the rolls cool for a few minutes before serving with sweet-and-sour sauce for dipping.

Chili Crunch Salmon Fresh Rolls

Makes 12 fresh rolls

For the rolls

1 pound (454 g) skinless farm-raised salmon fillet

1½ tablespoons Chili Crunch (page 302, or store-bought)

1 tablespoon brown sugar

1 tablespoon oyster sauce

1 teaspoon toasted sesame oil

½ teaspoon kosher salt

½ teaspoon ground white pepper

6 ounces (170 g) rice vermicelli (see Note)

1 tablespoon extra-virgin olive oil, plus more if needed

12 (10-inch/25 cm) round store-bought rice paper wrappers (see Note, page 276)

1 large watermelon radish, thinly sliced

3 cups (200 g) thinly shredded Little Gem or romaine lettuce

1 cup (70 g) fresh mint leaves

For the dipping sauce

½ cup (120 ml) hoisin

½ cup (160 g) sesame paste or tahini

2 tablespoons sriracha

2 teaspoons toasted sesame oil

My childhood best friend, Amanda, was Vietnamese. Amanda and I initially connected because our last names were different by one letter (Cho and Chu), and we were the only Asian students in our grade (and I'm pretty sure in the entire elementary school at the time). We shared a passion for dancing (terribly, I might add) to music videos on MTV and taking turns eating at each other's houses. At Amanda's, I got an introductory course in homestyle Vietnamese food, including goi cuon (Vietnamese fresh rolls), beef pho, and balut (fertilized duck egg), and there was always an abundance of fresh herbs on her family's table. Even though the food at her house was completely different from the Chinese food my family prepared, I felt a sense of familiarity in Amanda's kitchen.

To this day, Vietnamese food has some of the most comforting and nostalgic flavors for me. I developed these rolls as an homage to those lunches at Amanda's house. You want to go heavy on the mint here, which serves as a cooling, crisp backdrop for the chili-crunch-marinated salmon. Salmon is inherently rich and flavorful, and the marinade complements those qualities with a kiss of heat and sweetness.

PREPARE THE SALMON: Cut the salmon against the grain at a steep angle into ½-inch-thick (1 cm) slices and transfer to a large bowl. Add the chili crunch, brown sugar, oyster sauce, sesame oil, salt, and white pepper and gently combine. Cover the bowl and allow the salmon to marinate at room temperature for 30 minutes or in the refrigerator for up to 24 hours.

MEANWHILE, SOAK THE NOODLES: Fill a large pot with water and bring to a boil over high heat. Cook the vermicelli according to the package directions. Drain the noodles and rinse under cold water. If the noodles are going to sit at all before you assemble the rolls, toss them with a little bit of olive oil to prevent sticking.

COOK THE SALMON: In a large pan, heat the olive oil over medium-high heat. Working in batches if needed, add the salmon to the pan and sear until crisp and browned around the edges, about 1 minute per side. Transfer the salmon to a plate and let cool completely.

(recipe continues)

ASSEMBLE THE ROLLS: Fill a large cake pan or pie dish (slightly larger than the rice paper wrappers) with tepid water (hot or warm water will make the wrappers too flimsy). Working with one at a time, submerge a wrapper in the water for 10 seconds and set it on a cutting board (the rice paper will continue to soften as it sits on the cutting board; do not oversoak). Place a piece of salmon in the center of the wrapper. Arrange 3 or 4 slices of radish on top of the salmon. Place a bundle of noodles just below the salmon and top the noodles with some lettuce and a few mint leaves. Lift the lower edge of the wrapper and fold it up and over the bundle of noodles and lettuce, then fold it up and over again over the salmon, making sure to tighten it around the filling. Fold the left and right corners of the wrapper tightly over the filling and then tightly roll up the wrapper and press the seam to seal. Place the assembled roll on a rimmed baking sheet or platter and repeat with the remaining wrappers and filling. Make sure to leave a little space between the rolls on the baking sheet to keep them from sticking.

MAKE THE DIPPING SAUCE AND SERVE: In a medium bowl, stir together the hoisin, sesame paste, sriracha, and sesame oil until smooth. Serve the rolls with the dipping sauce on the side.

NOTE: *If you can find rectangular sheets of portioned-out rice vermicelli, that's even better—they are designed specifically for fresh rolls.*

Joong

Makes 12 joong

36 dried bamboo leaves

5 cups (1.04 kg) sticky rice

1 cup (125 g) raw peanuts

1 pound (454 g) pork belly, cut into 1½-inch (4 cm) pieces

1½ teaspoons kosher salt

½ teaspoon Chinese five spice powder

3 lap cheong (Chinese sausages), quartered

12 Salted Egg Yolks (page 143)

Joong varies from family to family and region to region. Some versions are sweet, some are heavy on the mung beans, and some don't contain any meat at all. In my family, joong are bundles of sticky rice studded with tasty bits of Chinese sausage, salted pork belly, peanuts, and cured egg yolks, all wrapped up and steamed in bamboo leaves. My pau pau normally spends an entire week making mountains of these for our family every year for the Dragon Boat Festival. At the end of the week, her dining table is covered in bowls piled high with joong. But she is getting older, so I am ensuring her joong-making tradition continues.

Most people think joong are incredibly difficult to master, but the truth is, you just need time to prep your ingredients and more time to wrap each bundle. All in all, making joong is a two-day production at its shortest, so block out time in your calendar. If you have some friends to help you with wrapping, the process is relatively quick.

This recipe yields a modest number of joong—just a dozen. It's a manageable quantity, especially if this is your first time making them. But you can easily double, triple, or otherwise scale up the production to fit your needs and schedule best. Bamboo leaves are the trickiest ingredient to find, and there's really no substitute for them. You can get them in Chinese grocery stores, typically in the dried or preserved foods aisle (wherever the dried shiitake mushrooms are), or ask a store employee.

DAY 1

SOAK THE BAMBOO LEAVES: Place the bamboo leaves in a large stockpot or bowl filled with water. Gently bend the leaves so they are fully submerged; they have a tendency to float, so place a heavy bowl over them to help weight them down. Cover the pot and set aside to soak for 24 hours, switching out the water with fresh water after 12 hours.

SOAK THE RICE AND PEANUTS: Place the rice in a large bowl and add cold water to cover. Cover the bowl and soak for at least 12 hours and up to 24 hours. Place the peanuts in a medium bowl and add cold water to cover. Cover the bowl and soak for at least 12 hours and up to 24 hours.

MARINATE THE PORK: Place the pork belly in a resealable container. Add the salt and five spice and toss to coat the pork belly. Cover and refrigerate overnight.

DAY 2

SEAR THE PORK: Heat a large skillet over medium-high heat. Add the pork belly and sear until browned on two sides, about 3 minutes on either side. Transfer to a plate and allow to cool before assembling the joong.

ASSEMBLE THE JOONG: Cut twelve 30-inch-long (76 cm) pieces of kitchen twine. Drain the bamboo leaves from the water and pat them dry with paper towels or a clean kitchen towel. Drain the rice and peanuts.

Place 2 bamboo leaves on a work surface, overlapping them slightly. Fold the leaves in half at a diagonal and twist to create a little "cup." Add a scoop of rice and then layer on some of the peanuts, pork belly, lap cheong, and a salted egg yolk. Cover the layers with another scoop of rice. Wrap a third leaf around the "base" of the joong. While holding firmly, fold the exposed edge of the joong over and bend the top of the leaves down. Tightly wrap the twine around the joong a few times and tie the ends together to secure. (See photos, pages 282–283.) After you assemble each joong, place it in a large stockpot, tightly packing them together.

COOK THE JOONG: Fill the pot with cold water to cover (the joong should be submerged) and bring to a boil over high heat. Reduce the heat to low, cover, and simmer the joong for 5 hours. Keep an eye on the water level; if it gets too low, add more water to keep the joong submerged. (I boil some water in a kettle and add it to the pot as needed.)

SERVE: With tongs, remove the joong from the water and let cool for about an hour before serving. Simply eat these on their own by untying the string and unwrapping the leaves. Joong can be stored at room temperature for about a day, in the refrigerator for up to 5 days, or in the freezer in a zip-top bag for up to 6 months.

FREEZING AND REHEATING JOONG

My pau pau would make these just once a year, so before I started making joong on my own, my mom would freeze a dozen or so for me to pick up when I flew home to Ohio. I'd stuff them into my carry-on and would always get stopped at the Cleveland airport because on the scanner, their unique shape looks suspicious to TSA agents. I would explain them the same way every time and was always met with an "Oh, that sounds so good!" Once the joong safely made it to my freezer in the Bay Area, I would ration them over the course of a few months.

Stored in a resealable container (a zip-top bag works great), joong will keep in the freezer for up to 6 months. To reheat them from frozen, steam for about 45 minutes, or microwave for 8 to 10 minutes, until fully warmed through. To reduce the cooking time, plan ahead and allow the joong to defrost in the fridge overnight, then steam for about 20 minutes or microwave for 2 to 3 minutes.

How to Wrap Joong

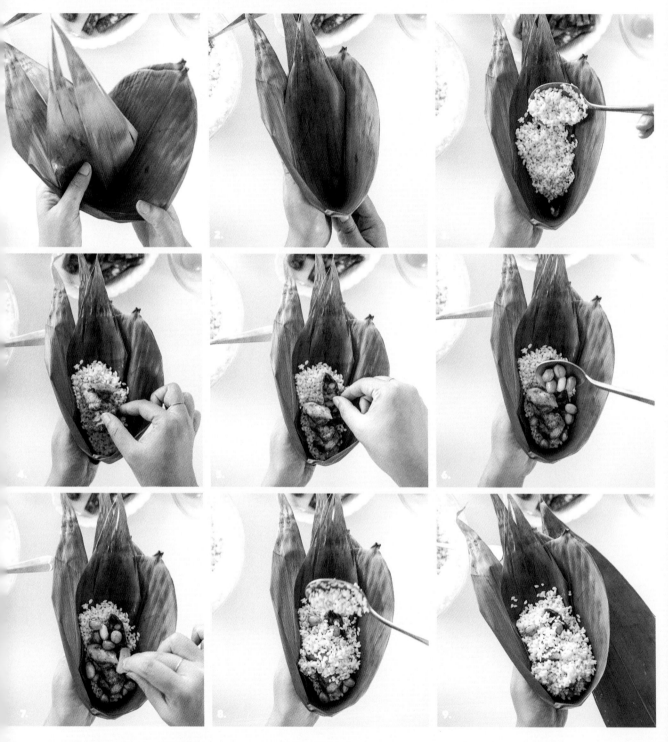

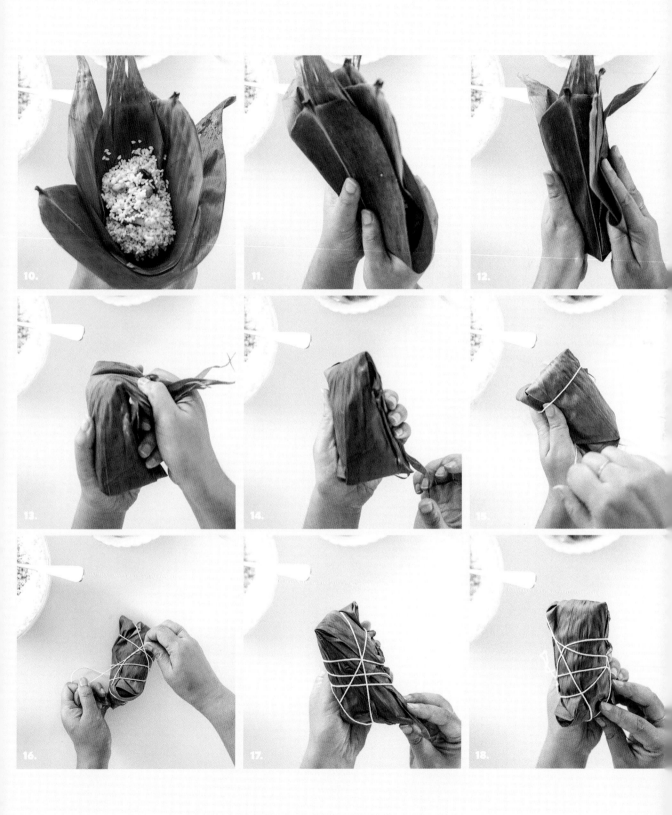

More Than Sides

To me, dinner feels incomplete without a scoop of steamed rice. On cold nights, a bowl of nourishing soup with floating bits of tofu and wispy strands of egg is a necessary warm-up lap for a bigger meal ahead. And my kitchen just doesn't feel stocked without jars of something crunchy, sour, fiery, and pungent waiting in the wings to pull a memorable meal together. The components in this chapter are essential for the recipes in this book. I hate using the term "side dishes" to describe them, because they're more than side dishes. Side dishes feel optional, meaning the main dish can stand alone without them. That's not the case here. Oxtail and Daikon Stew (page 205) needs a bed of steamed rice to soak up all the flavor you've developed, and you simply can't enjoy Sizzle Sauce Noodles (page 81) without making a batch of Sizzle Sauce. After making these foundational recipes a few times, you'll start to see how they connect the dots between the flavors and textures on your table.

Perfect Steamed Jasmine Rice

Serves 4 to 6

2 cups (420 g) jasmine rice

2½ cups (600 ml) water

Knowing how to properly cook rice is a basic part of life. Steamed jasmine rice has an intoxicating aroma that can perfume a whole house and signal that dinner is almost ready. Many people rely on the convenience of a rice cooker, but you don't need to. I consciously keep my "gadgets" and kitchen equipment to a minimum, and a good pot makes equally perfect rice. Both cooking options have been provided for you here; either way, it's easy steaming! Just be sure not to get too distracted during the first few minutes when the pot is on the burner, because as soon as you start to see bubbles on the surface of the water, it's time to lower the heat and place on the lid.

WASH THE RICE: Place the rice in a medium saucepan or the bowl of your rice cooker. Fill with cold water and wash the rice by swirling it with your hands and sliding the rice between your palms. The water will look cloudy. Drain the water and repeat the rinsing process one more time, draining out all the water. Add the 2½ cups (600 ml) fresh water.

To cook the rice in a saucepan: Bring the water to a simmer over medium-high heat. Reduce the heat to medium-low or low to maintain a very gentle simmer, cover, and steam the rice until the grains are plump and fluffy and no water remains in the pot, 15 to 17 minutes. Remove the lid, immediately fluff the rice with a spoon or rice paddle, and serve.

To cook the rice in a rice cooker: Set the bowl into the rice cooker and cover with the lid. Press the button to start, according to the model of your machine. The cooking time differs per rice cooker, but the rice will be done once the machine beeps or starts singing to you. Open the lid, immediately fluff the rice with a spoon or rice paddle, and serve.

HOW TO SAVE LEFTOVER RICE

If you have any leftover rice, store it in an airtight container in the fridge for up to 5 days. To reheat, simply microwave until fluffy and steamy again, 1 to 3 minutes. Leftover rice is best for making fried rice because chilling the rice brings the starches to the surface and draws out moisture. The Shrimpy Ketchup Fried Rice (page 65) makes great use of it!

Building Intuition, One Pot of Rice at a Time

Steamed rice was one of the first things I learned to cook. I was small enough that I needed to stand on a step stool at the sink so my short, chubby arms could reach the bowl of rice as I rinsed the starch away. My goong goong instructed me to wash the rice at least twice (triple-wash it if you have time) so the grains wouldn't be completely clumped together when cooked. He also taught me the "palm trick" as a way to measure the proper amount of water for the rice: He filled the bowl with water and stopped right when he thought there was enough. Then he stuck his hand in, palm down, and if the water reached his knuckles, there was enough. There was always just the right amount of water, and the rice always came out fluffy and perfect.

I do see some flaws in his method, though. Some hands are bigger than others, and the sizes of countless rice cookers or pots vary. Different varieties of rice require different quantities of water, and different cooking times, too. Admittedly, I think the key to his "trick" is the practice of building your intuition as a cook. When I make steamed rice, I rarely, and I mean *rarely*, measure the rice and water. The process is as instinctual as breathing. I have a favorite rice pot, and since I've made steamed rice so many times, I measure the rice with my heart, depending on how hungry I am or how many people I'm planning to feed, and then pour in the water and wait until I feel the approval of my ancestors to tell me to stop. For you, however, I developed the rice recipes in this book by measuring the amount of water I intuitively pour into my rice. Measure your rice and your water the first few times you prepare it and find your favorite rice cooker or saucepan, and I promise the more you make it, the stronger your rice intuition will be.

Gingery Brown Rice

Serves 4 to 6

2 cups (420 g) short-grain brown rice

2 tablespoons grated fresh ginger

2 teaspoons chicken bouillon powder (see Note)

3 cups (720 ml) water (see Note)

The next time you get a craving for a nutty, toothsome, and fiber-rich grain, this is the recipe for you. Brown rice gets a bad rap for being boring and bland and a second-rate choice (after white rice) when you're trying to be healthier. I implore you to track down some Japanese short-grain brown rice and incorporate grated fresh ginger and chicken bouillon (if you have some chicken stock, even better) into the pot as it steams. There's just enough additional flavor to bring a little zing and complement the earthiness of the rice without overpowering it. Short-grain brown rice is plumper and chewier than longer-grained varieties and cooks considerably faster, too.

WASH THE RICE: Place the rice in a medium saucepan or the bowl of your rice cooker. Give the rice a quick rinse (there is no need to wash it multiple times because it doesn't have the same level of starch as white rice). Drain and add the ginger, bouillon powder, and the 3 cups (720 ml) fresh water to the rice and give it a good stir.

To cook the rice in a saucepan: Bring the water to a simmer over medium-high heat. Reduce the heat to medium-low or low to maintain a very gentle simmer, cover, and steam the rice until the grains are plump and fluffy and no water remains in the pot, 23 to 25 minutes. Remove the lid, immediately fluff the rice with a spoon or rice paddle, and serve.

To cook the rice in a rice cooker: Set the bowl into the rice cooker and cover with the lid. Press the button to start, according to the model of your machine. The cooking time differs per rice cooker, but it will be done once the machine beeps or starts singing to you. Open the lid, immediately fluff the rice with a spoon or rice paddle, and serve.

NOTE: *You can replace the bouillon powder and water with 3 cups (720 ml) Scrappy Chicken Stock (page 300).*

Jade Rice

Serves 4 to 6

2 cups (420 g) jasmine rice

2½ cups (600 ml) plus
2 tablespoons water

¼ teaspoon kosher salt

1½ cups (40 g) fresh Thai
basil

½ cup (20 g) fresh cilantro

2 garlic cloves, peeled

1 tablespoon fish sauce

Rice is so neutral in flavor that it's often relegated to sidekick status. When you're in the mood for a vibrant, flavorful rice with main-character energy, this is the rice to make. A punchy puree of fresh herbs and fish sauce is folded into freshly steamed jasmine rice. With each turn, every grain of rice takes on a verdant hue and zesty coating of flavor. A scoop of this is a great partner to Lemon Togarashi Grilled Chicken (page 181), Coconut Short Ribs with Creamy Butternut Squash (page 206), and Triple Pepper Beef (page 57), to name just a few.

WASH THE RICE: Place the rice in a medium saucepan or the bowl of your rice cooker. Fill with cold water and wash the rice by swirling it with your hands and sliding the rice between your palms. The water will look cloudy. Drain the water and repeat the rinsing process one more time, draining out all of the water. Add the 2½ cups (600 ml) fresh water and the salt.

To cook the rice in a saucepan: Bring the water to a simmer over medium-high heat. Reduce the heat to medium-low or low to maintain a very gentle simmer, cover, and steam the rice until the grains are plump and fluffy and no water remains in the pot, 15 to 17 minutes. Remove the lid and immediately fluff the rice with a spoon or rice paddle.

To cook the rice in a rice cooker: Set the bowl into the rice cooker and cover with the lid. Press the button to start, according to the model of your machine. The cooking time differs per rice cooker, but the rice will be done once the machine beeps or starts singing to you. Open the lid and immediately fluff the rice with a spoon or rice paddle.

MEANWHILE, PUREE THE HERBS: In a food processor, combine the basil, cilantro, garlic, the 2 tablespoons water, and the fish sauce. Pulse until smooth, adding another tablespoon of water if necessary. Mix the herb sauce into the cooked rice and serve.

NO GRAIN OF RICE LEFT BEHIND

The crispy layer of rice at the bottom of the pot is the single best reason for cooking rice in a pot instead of in a rice cooker.

This method for ensuring some scorched bits of rice works best in a stainless-steel or enamel-clad saucepan or pot. After serving all the rice for your meal, leave a thin layer on the bottom of the pot. Set the pot over low heat and toast the rice until golden brown; the time will vary depending on your pot and how cooked your rice is, but it typically takes 8 to 12 minutes. Start scraping the rice off the bottom of the pot with a spoon; if it's stuck, toast it for a few more minutes. If the rice releases from the pot, turn off the heat and scrape all the rice out onto a plate. It's normal for the rice to break up into smaller chunks, but when the stars align, you will be able to remove the entire layer of rice like one big crispy rice cracker!

Everyday Tong

Serves 4 to 6

8 cups (1.92 L) water

2 small kohlrabi (250 g), peeled and thinly sliced

4 garlic cloves, smashed and peeled

1 tablespoon chicken bouillon powder

½ teaspoon kosher salt

½ teaspoon ground white pepper

8 ounces (227 g) silken tofu, cubed

1 tablespoon oyster sauce

2 green onions, thinly sliced

A classic Chinese dinner, whether at a restaurant or in your own home, starts with *tong*, the Chinese word for soup. A steamy bowl is treated like a first course to warm up the belly and aid digestion, which is super helpful when you know you're about to have a big dinner. Tong is also treated as a savory form of medicine, like a tonic or an elixir, to help cure whatever ails you. Dinner is ready when my mom yells "Yum tong aaa!" which signals everyone to scurry into the kitchen, grab a bowl, and help themselves to some steamy broth. Some nights, the tong is a traditional clear pork bone broth with winter melon, and other nights, a Country Ham and Corn Egg Drop Soup (page 297). On special occasions, my pau pau will brew an extra-medicinal tong with ginseng and other dried herbs I can't identify.

In my small household, we store the soup in the fridge for the week and warm up bowls before dinner or even in the morning to start the day. You can also alter the baseline recipe every time you make it. My everyday version includes ingredients I usually have in my kitchen, but if you can't find kohlrabi, simply replace it with carrots, chayote, or winter melon. Instead of silken tofu, you can add tofu knots or pieces of bean stick directly to the broth as it simmers. If tofu is not your thing or you're craving something meatier, add thin slices of raw chicken breast or cubes of pork to the tong to gently poach as it simmers. A spoonful of chicken bouillon powder is my shortcut for flavorful tong, but if you've prepared Scrappy Chicken Stock (page 300) or Tomato Kombu Broth (page 301), use it instead. Making tong is a personal practice and ritual, so make it your own.

In a large pot, combine the water, kohlrabi, garlic, bouillon, salt, and white pepper and bring to a boil over medium-high heat. Reduce the heat to medium-low or low, cover, and simmer until the vegetables are tender and the broth is flavorful, 30 minutes. Gently stir in the tofu and oyster sauce and simmer until the tofu is warmed through, 5 to 10 minutes. Turn off the heat, add the green onions, and allow the soup to cool for a few minutes before serving.

Store the leftover soup in an airtight container in the fridge for up to 5 days.

Egg Drop Soup

Crack 4 large eggs into a medium bowl. While gently stirring the hot soup, pour in the eggs one at a time. Continue to stir the soup for a few moments more to create wispy trails of egg. Turn off the heat and allow the soup to cool for a few minutes before serving. This method will give you thin wisps of egg whites and bigger pockets of poached egg yolks, which I always make sure to find when serving myself the tong. For extra-wispy egg drop soup, whisk the eggs first before stirring them into the soup, or use only egg whites.

Country Ham and Corn Egg Drop Soup

Serves 4 to 6

2 ears corn, husked

8¼ cups (1.98 L) water

6 ounces (170 g) country ham, diced

2 tablespoons oyster sauce

1 tablespoon chicken bouillon powder

1½ teaspoons ground white pepper

1 teaspoon kosher salt

¼ cup (30 g) cornstarch

4 large eggs

4 green onions, thinly sliced

This recipe is what happens when Cantonese corn soup starts a new life in America. Corn soup is a quintessential "house soup" in many Chinese homes and restaurants. It has a silky, chowderlike texture, delicate strands of egg, lovely sweetness, and lingering heat from a generous amount of white pepper. I'm not sure when my parents started adding cubes of country ham to their corn soup, but as far back as I can remember, I was hunting through the depths of my bowl, looking for the meaty chunks of ham. Country ham is cured, so it's salty and smoky, an amazing flavor contrast to the natural sweetness of the corn. In summer (soup season never ends!), when corn is in its prime, seize the opportunity to unlock even more flavor by boiling the corncobs in the broth first. When it's not exactly corn season, which is also the more typical soup season, simply adding 2 cups of canned or frozen corn will still be delicious.

SIMMER THE SOUP: Cut the corn kernels off the cobs and set aside; place the cobs in a large pot. Add 8 cups (1.92 L) of the water and bring to a boil over medium-high heat. Reduce the heat to maintain a simmer, cover, and cook until the broth tastes sweet and very corny, about 15 minutes. Discard the cobs. Add the corn kernels, ham, oyster sauce, bouillon, white pepper, and salt to the pot, stir, and simmer for 15 minutes more.

THICKEN THE SOUP: In a small bowl, whisk together the remaining ¼ cup (60 ml) water and the cornstarch to make a slurry. While gently stirring the soup, pour in the slurry and cook, stirring, until the soup thickens slightly, 2 to 4 minutes.

Crack the eggs into a bowl (you can use the one you used for the slurry). While gently stirring the soup, pour in the eggs one at a time. Stir the soup for a few moments more to create wispy trails of egg. Add the green onions and stir to incorporate them into the soup. Turn off the heat and allow the soup to cool for a few minutes before serving.

Hot-and-Sour Soup

Serves 4 to 6

8¼ cups (1.98 L) water

4 medium tomatoes, roughly chopped

2 serrano peppers, thinly sliced

⅓ cup (80 ml) rice vinegar, plus more if needed

2 tablespoons oyster sauce

1 tablespoon chicken bouillon powder

1 tablespoon soy sauce

1 tablespoon kosher salt

1 teaspoon ground white pepper

8 ounces (227 g) firm tofu, cut into small cubes

4 ounces (57 g) fresh wood ear mushrooms (or 1 ounce/28 g dried, rehydrated; see page 247), thinly sliced

6 ounces (170 g) beech mushrooms, torn into smaller clusters

¼ cup (30 g) cornstarch

4 green onions, thinly sliced

Sharp and tangy hot-and-sour soup is a takeout favorite that is, in my opinion, best made at home. To me, a good hot-and-sour soup should make your nose tingle ever so slightly when you smell it, and making it at home means you can control how hot and sour it is. I got this recipe from my parents, because the hot-and-sour soup at the family restaurant was considered to be the very best, but I still took some liberties with it. Tomatoes make a surprise appearance; their acidity and brightness are a key element in this version of the soup. Serrano peppers are not the typical spicy pepper used in a Chinese hot-and-sour soup, but their inherent vegetal flavor works really well here, and they are more consistently spicy than jalapeños (in my opinion). This soup will wake you up and make you sweat a little, but you'll want to come back for another bowl or two.

SIMMER THE SOUP: In a large pot, combine 8 cups (1.92 L) of the water, the tomatoes, serranos, vinegar, oyster sauce, bouillon, soy sauce, salt, and white pepper. Bring to a boil over medium-high heat. Reduce the heat to maintain a simmer, cover, and cook until the tomatoes are broken down, about 15 minutes. Taste the soup and add a splash more vinegar if you like your soup a little more sour. Add the tofu and mushrooms, stir to combine, and simmer for about 5 minutes to warm them through.

THICKEN THE SOUP: In a small bowl, whisk together the remaining ¼ cup (60 ml) water and the cornstarch to make a slurry. While gently stirring, pour the slurry into the soup. Continue to stir until the soup thickens slightly, 2 to 3 minutes. Add the green onions and stir them into the soup. Turn off the heat and allow the soup to cool for a few minutes before serving.

Scrappy Chicken Stock

**Makes about 8 cups
(1.92 L)**

1 pound (454 g) chicken
feet or wings (or the
carcass from Shacha Roast
Chicken, page 193)

12 cups (2.88 L) water

1 yellow onion, halved

1 large carrot

1 small sheet kombu

4 large garlic cloves,
peeled

2 tablespoons kosher salt

½ teaspoon ground white
pepper

I'm not necessarily one to save all my onion skins, root vegetable nubs, and animal bones in the freezer to make a hodgepodge stock. But I do love a rich chicken stock and make this scrappy version using staple ingredients from around the kitchen. Using chicken feet (a cut of chicken wasted far too often), wings, or both will result in a more full-bodied stock, because they are loaded with collagen and fat. It's a good sign if the stock has a jiggly consistency when it's chilled. After making Shacha Roast Chicken (page 193), use the carcass for stock. It will be less fatty than using chicken feet or wings, but it's a great way to extract every ounce of flavor from the chicken.

Steam your rice in this flavorful stock for a more enriched grain, and use it to replace the bouillon and water in recipes that call for chicken bouillon.

In a large pot, combine the chicken, water, onion, carrot, kombu, garlic, salt, and white pepper. Bring to a boil over medium-high heat. Reduce the heat to maintain a simmer and cook, uncovered, until the stock is very golden, rich, and flavorful, 1 to 2 hours (the longer the better). Turn off the heat and allow the stock to cool. Scoop out all the solids with a spider and discard; for extra-smooth stock, strain through a fine-mesh sieve. Divide the stock between two 1-quart (960 ml) tall containers, cover, and store in the fridge for up to 5 days or in the freezer for up to 3 months.

Tomato Kombu Broth

Makes about 8 cups (1.92 L)

12 cups (2.88 L) water

2 pounds (908 g) tomatoes (the best you can find)

1 big sheet kombu

1 tablespoon kosher salt

It is shocking how flavorful this broth tastes, especially because you need only four ingredients (one of which is water) *and* it's vegan. Ripe tomatoes and kombu are brimming with umami but support each other with elements the other lacks: the tomatoes are refreshing and lend acid and sweetness, while the kombu provides a savory brininess in the broth. Taking inspiration from Japanese dashi, simmering a sheet of kombu releases a natural salinity and unique MSG-like flavor into the stock without the addition of MSG (not that there's anything wrong with MSG). This broth is the base for Shrimp Noodle Soup for the Soul (page 104) and transforms Chicken, Corn, and Jalapeño Wontons (page 240) into a summery wonton soup. As with Everyday Tong (page 294), you can easily turn this into an egg drop soup as well (see page 295).

In a large pot, combine the water, tomatoes, kombu, and salt. Bring to a boil over medium-high heat. Reduce the heat to maintain a simmer and cook, uncovered, until the tomatoes are broken down and the stock is dark amber in color, 1 to 2 hours. Turn off the heat and allow the broth to cool. Discard the kombu and use a slotted spoon to strain out the tomatoes. Divide the stock between two 1-quart (960 ml) tall containers, cover, and store in the fridge for up to 5 days or in the freezer for up to 3 months.

Chili Crunch

Makes 1½ cups (360 ml)

2 tablespoons pepitas

2 tablespoons roughly chopped red-skinned peanuts

1 tablespoon white sesame seeds

2 tablespoons crushed red chili flakes

1 tablespoon fermented black beans

2 teaspoons crushed Sichuan peppercorns

1 teaspoon smoked paprika

1 cup (240 ml) grapeseed oil

½ cup (60 g) minced garlic (from about 2 heads)

My kitchen cabinets contain about a dozen different chili oils and chili crisps. On a trip to Mexico City, I fell in love with salsa macha, which is remarkably similar to a classic Chinese chili oil but smokier and nuttier. So I crafted my own version that combines everything I love about these spicy, unctuous condiments.

Chili oil, chili crisp, and chili crunch are all names for this condiment that are often used interchangeably based on its texture. My chili crunch is heavy on the fried garlic and chock-full of seeds and nuts, has a hint of smokiness, will make your mouth buzz a little (from the Sichuan peppercorns), and is satisfyingly spicy without melting your face off. Use chili crunch on everything: spoon it onto your morning eggs, toss it with noodles and a little Chinkiang vinegar, roast potatoes with it, or mix it into popcorn.

TOAST THE SEEDS: In a medium skillet, toast the pepitas, peanuts, and sesame seeds over medium heat, stirring occasionally, until aromatic, 4 to 5 minutes. The seeds will crackle and pop. Take care not to burn them, which would give the chili crunch a bitter taste. Transfer the mixture to a heatproof medium bowl. Stir in the chili flakes, black beans, Sichuan peppercorns, and paprika. Set a fine-mesh strainer over the bowl.

FRY THE GARLIC: In a medium saucepan, heat the grapeseed oil over medium-low heat. Add the garlic and gently fry until lightly golden brown, 7 to 9 minutes. Carefully pour the oil and garlic into the strainer set over the bowl. The contents of the bowl will sizzle and the garlic caught in the strainer will have a chance to crisp up. Allow the garlic to fully cool and get crisp before adding it to the bowl.

STORE: Give the chili crunch a stir to combine all the ingredients. It is ready to use immediately and can be stored in an airtight container at room temperature for up to 1 month. The flavor will continue to develop and deepen.

XO Sauce

Makes about 1½ cups (360 ml)

⅓ cup (30 g) small to medium dried scallops

⅓ cup (27 g) small to medium dried shrimp

2 tablespoons crushed red chili flakes

1 tablespoon soy sauce

1 tablespoon sugar

1 cup (240 ml) neutral oil, such as grapeseed

1 tablespoon minced garlic

XO sauce is a condiment that's traditionally made with dried scallops, dried shrimp, and cured pork. It has a touch of heat and sweetness, with a pronounced brininess from the dried seafood. "XO" originally stood for "extra old," alluding to its being aged and considered a luxury ingredient warranting a high price. There aren't many store-bought XO sauces, so if you want to enjoy it in your kitchen, you need to make it yourself! My version omits the cured pork to focus instead on the dried scallops and shrimp, both easily found at your local Chinese or Asian market. Just like Chili Crunch (opposite), this condiment will taste good on practically anything, but it is especially good drizzled on XO Scallop Jook (page 210) and Extra-Special XO Nian Gao (page 99).

REHYDRATE THE DRIED SEAFOOD: In a medium bowl, combine the dried scallops and shrimp and add boiling water to cover. Cover the bowl with a plate or plastic wrap. Let the dried shellfish soak until hydrated, 45 minutes to 1 hour.

Drain the scallops and shrimp and pat dry with a clean kitchen towel, then transfer to a food processor. Pulse a few times, just until crumbly with wispy strands of scallop.

In a medium heatproof bowl, stir together the chili flakes, soy sauce, and sugar to combine. Set a fine-mesh strainer over the bowl.

FRY THE SEAFOOD AND GARLIC: In a medium saucepan, heat the oil over medium-low heat. Line a plate with paper towels. Carefully add the dried scallops and shrimp to the hot oil and fry, stirring often, until starting to crisp and turn lightly golden brown, 3 to 4 minutes. Add the garlic and cook, stirring continuously, until everything is golden brown, 5 to 6 minutes. The oil will foam up from the protein in the scallops and shrimp, so make sure to keep stirring. Remove from the heat and pour the oil through the strainer into the bowl with the soy mixture. Spread the fried seafood and garlic into a single layer on the paper towel–lined plate and allow them to fully cool and crisp, then return them to the bowl with the oil and stir. Transfer the sauce to an airtight container and store in the fridge for up to 3 months.

Black Bean and Garlic Paste

**Makes about ⅓ cup
(70 g)**

3 tablespoons fermented
black beans, preferably
Yang Jiang brand

3 tablespoons minced
garlic

3 tablespoons extra-virgin
olive oil

This isn't quite a sauce, but it quickly becomes a bold and robust
one once it hits the pan with some oil. The black beans are
actually salted fermented soybeans, which have an intensely
pungent flavor. You'll want to keep a steady supply of black bean
and garlic paste in your fridge, because a spoonful pairs perfectly
with any vegetable, especially ong choy (page 120) and gai lan.
And you can't go wrong adding some to a clean-out-the-fridge-
style stir-fry for instant flavor.

My mom advises making small batches of black bean and
garlic paste at a time, because in her opinion, you don't want it
sitting around in your fridge for too long. Fresh is best, but with a
good layer of olive oil on top, the paste will keep in the fridge for
a month.

Place the black beans in a small heatproof bowl and add hot water
to cover. Soak the beans until plump, about 5 minutes. Drain and
pat dry. On a cutting board, combine the black beans and garlic.
Finely chop the black beans, gradually incorporating the garlic
to form a thick paste. Transfer to a small airtight container and
pour the olive oil over the top (do not stir). Cover and store in the
refrigerator for up to 1 month.

Sizzle Sauce

Makes about 1½ cups (360 ml)

3 cups (170 g) finely chopped green onions (about 2 bunches)

1¼ cups (300 ml) grapeseed oil

1 (2-inch/5 cm) piece fresh ginger, peeled and minced

2 garlic cloves, minced

½ teaspoon kosher salt

It is very common in Chinese cooking to add some drama to your meal by pouring hot oil over a mixture of spices and aromatics, which quickly cooks them and blooms their flavors, resulting in a very satisfying sizzle. You do this as part of making Chili Crunch (page 302) and XO Sauce (page 303), and often as a final touch (done tableside) when serving steamed fish. This sizzle sauce is different in that all the sizzling is done in the pan. It lacks the awe of a tableside show but delivers a more impactful flavor and keeps well in the fridge. The hot oil will coax out more depth and sweetness from the green onions especially. The extra step of blending the infused oil with the aromatics releases even more flavor and emulsifies the sauce into something creamy and irresistible. Use this for Sizzle Sauce Noodles (page 81), spread it over toasted bread, marinate some chicken in it to grill later, or simply eat it with steamed rice and a fried egg.

SIZZLE THE AROMATICS: In a medium skillet, combine the green onions, grapeseed oil, ginger, and garlic. Warm over medium heat until the aromatics begin to sizzle, then cook, stirring occasionally, until the green onion greens start to crisp and lightly brown, about 10 minutes. Turn off the heat and allow to cool for about 10 minutes.

BLEND AND STORE: Carefully transfer the oil and aromatics to a blender. Add the salt and blend for a few moments until mostly smooth. Transfer the sizzle sauce to a jar and allow to fully cool. Cover and store in the fridge for up to 2 weeks.

Dumpling Dip

**Makes about ¾ cup
(180 ml)**

½ cup (120 ml) seafood soy
sauce, preferably Amoy

2 tablespoons apple cider
vinegar

2 teaspoons toasted
sesame oil

1 teaspoon maple syrup

1 teaspoon crushed red
chili flakes

Sweet, salty, tangy, and a touch spicy, this dip is a dumpling's best friend. The recipe is loosely based on my mom's dumpling dipping sauce, and she swears the secret to why it's so good is Amoy brand seafood soy sauce. Not all soy sauces are the same; this particular one is a little thinner, sweeter, and less salty than a typical soy sauce, which contributes to the lightness of the dipping sauce. You can use whatever soy sauce you have access to, of course, but if you happen to find this Amoy variety, don't pass it up.

In a medium bowl, stir together the soy sauce, vinegar, sesame oil, maple syrup, and chili flakes to combine. Serve immediately, or transfer to an airtight container and store in the fridge for up to a few weeks.

Pineapple Sweet-and-Sour Sauce

Makes about 1½ cups (360 ml)

1 cup (240 ml) pineapple juice

¼ cup (50 g) sugar

¼ cup (60 ml) rice vinegar

2 tablespoons ketchup

1 tablespoon cornstarch

1 teaspoon crushed red chili flakes

½ teaspoon kosher salt

You know how a flavor can instantly transport you to such a specific moment in time that you almost feel like you're there? This sweet-and-sour sauce does that for me. When I was a kid, running around my grandparent's restaurant, I would eat an egg roll as an afternoon snack. I would cut the egg roll in half lengthwise, scoop out all the filling, and then dunk the blistered wrapper into a cup of the house-made sweet-and-sour sauce. I vividly remember the orange hue of the sauce and its bright flavor.

This sweet-and-sour sauce is punchy and not too sweet, with a luscious consistency. It's a go-to dipping sauce for anything crispy, like the Chicken and Cabbage Spring Rolls (page 263), and provides a pop of acidity to fried pork chops (page 62).

In a medium saucepan, whisk together the pineapple juice, sugar, vinegar, ketchup, cornstarch, chili flakes, and salt. Warm over medium heat, stirring continuously, until thick and glossy, 5 to 6 minutes. Transfer to an airtight container and allow to fully cool. Cover and store in the fridge for up to 2 weeks.

Party Pickles

Makes 4 cups (800 g)

⅓ pound (150 g) purple daikon radish (or regular daikon), cut into batons (see page 27)

⅓ pound (150 g) carrots, cut into batons (see page 27)

½ medium red onion, thinly sliced

1 Fresno chili, thinly sliced into rings

1 tablespoon kosher salt

1 tablespoon soy sauce

1 cup (240 ml) water

1 cup (240 ml) rice vinegar

¼ cup (50 g) sugar

It's not uncommon to find a jar of these party pickles in my fridge. For some color, crunch, and tartness, I like to set the jar out on the table to share or pluck out a few pickles as a snack throughout the day. These are a more colorful variation of Vietnamese pickled daikon and carrots, making them essential for Banh Mi Pasta Salad (page 164). You'll also find communal jars of pickled daikon at some Chinese restaurants, meant to be eaten as a palate cleanser. My version are affectionately called party pickles because there's something in the jar for everyone, and the medley of colors and flavors brings some life to the dinner table.

ARRANGE THE VEGETABLES: In a large bowl, combine the daikon, carrots, onion, chili, salt, and soy sauce.

MAKE THE BRINE: In a medium saucepan, combine the water, vinegar, and sugar and heat over medium heat until the sugar dissolves. Pour the vinegar mixture over the vegetables and stir gently with chopsticks. Let the vegetables sit in the brine at room temperature until fully cooled, about 1 hour. Transfer the pickles and brine to a jar or airtight container and refrigerate for at least 2 hours before using. The pickles will keep for up to 3 weeks.

Fried Garlic

Makes about ½ cup (50 g) fried garlic and 1⅓ cups (320 ml) allium oil

1½ cups (360 ml) grapeseed oil

½ cup (75 g) minced garlic cloves (from about 2 heads)

Keep a jar of fried garlic in your pantry to use when a dish needs a crunchy, pungent savory sprinkle.

FRY THE GARLIC: Set a fine-mesh strainer over a heatproof container and line a large plate with paper towels. In a medium saucepan, heat the grapeseed oil over medium-low heat until warm, then carefully transfer the garlic to the oil. Fry the garlic, stirring frequently with chopsticks, just until the moment it turns golden brown, 6 to 7 minutes. Garlic can go from golden brown to burnt very quickly!

STRAIN THE GARLIC: Pour the oil and garlic into the strainer. Transfer the fried garlic to the paper towel–lined plate and spread it into an even layer. Allow the garlic to crisp up and cool completely, then transfer it to an airtight container and store at room temperature for up to 2 months. The resulting allium oil can be cooled and stored in an airtight container at room temperature for a few months and used to fry more garlic or to add flavor in other recipes.

Fried Shallots

Makes about 1 cup (80 g) fried shallots and 1⅓ cups (320 ml) allium oil

2 or 3 shallots (140 g)

1 tablespoon rice flour

1½ cups (360 ml) grapeseed oil

If you like French's crispy fried onions, you'll love these homemade fried shallots. They are lighter and crispier and retain the sweetness of a fresh shallot. Use them to top jook (page 210), salads, and even the occasional green bean casserole. A very sharp knife is important for getting the most uniformly thin slices so everything fries evenly. If you're comfortable using a mandoline, you can use that to slice the shallots instead.

SLICE THE SHALLOTS: Trim off the ends of the shallots; peel off and discard the outer layer. Slice each shallot into thin rounds with a very sharp knife or mandoline. Transfer the shallots to a medium bowl and add the rice flour. Toss to lightly coat the shallots.

FRY THE SHALLOTS: Set a fine-mesh strainer over a heatproof container and line a large plate with paper towels. In a medium saucepan, heat the grapeseed oil over medium heat. When the oil is warm, carefully transfer the shallots to the oil and fry, stirring frequently with chopsticks, just until the moment they turn golden brown, 7 to 9 minutes (if they are browning quickly, reduce the heat to medium-low).

STRAIN THE SHALLOTS: Pour the oil and shallots into the strainer. Transfer the fried shallots to the paper towel–lined plate and spread them into an even layer. Allow the shallots to crisp up and cool completely, then transfer them to an airtight container and store at room temperature for up to 1 month. The resulting allium oil can be cooled and stored in an airtight container at room temperature for a few months and used to fry more shallots or to add flavor to other recipes.

Finding Common Ground

Grandparents, parents, and children grow up in vastly different environments, with ever-changing cultural circumstances, yet they usually exist within a lifetime of each other. My goong goong grew up in Southern China, for instance, with a single mother, and when he got older, he moved from Hong Kong to Ohio with his entire family (his mother, wife, and five young children). At a very young age, my mom also had to assimilate herself into a whole new world, navigating life in America with few resources while helping to support her immigrant parents and the family she raised with my dad. Comparatively, my life is far less challenging. I never had to translate for my parents or financially support them. But there is a definite feeling of friction between immigrants and their first-generation American-born children. That conflict often presents itself as choosing the life you want versus the life your family thinks you should pursue after they worked to help create it for you.

One of the greatest gifts my parents have given me is the space to be myself and follow my own path. Admittedly, this took some convincing at times. We have a very good relationship, but not a perfect one. (Is there such thing as a perfect relationship, honestly?) I see it as a constant practice of trying to understand them. When you're raised in an immigrant family, you have unspoken pressures and expectations (even more so when you're the eldest grandchild and the first to be born in America, as

I am). Moving away, traveling the world, and ultimately focusing on yourself is a luxury that many children of immigrants don't get to experience. When we do pursue our own interests, our decisions often coexist with a deep, heavy feeling of guilt. For some, this pressure is purely internalized, while for others, it may come directly from the generations before them. There's always the reality that our families gave so much to us and struggled so we could make our dreams a reality. But we have the opportunity to experience life in a way our parents and grandparents didn't.

All that said, I take issue with the tired narrative of the overly strict Asian parent. The stereotype may ring true for many kids, but my parents, Wanda and Tai, were not like that. It's not that they didn't want my brother and me to do well in school, but their mantra was closer to "Try your best" than "Be the best." As parents, they are painfully goofy, selfless, and exceedingly generous. When I'm with them, I always feel cared for. Their love is evident in the way my mom peels a pomelo for me as an afternoon snack and never lets a dish stay dirty in my sink, and how without fail, my dad will offer me his entire bowl of beef pho (or any meal, for that matter) if I mention that his food looks better than what I ordered (I never actually take him up on it).

My family has always adhered to a fairly rigid "work hard and don't do anything risky" mentality, a remnant of their early days in America when that perspective protected them. My goong goong worked hard to build a restaurant business that provided for his family. He cooked exceptional Chinese food, never took shortcuts, and was always generous with his staff. His motto in business (and in life) was "Put your people first." This is a sentiment shared by immigrant families everywhere, because you're not guaranteed much in life, but you will always have your family.

As a result, thinking of others before myself is ingrained in me. But over time, I've worked on prioritizing my own happiness without that heavy feeling of guilt. Leaving my safe career as an architectural designer to pursue a career in food writing and media was a turning point. My parents were worried at first, naturally, and questioned whether I could financially support myself in San Francisco and if I'd have steady work in the future. I honestly didn't know, but I asked them to trust me. Eventually, they did. Choosing a career born of my own passions and interests was liberating and empowering. And chief among its joys is that I get to share the experience with my family by telling their stories to a whole new audience of readers and home cooks and, of course, by feeding them the results of the recipes I develop.

As it is for countless families, food is our common ground. Cooking with them—not just watching on the sidelines or prepping a few vegetables, but really cooking as a team with different perspectives and techniques—used to be challenging. I would often excuse myself and choose to be a spectator instead, so I wouldn't get in their way or vice versa. Now

the hum of a house filled with people I love and the feeling of harmony in the kitchen while I prepare a dessert and my mom fries spring rolls as my dad stir-fries greens beside her is everything I ever could've dreamed of. Cooking together helps soothe the tensions between generations. I understand my family much more through eating and preparing their favorite dishes, and they, in turn, get a chance to understand me on a deeper level by tasting the recipes I create all on my own.

I Love You, Here's Some Fruit

The very act of peeling, seeding, and slicing fresh fruit is a distinct love language, a simple and quiet gesture of care, especially in an Asian family. Sharing fruit is seen as an act of affection. For many families, including mine, it stems from a time when seasonal fruit was a small yet somewhat accessible luxury. Oranges were the only fruit my grandparents could afford during their early years in America, but when they found a deal on cherries or plums at the market, they would proudly bring home an abundance of them so everyone could experience the sweetness. Asian people are also not particularly known for communicating their feelings verbally, so when words fail, a plate of peeled and sliced mango is an easy way of saying "I love you" or even "I'm sorry."

In-season ripe fruit is beautiful on its own—it is nature's candy, after all. But fruit is also the star of the show when it comes to baking the Malty Banana Cream Pie of your family's dreams, or when it's cooked down into a syrup and turned into vibrant Blueberry and Black Sesame Tang Yuan. Whether suspended in gelatin, layered in an icebox cake, or artfully arranged atop a pie or cake, fresh fruit can take on new dimensions as the grand finale to a memorable meal.

Fruit on Ice (Lime Granita)

Serves 4 to 6

1½ cups (360 ml) water

⅓ cup (80 ml) freshly squeezed lime juice (from 5 to 6 limes)

⅓ cup (67 g) sugar

2 to 3 cups sliced or cut seasonal fruit (whatever looks best at the market or farm stand; see page 318)

"Fruit on Ice" might sound like a potentially entertaining skating event, but in truth, it's a slightly more refined way to present the most common Chinese dessert: chilled fruit. After a robust meal of spicy dumplings and oil-slicked noodles, a platter of sliced oranges or other seasonal fruit provides a refreshing respite. Take the opportunity to compose fruit on ice like a still life, with a variety of your favorite Asian fruits, like longan and mangosteen. There's also something beautifully understated about a platter of thin wedges of apple and stone fruit. The ice underneath in this case is lime granita, which is not only easy to make but also very practical. It chills the fruit while adding crunch, sweetness, and tartness to each bite.

MAKE THE GRANITA: In a medium saucepan, combine the water, lime juice, and sugar. Heat over medium heat, stirring, until the sugar dissolves completely. Turn off the heat and allow to cool for 15 minutes. Transfer the mixture to a heatproof container (a square baking pan works great here) and cover with a lid or plastic wrap. Freeze until mostly solid, about 2 hours, then scrape the lime ice with a fork to create flakes. Freeze for 30 minutes more and then repeat the scraping process every 30 minutes, once or twice more, until all the ice is scraped and fluffy. Keep the granita in the freezer until ready to serve.

ARRANGE THE FRUIT AND SERVE: Just before serving, give the granita one last fluff, then transfer it to a chilled platter, top with the fruit of your choice, and serve.

ABUNDANCE!

Here are a few of my favorite fruits that would make for a spectacular platter of fruit on ice, with recommendations for how to slice and serve them.

ASIAN PEAR | Cut in half, scoop out the core with a spoon, and cut into thin wedges.

FUYU PERSIMMON | Trim off the stem end and cut into ¼-inch-thick (6 mm) slices from the base to the stem, then cut the slices in half.

LONGAN AND LYCHEE | Peel the fruit fully or halfway and have your guests eat around the seed inside.

MANGOSTEEN | Place the fruit on its side on a cutting board and firmly press down with your palm until it breaks open. Peel the fruit fully or halfway, exposing the cloves of flesh inside. Advise your guests that some of the cloves may have a seed they'll need to eat around.

MELONS | Cut the melon in half and remove the seeds. Scoop out the flesh with a melon baller, or peel and cut into chunks.

ORANGES | Trim the top (stem end) and bottom to expose the fruit and stand the orange flat on your cutting board. Cut away the peel from the sides, following the curve of the fruit with your knife. Trim away any remaining pith and cut the fruit into ¼- to ½-inch-thick (6 to 12 mm) slices.

STONE FRUITS (PEACHES, PLUMS, CHERRIES) | Cut in half, scoop out the pit with a spoon or pull it out with your fingers, and cut the flesh into thin wedges or chunks (leave cherries in halves).

Mango Pomelo Sago

Serves 4 to 6

3 ripe Champagne mangoes (about 400 g)

2 cups (480 ml) water

¼ cup (60 ml) sweetened condensed milk

½ cup (80 g) dried sago pearls

1 pomelo, peel and pith removed (see page 322)

You simply cannot survive the heat of Hong Kong without frequenting a dessert café every day. You'll find ice cream and waffles at these cafés, but their primary focus is dessert soups. The creamy base (or broth, if you will) is most often made with sesame paste, coconut milk, or blended fruit, which is then topped with fresh fruit, ice cream, sticky rice (page 336), mochi, taro, sweet red beans, grass jellies—the list could go on forever. Regardless of the topping, the soup is at once cooling, refreshing, and texturally exciting.

I have a deep love for classic mango pomelo sago. It's like a thin mango smoothie with tiny tapioca pearls (sago) and big chunks of mango and juicy pomelo that burst with each spoonful. If pomelo is a little bitter on your palate, you can keep it a strictly mango sago, or add diced peaches or berries instead. A small amount of sweetened condensed milk in the mango puree makes it creamy yet not at all cloying. Use the ripest mangoes you can find to avoid the need to add more sugar.

BLEND THE MANGO: Peel, pit, and cube 2 of the mangoes. In a blender, combine the cubed mangoes, the water, and the condensed milk. Blend until very smooth. Transfer the mixture to an airtight container, cover, and chill in the fridge for at least 1 hour and up to 5 days.

COOK THE SAGO: Meanwhile, bring a saucepan of water to a boil. Pour in the sago pearls and give the pot one gentle stir to prevent them from sticking to the bottom. Boil without stirring (which can cause the sago to break down), until the sago is translucent, 20 to 22 minutes. Drain the sago in a fine-mesh strainer and rinse under cold water. If not serving right away, transfer the sago to an airtight container and add water to cover. Store in the fridge for up to 5 days (the sago will gradually absorb the water in the container).

SERVE: Peel, pit, and cube the remaining mango. With a slotted spoon, divide the sago into serving bowls, pour in the mango mixture, and top with the fresh mango cubes and the pomelo.

How to Peel a Pomelo

The first thing I do to prepare for Lunar New Year is buy a pomelo. Leading up to the holiday, Asian markets are bursting with these giant pale green orbs. The pomelo is the biggest and one of the three original citrus fruits (along with mandarin oranges and citrons). Like all citrus, pomelos are a sign of good luck, and families will happily display the fruit around the house for some festive cheer. Pomelos typically need a few days or even a week or two to ripen after purchase. You'll know when one is ready by smelling it. It should smell strongly floral. The flavor is similar to grapefruit but much sweeter. I love them so much and can easily put back a whole pomelo on my own.

Cutting into a pomelo for the first time can be a little confusing. There is *a lot* of pith to work through before you get to the juicy segments within. Instead of cutting it into wedges or suprêmeing it, like you would an orange, this is the best way to peel a pomelo.

1. Start by cutting off the very top (stem end) of the pomelo until you can just barely see the flesh inside. It normally takes a few exploratory cuts to figure out how deep the pith goes (it could be 1 inch/2.5 cm thick or more), but it's not a big deal if you cut too far in.
2. Cut vertical slits, about 1 inch (2.5 cm) apart, down the sides of the fruit, cutting into the peel until just before you hit the flesh.
3. Working around the fruit, dig your fingers into the pith at the top and pull the peel away from the flesh. The rind will remain intact at the bottom, so you'll be left with a flower-shaped pomelo peel. (I have a tradition that whoever peels the pomelo can force anyone else to wear it as a hat during dinner.)
4. Now that you've removed the peel, pull the fruit apart, separate the segments, and peel away the membrane surrounding each segment. It takes a lot of work to get to the juicy fruit, but it's always worth it.

Orange Lychee Jell-O

Serves 6

1 (20-ounce/565 g) can lychees in syrup, drained (reserve the syrup)

1 cup (240 ml) freshly squeezed orange juice

1½ tablespoons unflavored gelatin powder

1 orange, cut into slices and segments (see page 319)

When was the last time you enjoyed Jell-O? Colorful cups of Jell-O were a highlight of my Midwestern childhood lunch boxes. Making slightly fancy gelatin cups with pieces of fresh fruit will make you feel like a kid again. Here the syrup from canned lychees (never let it go to waste!) is used to sweeten the mix. Lychees and orange segments suspended in gelatin look graceful and sophisticated; the approach is inspired by Chinese osmanthus jellies, which typically have bits of goji berry and osmanthus flowers suspended inside. If you're having friends over, this is a great make-ahead dessert option; watch your guests' faces light up when you say there's Jell-O for dessert.

SIMMER THE GELATIN: In a medium saucepan, whisk together 1 cup (240 ml) of the lychee syrup, the orange juice, and the gelatin powder. Allow the gelatin to bloom until the mixture thickens, 5 to 10 minutes. Heat over medium heat until the mixture just starts to simmer. Turn off the heat and let cool until warm, about 15 minutes.

ADD THE FRUIT AND LET SET: Arrange the lychee and orange segments in six individual 6- to 8-ounce (180 to 240 ml) cups or ramekins. Pour the gelatin mixture into the cups over the fruit. Cover the cups with plastic wrap and chill in the fridge until set, 3 to 4 hours. Serve or store in the fridge for up to 5 days.

Tofu Pudding
with Figs and Ginger Syrup

Serves 6

For the tofu pudding

2 cups (480 ml) unsweetened soy milk

¼ cup (50 g) granulated sugar

2 teaspoons unflavored gelatin powder

1 teaspoon vanilla bean paste or extract

For the syrup

½ cup packed (100 g) brown sugar

½ cup (120 ml) water

1 (2-inch/5 cm) piece fresh ginger, peeled and cut into matchsticks

6 ripe figs, cut into wedges

Tofu pudding is one of the most underrated Chinese desserts. The pudding is made from soy milk (soybeans being the foundation of tofu) set with a thickener, which gives it a texture similar to silken tofu. The dessert is normally served with syrup, but I love the way that jammy ripe figs, with their honeylike interior, amplify the deep flavor of the brown sugar ginger syrup that's drizzled over the top. When it's not fig season, dark fruits like blackberries, mulberries, and plums make excellent substitutes, even if they aren't traditional toppings.

The most important factor in the success of this recipe is the soy milk, which you should buy from an Asian grocery store. I wouldn't even consider using the versions of soy milk sold in most American grocery stores, as it's not remotely the same. The texture and flavors are just off. But if you can't find Asian soy milk, or you're looking to save time and don't want to make the pudding entirely from scratch, use silken tofu instead. The texture is close enough. In that case, all you have to do is make the syrup and slice some fruit.

MAKE THE TOFU PUDDING: In a medium saucepan, whisk together the soy milk, granulated sugar, gelatin, and vanilla. Bring to a simmer over medium heat, then immediately turn off the heat and let cool until warm to the touch. Transfer to an airtight container, cover, and chill in the fridge until set but still jiggly, at least 3 to 4 hours and up to overnight.

SIMMER THE SYRUP: In a small saucepan, combine the brown sugar, water, and ginger. Bring to a simmer over medium heat, stirring to dissolve the sugar completely, then simmer for about 5 minutes, until the syrup has thickened. Turn off the heat and let the syrup cool completely.

TOP WITH FRUIT AND SERVE: Scoop thin layers of the chilled tofu pudding into six individual 6- to 8-ounce (180 to 240 ml) cups or ramekins. Pour the syrup over the pudding and top with the sliced figs.

Blueberry and Black Sesame Tang Yuan

Makes 18 dumplings

For the filling

½ cup (125 g) black sesame paste

2 tablespoons unsalted butter, at room temperature

2 tablespoons sugar

For the dough

⅔ cup (3 ounces/85 g) fresh or frozen blueberries

½ cup (120 ml) water

2 tablespoons sugar

1 cup plus 3 tablespoons (142 g) glutinous rice flour, plus more as needed

Lunar New Year is a fifteen-day-long celebration. The Lantern Festival falls on the last day, when the tradition is to light loads of lanterns, set off some firecrackers, watch a lion dance or two, and eat tang yuan. These chewy glutinous rice balls are filled with sweet nuts and, on some occasions, a savory combo of cabbage and mushrooms. The round shape of the dumplings mimics the moon and represents wholeness, which is a big theme of Lunar New Year. I first tried tang yuan at my ma ma's (paternal grandmother's) apartment in Hong Kong, and I have a very fuzzy memory of asking for a second bowl, followed by a third.

This tang yuan dough is made with a blueberry syrup to give it a violet color and faint berry flavor. When paired with the black sesame paste, it tastes like sophisticated peanut butter and jelly. The black sesame paste is blended with softened butter so that when the tang yuan boils away, the filling turns into a sweet and nutty molten dumpling belly.

MIX THE FILLING: In a medium bowl, combine the sesame paste, butter, and sugar with a flexible spatula until very smooth. Cover and chill in the fridge until firm but scoopable, about 1 hour. Line a plate or quarter sheet pan with parchment paper. Scoop heaping teaspoons of the filling onto the plate and freeze until solid, 20 to 30 minutes. (This step makes rolling the dumplings much easier.)

SIMMER THE SYRUP: In a small saucepan, combine the blueberries, water, and sugar. Bring to a simmer over medium heat. As the blueberries plump and darken in color, smash them with the back of a wooden spoon or spatula (the water will turn dark purple). Simmer until the mixture is syrupy, 4 to 5 minutes. Turn off the heat and let cool for a few minutes.

KNEAD THE DOUGH: Place the rice flour in a medium bowl. Pour in the blueberry syrup, mixing with a flexible spatula to form a shaggy dough. Scrape any dough stuck on the spatula back into the bowl. Cover the bowl with a plate and allow the dough to rest and cool for 10 minutes (the steam will fully hydrate the dough).

(recipe continues)

Turn the dough out onto a clean work surface and knead until very smooth, about 1 minute. The dough should be tacky like Play-Doh, not sticky. If it sticks to your hands, add another tablespoon of rice flour at a time until it no longer sticks.

ASSEMBLE THE DUMPLINGS: Divide the dough into 18 equal pieces (about ½ ounce/13 to 14 g each; use a digital scale if you have one). Roll one piece of dough between your palms into a small ball. Dust it with a little extra rice flour and flatten it between your palms into a 1½-inch-diameter (4 cm) round. Place a ball of frozen sesame paste in the center and pinch the edges of the dough together to completely enclose the filling. Set the dumpling on a plate and repeat with the remaining dough and filling.

BOIL THE DUMPLINGS: Bring a large pot of water to a boil. Working in batches of 6, carefully drop the dumplings into the water. Give the pot a gentle stir to keep them from sticking to the bottom. Boil until the dumplings float to the surface, 3 to 4 minutes. With a slotted spoon, scoop the dumplings into serving bowls (3 per serving) and spoon a few tablespoons of the boiling liquid into the bowls so the dumplings don't stick to each other or to the bowl. Repeat with the remaining dumplings. Serve warm.

HOW TO FREEZE AND REHEAT TANG YUAN

Freeze any extra tang yuan before boiling on a small plate or quarter sheet pan until solid, then transfer to a zip-top bag and store in the freezer for up to 3 months. To reheat, bring a large pot of water to a boil and boil as you would fresh tang yuan, allowing a few extra minutes of cooking time.

Raspberry and White Rabbit Cookies

Makes 8 big cookies

12 tablespoons (1½ sticks/ 170 g) unsalted butter

1 cup (135 g) all-purpose flour

½ teaspoon kosher salt

¼ teaspoon baking soda

12 White Rabbit candies (65 g), unwrapped

½ cup (100 g) granulated sugar

¼ cup packed (50 g) brown sugar

1 large egg

2 teaspoons vanilla bean paste or extract

¾ cup (110 g) fresh raspberries

1½ teaspoons flaky sea salt

There's a lot going on in this crave-worthy cookie—crispy edges, rich butterscotch flavor, bright raspberries, chewy puddles of White Rabbit candy, and an aggressive amount of flaky salt—but everything is in balance. White Rabbit is an iconic Chinese candy that tastes like sweetened condensed milk; you can buy it at any Chinese or Asian grocery store. These cookies are best eaten warm, while the candies are still gooey and the berries are jammy. The dough freezes beautifully, so you can stash away any extra portions in the freezer and be that much closer to having freshly baked cookies whenever the craving strikes.

BROWN THE BUTTER: In a medium saucepan, melt the butter over medium-low heat. Use a flexible spatula to stir the melted butter continuously until it turns a deeper brown with golden brown milk solids, 6 to 8 minutes. (Watch closely, as butter can burn quickly. If the butter starts to brown too quickly, reduce the heat.) Transfer the brown butter to a large bowl and let cool completely, 20 to 25 minutes.

WHISK THE DRY INGREDIENTS: In a medium bowl, whisk together the flour, kosher salt, and baking soda.

SOFTEN THE CANDY: Place the candies in a heatproof medium bowl and microwave at 50 percent power for 40 seconds to soften them. They should have a little give when you press on them; if they don't, microwave for 10 seconds more. (If you don't have a microwave, spread the candies on a small baking sheet lined with parchment paper and soften them in a 300°F (149°C) oven for 2 to 4 minutes.) Transfer the softened candies to a cutting board and carefully pull them apart into longer strands, breaking some of them apart.

MIX THE DOUGH: Add the granulated sugar and brown sugar to the cooled brown butter and whisk until smooth. Add the egg and vanilla and whisk until very smooth and lightened in color, about 1 minute. Add the flour mixture and combine with a flexible spatula until only a few dry streaks remain. Scatter the raspberries and candy pieces over the dough and gently mix until just combined. The raspberries will break down a bit when you mix them in. For more photogenic cookies, save a few pieces of the candies to stick into the cookies right before baking. Cover and chill the dough until firm but scoopable, at least 1 hour and up to 24 hours.

WARM UP: Preheat the oven to 350°F (177°C) and line two large rimmed baking sheets with parchment paper.

BAKE THE COOKIES: Scoop 3-tablespoon portions of dough (a disher or cookie scoop is handy for this) onto the prepared baking sheets, spacing them at least 3 inches (7.5 cm) apart. If you're using a spoon for this, try your best to form the dough into even rounds on the baking sheets. Sprinkle flaky salt over the top of each cookie.

Bake the cookies until golden brown around the edges, 14 to 16 minutes. Allow the cookies to cool on the pan for 10 minutes before serving or transferring to a wire rack to cool completely.

HOW TO FREEZE COOKIE DOUGH

Line a quarter sheet pan with parchment paper. Scoop the dough into 3-tablespoon portions and place it on the prepared pan. Loosely cover with plastic wrap and freeze until solid. Transfer the dough balls to a zip-top bag, press out any air, and store in the freezer for up to 3 months. (If you're planning on baking these in the next day or two, you can just store them in the fridge.) Before baking the cookies, allow the frozen cookie dough to thaw on the counter for at least 30 minutes (or pull it from the fridge about 15 minutes before baking). Bake as you would fresh cookie dough, allowing an extra minute or two of baking time.

Passion Fruit and Hojicha Icebox Cake

Serves 6 to 8

1½ cups (350 g) fresh or frozen passion fruit pulp

Finely grated zest of 1 orange

2 cups (480 ml) heavy cream

¾ cup (75 g) confectioners' sugar

1 tablespoon hojicha powder

9 to 12 cream crackers (preferably Hup Seng) or graham crackers

When I would visit my grandparents' house as a child, I could always count on finding a box of ice cream in the freezer. Yes, a box—not a pint. My goong goong would completely unfold the walls of the box (which turned into a plate of sorts) and cut the big brick of ice cream into slices. Sometimes it was plain vanilla and other times it was Neapolitan, with layers of chocolate, vanilla, and strawberry. For some crunch, I would top my slice with crushed-up animal crackers or cream crackers, if they were on hand. (This was one of my earliest forays into recipe development, I'm sure.)

Those memories inspired this icebox cake, with its layers of tart passion fruit, ethereal hojicha (a roasted green tea similar to matcha), whipped cream, and cream crackers (I like Hup Seng cream crackers because the tin they're packaged in makes a great decorative element in my kitchen). While the icebox cake sets in the freezer, the crackers absorb the moisture from the whipped cream and get slightly mushy, but in the best cookies-and-cream-ice-cream kind of way.

REDUCE THE PASSION FRUIT: In a medium saucepan, combine the passion fruit pulp and orange zest. Bring to a simmer over medium-low heat. Simmer, stirring occasionally, until thick, 15 to 18 minutes. Allow the mixture to cool for a few minutes, then transfer to a heatproof container. Cover with a lid and chill in the fridge until cooled completely (it will continue to thicken as it cools), at least 1 hour and up to 5 days.

WHIP THE CREAM: In the bowl of a stand mixer fitted with the whisk attachment, combine the cream, confectioners' sugar, and hojicha powder. Whip on medium speed just until medium-stiff peaks form, 3 to 5 minutes.

ASSEMBLE THE CAKE: Line the long sides of a 9 by 5-inch (23 by 13 cm) loaf pan with parchment paper, leaving a few inches of overhang on either side for lifting. With an offset spatula, spread a quarter of the cream mixture over the bottom of the loaf pan. Drizzle a quarter of the passion fruit over the cream. Arrange a single layer of the crackers over the passion fruit, cutting them as needed to make an even layer. Repeat to form more layers of cream, passion fruit, and crackers, dividing them evenly and ending with a layer of cream and a drizzle of passion fruit. Cover the pan with plastic wrap and freeze until solid, at least 4 hours and ideally overnight.

SERVE: Using the overhanging parchment, lift the cake out of the pan and transfer it to a cutting board. Remove the parchment, slice the cake, and serve. (Running a sharp knife under hot water will give you very clean cuts.) Store any remaining cake in the freezer, wrapped or covered well; it will keep for up to 2 weeks.

Grilled Peaches and Coconut Sticky Rice

Serves 4 to 6

1 (13.5-ounce/400 ml) can full-fat coconut milk

1 tablespoon sugar

½ teaspoon kosher salt

¾ cup (165 g) sticky rice

¼ cup (55 g) short-grain purple sticky rice (or more regular sticky rice)

Neutral oil, such as grapeseed, for grilling

3 medium peaches, halved and pitted

2 tablespoons unsalted butter, melted

Here's a delightful, slightly smokier twist on the ever-popular Thai mango sticky rice. The magic happens when you grill ripe peach halves, allowing the flames to impart a smoky char as they intensify the natural sweetness of the fruit. The jammy caramelized peaches make a wonderful foil to the salty-sweet coconut sauce and chewy rice. Keep this dish in mind when you're looking for a dessert to top off a backyard barbecue while the grill is still hot. There's also something special about serving this dessert family-style, with the rice and peaches spread out on a big platter for everyone to scoop into. It makes a delicious, beautiful mess.

MAKE THE COCONUT SAUCE: In a medium saucepan, stir together ½ cup (120 ml) of the coconut milk, the sugar, and the salt with a flexible spatula. Bring just to a simmer over medium-low heat, then cook at a gentle simmer, stirring continuously, until the mixture is thick and glossy, 5 to 7 minutes. Remove from the heat and allow the sauce to cool in the pan (or transfer it to a small cup or bowl).

COOK THE RICE: In a medium saucepan, rinse the rice to remove some of the starch, then drain. Add the remaining coconut milk to the pan and bring to a simmer over medium-high heat. Reduce the heat to medium-low, cover, and simmer gently until the rice is plump and tender, 15 to 18 minutes. Turn off the heat and let the rice steam, covered, for 5 minutes. Remove the lid, fluff the rice, and allow to cool for a few minutes.

GRILL THE PEACHES: Preheat the grill to medium-high (between 450° and 500°F/232° and 260°C) for at least 30 minutes. Pour some oil onto a bundle of paper towels and, holding them with tongs, rub them over the grill grates to lightly coat with oil.

Brush the cut faces of the peaches with melted butter and place them cut-side down on the grill grates over direct heat. Grill the peaches are until caramelized and (you will see grill marks), 4 to 5 minutes. Flip the peaches, brush with more butter, and grill on

the other side just to soften slightly, 1 to 2 minutes. Transfer the grilled peaches to a plate.

ASSEMBLE AND SERVE: Pour about half the coconut sauce into a deep serving platter. Scoop the rice onto the platter, into either one big mound or multiple smaller mounds, and arrange the peaches on top. Drizzle the remaining coconut sauce over the rice and peaches and serve.

Sesame Persimmon Galette

Serves 8

For the dough

1¾ cups (229 g) all-purpose flour, plus more as needed

12 tablespoons (1½ sticks/170 g) unsalted butter, cut into cubes and chilled

¼ teaspoon kosher salt

⅓ cup (80 ml) cold water

For the filling

½ cup (130 g) sesame paste or tahini

2 tablespoons honey

2 tablespoons confectioners' sugar

1 teaspoon vanilla bean paste or extract

½ teaspoon ground cinnamon

½ teaspoon ground ginger

¼ teaspoon kosher salt

5 semi-ripe Fuyu persimmons (about 1½ pounds/730 g), cut into thin wedges and seeded (if necessary)

For the topping

1 large egg, whisked

1 tablespoon sesame seeds

For the glaze

¼ cup (60 ml) water

¼ cup (50 g) granulated sugar

Persimmons taste like fall, with subtle hints of vanilla and cinnamon. Some varieties of persimmon (like Fuyus) can be eaten when they're still crisp like an apple, while others (like Hachiyas) can only be eaten when they're beyond ripe and extremely soft to the touch.

This galette is a favorite way to make use of an abundance of persimmons (or other fruits), regardless of the season. It's best made with semi-ripe Fuyu persimmons, which should have a very slight give to them if you press on their skin but should not yet be squishy. A layer of honey-sweetened tahini grounds the persimmons (both physically and flavorwise), and the buttery crust hugs everything together as the fruit releases its natural sugars. Serve while still warm from the oven with a scoop of ice cream or malty whipped cream (page 345) on top.

MAKE THE DOUGH: Place the flour, butter, and salt in a food processor. Pulse a few times just to form a few clumps. With the food processor running, slowly pour in the cold water until the dough just comes together (this should take no more than 30 seconds). Transfer the dough to a clean countertop and briefly knead just to bring it together. Pat the dough into a 6-inch (15 cm) disc and wrap in plastic wrap. Chill in the fridge for at least 2 hours and up to 5 days.

ASSEMBLE AND BAKE THE GALETTE: Preheat the oven to 400°F (204°C) and line a large rimmed baking sheet with parchment paper. In a medium bowl, whisk together the sesame paste, honey, confectioners' sugar, vanilla, cinnamon, ginger, and salt until smooth and thick.

On a lightly floured surface, roll out the dough into a 13-inch (33 cm) round. Transfer the dough to the prepared baking sheet. Spread the sesame paste mixture over the dough, leaving a 1-inch (2.5 cm) border. Arrange the persimmon wedges over the sesame paste mixture. Fold the border of the dough over the filling, leaving the center exposed. Brush the dough with the egg and sprinkle with the sesame seeds. Bake the galette until the crust is golden brown and the fruit is tender, 28 to 32 minutes.

MAKE THE GLAZE: In a small saucepan, combine the water and granulated sugar. Warm over medium heat, stirring, until the sugar dissolves, then bring to a simmer and cook until the mixture thickens, 3 to 5 minutes. Turn off the heat and let the glaze cool.

SERVE: Remove the galette from the oven and immediately brush the persimmons with the glaze. Slice and serve the galette while still warm, or allow to cool completely and serve at room temperature.

Pistachio Pear Baked Nian Gao

Serves 8

1 cup (125 g) raw pistachios

4 tablespoons (½ stick/57 g) unsalted butter

1 (13.5-ounce/400 ml) can full-fat coconut milk

½ cup packed (100 g) brown sugar

2 large eggs

1 teaspoon vanilla bean paste or extract

2 cups (260 g) glutinous rice flour or mochiko flour

1 tablespoon baking powder

1 teaspoon ground cinnamon

½ teaspoon ground ginger

½ teaspoon ground cardamom

½ teaspoon kosher salt

Nonstick cooking spray

1 Bosc or Bartlett pear, cut into thin wedges and cored

Nian gao is a traditional steamed sticky rice cake used to celebrate Lunar New Year, symbolizing growth and advancement. The classic version made with glutinous rice flour and brown sugar is a little too sticky for my taste. So for this recipe, I drew inspiration from Hawaiian butter mochi and mochi muffins, which have a similar foundation of sweet rice flour but are enriched with butter and coconut milk. They are also baked rather than steamed. The result is nian gao that is chewy with a slightly sticky core and a crisp, toasty crust. Pistachios, warming spices, and pear take this cake into cozy-winter-baking territory.

TOAST THE PISTACHIOS: Preheat the oven to 325°F (163°C). Spread the pistachios on a rimmed baking sheet and bake until fragrant and lightly toasted, 8 to 10 minutes, giving the pan a quick shake halfway through. Let the pistachios cool completely, then transfer to a food processor. Pulse until roughly chopped, about 1 minute. Reserve ¼ cup (30 g) for the topping. Pulse the remaining pistachios until very finely chopped, 2 to 3 minutes more. If the pistachios accidentally end up as pistachio butter, don't worry, it won't negatively impact the cake!

MIX THE BATTER: In a medium saucepan, melt the butter over medium heat, then turn off the heat and whisk in the coconut milk, finely chopped pistachios, brown sugar, eggs, and vanilla until smooth. In a medium bowl, whisk together the rice flour, baking powder, cinnamon, ginger, cardamom, and salt. Add the flour mixture to the butter mixture and whisk until thick and smooth.

BAKE THE CAKE: Coat a 10-inch (25 cm) cast-iron skillet or round cake pan with nonstick spray. Pour the batter into the pan and arrange the pear slices on top in a sunflower pattern (or whatever pattern you like, but try not to overlap the fruit too much because it will prevent the batter underneath from fully baking). Sprinkle the reserved chopped pistachios around the outer edge of the pan and in the center of the batter. Bake until the edges are crisp and golden brown and the cake is set in the center, 35 to 38 minutes.

Transfer the cake to a wire rack to cool before serving. Cover any remaining cake and store on the counter for up to 1 day, then transfer to the fridge, where it will keep for up to 5 days more.

Soy Caramel Apple Crisp

Serves 6 to 8

1 cup (200 g) granulated sugar

6 tablespoons (¾ stick/85 g) unsalted butter, cut into cubes

½ cup (120 ml) heavy cream, at room temperature

1½ tablespoons soy sauce

For the topping

½ cup (60 g) rolled oats

2 tablespoons all-purpose flour

2 tablespoons brown sugar

½ teaspoon kosher salt

½ teaspoon Chinese five spice powder

4 tablespoons (½ stick/57 g) unsalted butter, cut into small cubes and chilled

For the filling

6 Fuji apples (about 2¼ pounds/1 kg)

1 tablespoon cornstarch

1½ teaspoons Chinese five spice powder

¼ teaspoon kosher salt

Ice cream, for serving

This crisp is built around two dessert standbys: apples and caramel sauce. Wherever you are, no matter what time of year it is, you can usually find decent apples. And once you learn to make caramel sauce from scratch, you'll realize that the process is amazingly simple, easy to remember, and adaptable. Combining the two creates a dessert that at first tastes familiar and traditional—until you notice the salty, earthy undertones courtesy of the splash of soy sauce in the caramel. The recipe intentionally makes more soy caramel sauce than you need; you can drizzle some of the extra caramel on top of the crisp, or dip apple wedges into it as a snack while the crisp bakes, which you will definitely want to do.

MAKE THE CARAMEL SAUCE: In a medium saucepan (preferably stainless steel), melt the granulated sugar over medium heat, stirring continuously with a flexible spatula, until it's a light amber color, 7 to 9 minutes. The sugar will initially clump up, but keep stirring and it will eventually melt. Reduce the heat to medium-low and add the butter cubes (the sugar will bubble up a little). Stir until the butter is melted and incorporated completely. Stir in the cream (again, a little bubbling will occur at first) until combined, then stir in the soy sauce. When everything is incorporated and the sauce is smooth, remove from the heat and allow it to cool to room temperature. (If you're not using the sauce immediately, transfer it to an airtight container, cover, and refrigerate until ready to use, up to 2 weeks. The caramel will firm up as it chills; reheat it until pourable before serving, if needed.)

MIX THE TOPPING: In a medium bowl, combine the oats, flour, brown sugar, salt, and five spice. Add the cold butter, rubbing it into the oat mixture with your fingertips to form crumbs.

ASSEMBLE AND BAKE THE CRISP: Preheat the oven to 350°F (177°C).

Core the apples and chop into roughly ½-inch (1 cm) chunks. Place them in an 8- to 10-inch (20 to 25 cm) baking dish (oval, round, or square works fine) and add ⅔ cup (160 ml) of the caramel sauce, the cornstarch, five spice, and salt. Toss until well coated. Spread the apples into an even layer in the dish and sprinkle with the oat

topping. Bake until the apples are very tender, the caramel is gently bubbling, and the topping is crisp, 45 to 50 minutes. Transfer the crisp to a wire rack to cool for a few minutes before serving.

SERVE: Serve the crisp with ice cream and a drizzle of extra caramel sauce.

Malty Banana Cream Pie

Serves 8 to 10

⅓ cup (68 g) granulated sugar

¼ cup (30 g) cornstarch

3 large eggs

1 tablespoon vanilla bean paste or extract

½ teaspoon kosher salt

2 cups (480 ml) whole milk

4 tablespoons (½ stick/57 g) unsalted butter, cut into cubes

For the dough

1¾ cups (229 g) all-purpose flour, plus more as needed

12 tablespoons (1½ sticks/170 g) unsalted butter, cut into cubes and chilled

¼ teaspoon kosher salt

⅓ cup (80 ml) cold water

For the whipped cream

1½ cups (360 ml) heavy cream

½ cup (80 g) malt powder

¼ cup (30 g) confectioners' sugar

Pinch of kosher salt

For assembly

4 bananas, peeled and sliced

⅓ cup (35 g) chocolate malt balls, roughly chopped

For as long as I can remember, my dad's birthday has been celebrated with banana cream pie. He's a man who doesn't need much and hates getting gifts, but he's always grateful for a home-baked treat and a box of his favorite candies: Maltesers (the British equivalent of American Whoppers). He grew up eating the chocolate-covered malt balls in Hong Kong. This extra-special banana cream pie has the flavors of his beloved Maltesers woven in. The flaky pie shell is just thick enough to maintain the right balance of crust to filling. The pastry cream is luscious and heavy on the vanilla. And the whipped cream is flavored with malted milk powder, which makes it distinctly (but not overly) nutty and so irresistible that you could eat it by the spoonful, straight out of the bowl. A sprinkle of chopped malt balls over a tall slice of pie provides the final sweet touch.

MAKE THE PASTRY CREAM: In a medium bowl, whisk together the granulated sugar, cornstarch, eggs, vanilla, and salt until smooth. In a small saucepan, warm the milk over medium heat until it just starts to steam. Turn off the heat.

While whisking continuously, slowly pour ½ cup (120 ml) of the warm milk into the egg mixture in a steady stream, then whisk until very smooth. Pour the mixture into the saucepan with the remaining milk. Heat over medium-low heat, whisking continuously, until the custard thickens enough that the whisk leaves a trail, 12 to 15 minutes. Whisk in the butter until melted and incorporated. Transfer the custard to a medium bowl and cover with plastic wrap, pressing it directly against the surface of the custard to prevent a skin from forming. Chill in the fridge for at least 2 hours and up to 5 days.

MAKE THE DOUGH: Place the flour, butter, and salt in a food processor. Pulse a few times, just until a few clumps are formed. While the food processor is running, slowly pour in the cold water and process just until the dough comes together, about 30 seconds. Transfer the dough to a clean work surface and briefly knead to bring together. Pat the dough into a 6-inch (15 cm) disc and wrap tightly in plastic wrap. Chill in the fridge until very firm, at least 2 hours and up to 5 days.

(recipe continues)

BAKE THE CRUST: Preheat the oven to 425°F (218°C). On a lightly floured work surface, roll out the disc of dough into a 13-inch (33 cm) round. Gently fold the dough into quarters and transfer it to a 9-inch (23 cm) pie dish. Unfold the dough and fit it into the dish, tucking the edges of the dough under to form a thick outer edge that slightly overhangs the lip of the dish. Crimp the edges with your fingertips and prick the bottom of the crust a few times with a fork. Press a sheet of parchment paper over the dough and fill with pie weights, dried beans, or uncooked rice (I use about 2 cups/220 g of rice). Bake until the crust is just starting to brown, 15 to 18 minutes. Remove the parchment and weights (save the rice to reuse for another pie, or steam it for dinner). Bake until the crust is flaky and golden brown, 12 to 15 minutes more. Transfer it to a wire rack to cool completely.

MAKE THE WHIPPED CREAM: Place the heavy cream, malt powder, confectioners' sugar, and salt in the bowl of a stand mixer fitted with the whisk attachment. Whip on medium speed until medium-stiff peaks form, 3 to 5 minutes (take care not to overmix; you want soft mounds of whipped cream here for spreading).

ASSEMBLE THE PIE AND SERVE: Arrange a layer of banana slices (about 1½ bananas' worth) over the bottom of the crust. Spoon half the pastry cream over the bananas, spreading it evenly and filling in any gaps between the banana slices. Arrange another layer of banana slices (again, about 1½ bananas) over the pastry cream and spread the remaining pastry cream on top. Dollop the whipped cream over the pastry cream and swirl it with the back of a spoon. Top with the remaining banana slices and sprinkle with the chopped malt balls. Serve immediately, or tent loosely with foil and chill in the fridge until ready to serve, up to 4 days.

Lucky Cheesecake with Kumquats

Serves 8 to 10

1½ (8-ounce/226 g) packages cream cheese, at room temperature

½ cup (113 g) sour cream, at room temperature

4 large eggs, separated, at room temperature

1 teaspoon vanilla bean paste or extract

½ teaspoon almond extract

½ teaspoon kosher salt

1 cup (200 g) sugar

1½ cups (8 ounces/226 g) kumquats, thinly sliced and seeded

A lucky cheesecake is not a Japanese-style soufflé cheesecake. It's not a burnt Basque cheesecake, either. And it's definitely not a New York–style cheesecake. It combines elements from all three. There's no crust; it simply doesn't need it. The texture is cloudlike without losing any of the creamy body, and there's a hint of almond flavor. As it bakes, the top of the cheesecake will puff up and dome (thanks to the whipped egg whites), but it will deflate as it cools, creating a dip in the center with raised edges. Normally, deflation is an alarming sign when you're baking a cake, but here it's exactly what you're aiming for.

What makes this cheesecake lucky? It's the sheer amount of kumquats on top. Having a bountiful kumquat tree for Lunar New Year is a major flex, because in Chinese, the fruit's name sounds a lot like the word for gold, essentially promising you're going to be prosperous in the new year. If only life were as easy as simply eating auspicious fruit, am I right? Kumquats are like nature's Sour Patch Kids. The skin and pith are edible, so you can pop the whole fruit into your mouth and enjoy the initial burst of sweetness and the puckering tartness that soon follows. Here the tiny citrus are sliced into coins and thrown into the crater of the cheesecake. The more kumquats on the cheesecake, the brighter and luckier the future!

LINE THE PAN: Preheat the oven to 325°F (163°C). Press a large sheet of parchment paper into an 8-inch (20 cm) round cake pan, making sure the parchment paper overhangs the edge by about 3 inches (7.5 cm).

PREPARE THE BATTER: In a large bowl, stir the cream cheese with a flexible spatula until very smooth. Add the sour cream, egg yolks, vanilla, almond extract, and salt and mix until very smooth.

In the bowl of a stand mixer fitted with the whisk attachment, whip the egg whites on medium speed until frothy, about 2 minutes. Increase the speed to medium-high and slowly add the sugar in a steady stream. Whip until the egg whites reach medium peaks (when you lift the whisk out of the bowl, the meringue should mostly hold its shape but the peak should curl a little; take care not to overwhip), 6 to 8 minutes.

(recipe continues)

Add about one-third of the meringue to the cream cheese mixture and gently fold it in. Repeat with another one-third of the meringue. Add the remaining meringue and fold just until there are no white streaks of meringue showing.

BAKE THE CHEESECAKE: Pour the batter into the prepared pan and bake until the cheesecake is lightly golden brown and fluffy but still a little jiggly in the center, 65 to 75 minutes. Don't worry if there are cracks on the surface; they are natural. Turn off the oven and allow the cheesecake to cool in the oven until just warm to the touch, 30 to 45 minutes (it will deflate during this time). Transfer the cheesecake to a wire rack and cool completely in the pan.

CHILL THE CHEESECAKE: Cover the cheesecake with foil or plastic wrap and chill in the fridge for at least 4 hours and up to 4 days before serving.

TOP WITH KUMQUATS AND SERVE: Remove the cheesecake from the pan using the overhanging parchment and set it on a large plate or platter. Place the sliced kumquats in a pile in the center of the cheesecake and serve. Store any leftover cheesecake, covered, in the fridge for up to 5 days.

Cleveland-ish Cassata Cake

Serves 8 to 10

For the pastry cream

¼ cup (50 g) granulated sugar

2 large eggs

2 tablespoons cornstarch

1 teaspoon vanilla bean paste or extract

½ teaspoon kosher salt

1¼ cups (300 ml) whole milk

2 tablespoons unsalted butter, cut into cubes

For the fruit layer

2½ pounds (1.13 kg) strawberries, plus a few more for topping

For the sponge cake

1 cup (120 g) cake flour

2 tablespoons cornstarch

1½ teaspoons baking powder

¼ teaspoon kosher salt

6 large eggs, separated

¼ teaspoon cream of tartar

¾ cup (150 g) granulated sugar

⅓ cup (80 ml) extra-virgin olive oil

1 teaspoon vanilla bean paste or extract

(ingredients continue)

You might be wondering what an Italian cake with roots in Cleveland, Ohio, is doing in a Chinese American cookbook. Cleveland-style cassata cake is somewhat different from the Italian standard. In Italy, the cake layers are soaked in liqueur, layered with sweetened ricotta filling, and covered with whipped cream and fruit. This creation from Corbo's Bakery is a sponge cake layered with custard and macerated strawberries. It's not as sweet or heavy as many American layer cakes, so it reminds my mother of the airy cream cakes from Chinese bakeries in Hong Kong. She loved the cake so much that when my parents had their wedding in Hong Kong, she had the Chinese bakers create a Cleveland cassata cake. Over the years, cassata cake has continued to appear at family birthdays and graduations.

This cake has several components that take time to prepare. It's a project, but absolutely worth it. The sponge cake is airy, the whipped cream is fortified with crème fraîche (which makes it sturdy and gives it a gentle tang), and the strawberries are roasted to concentrate their natural sweetness, rather than macerated with additional sugar. You can decorate the cake to look as rustic or refined as you want.

MAKE THE PASTRY CREAM: In a medium bowl, whisk together the granulated sugar, eggs, cornstarch, vanilla, and salt until smooth. In a medium saucepan, warm the milk over medium heat until it just starts to steam. Turn off the heat.

While whisking continuously, slowly pour ½ cup (120 ml) of the warm milk into the egg mixture in a steady stream, then whisk until very smooth. Pour the egg mixture into the saucepan with the remaining milk. Heat over medium-low heat, whisking continuously, until the custard thickens enough that the whisk leaves a trail, 12 to 15 minutes. Whisk in the butter until melted and incorporated. Transfer the custard to a medium bowl and cover with plastic wrap, pressing it directly against the surface of the custard to prevent a skin from forming. Chill in the fridge for at least 2 hours and up to 5 days.

ROAST THE BERRIES: Preheat the oven to 325°F (163°C) and line a large rimmed baking sheet with parchment paper. Set aside a few strawberries for decorating. Hull the remaining strawberries and

For the whipped cream

2 cups (480 ml) heavy cream

½ cup (60 g) confectioners' sugar

1 teaspoon almond extract

½ teaspoon kosher salt

1 cup (240 g) crème fraîche

cut them into ½-inch-thick (1 cm) slices. Arrange the strawberry slices on the prepared baking sheet in a single layer. Roast until very tender and jammy, 60 to 65 minutes. Transfer the baking sheet to a wire rack and allow the strawberries to cool completely. Increase the oven temperature to 350°F (177°C).

MIX THE CAKE BATTER: Cut rounds of parchment to line the bottoms of three 8-inch (20 cm) round cake pans. In a medium bowl, whisk together the cake flour, cornstarch, baking powder, and salt.

Place the egg whites and cream of tartar in the bowl of a stand mixer fitted with the whisk attachment. Place the egg yolks in a separate large bowl. Whip the egg whites on medium speed until foamy, 1 to 2 minutes. Increase the speed to medium-high and slowly add ¼ cup (50 g) of the granulated sugar in a steady stream. Whip until the egg whites reach stiff peaks, 5 to 7 minutes.

Add the remaining ½ cup (100 g) sugar, the olive oil, and the vanilla to the bowl with the egg yolks. Vigorously whisk by hand until pale and smooth, 1 to 2 minutes. Using a flexible spatula, scoop out about 1 cup (50 g) of the beaten egg whites and fold them into the egg yolk mixture until fully incorporated. Fold the remaining egg white mixture into the yolk mixture in three additions, alternating with the flour mixture, reaching to the bottom and around the sides of the bowl as you fold so that no traces of flour remain. Take care not to deflate the beaten whites as you fold.

BAKE THE CAKE LAYERS: Divide the batter evenly among the prepared pans. Bake until the tops of the cakes are lightly golden brown and a toothpick inserted into the center comes out clean, 15 to 18 minutes. Transfer the pans to a wire rack and let the cakes cool until they deflate, so their tops are flat, 1 to 2 minutes. Invert the cakes onto the rack (this will prevent the cakes from deflating too much) and let cool completely. To release the cakes, flip them back over and run a small offset spatula around the edges of the cake, then carefully tip the cake layer out of the pan and peel off the parchment paper.

WHIP THE CREAM: Place the heavy cream, confectioners' sugar, almond extract, and salt in the bowl of a stand mixer fitted with the whisk attachment. Whip on medium speed until medium-stiff peaks form, 3 to 5 minutes. Fold in the crème fraîche with a flexible spatula until smooth.

ASSEMBLE THE CAKE: Transfer about half the whipped cream to a piping bag fitted with a round tip (about ¾ inch/2 cm in diameter).

Pipe a small dollop of the whipped cream in the center of a cake board or plate (to anchor the cake in place). Center a cake layer on top and use an offset spatula to spread a thin layer of whipped cream over the cake. Pipe a border of whipped cream around the edge of the cake. Spread the pastry cream over the whipped cream, staying within the border. Arrange half of the roasted strawberries over the custard in an even layer, then top with another cake layer. Repeat this layering until the third cake layer is on top. Spread whipped cream over the top of the cake and arrange the fresh strawberries on top. Pipe a border of whipped cream around the top or base of the cake (decoration is up to you). Place the cake in a cake box and chill in the fridge for at least 1 hour and up to 1 day before serving. Cover any leftover cake and store in the fridge for up to 4 days. Press a piece of plastic wrap against the exposed cake on the cut side to keep it extra fresh.

Menu Sets

If you go out to dinner at a Chinese restaurant, you'll likely see a page at the back of the menu dedicated to set dinners. These are determined by how many people you have in your party and make ordering less of an ordeal when you have lots of opinionated people at the table. I've crafted a few set menus of my own based on group size, occasion, and overall vibe. Not only do the flavors in each set work well together, the recipes are also strategic with timing and availability of stovetop and oven space. I generally plan to serve at least one dish per person, plus an extra dish just in case (it's better to have more than not enough). For large meals, I've used an asterisk to mark recipes that can be made a day or two in advance to lighten the load. There are infinite menu possibilities within this book, but these set menus are a good place to start.

DINNER FOR TWO

HOUSE SPECIAL

Perfect Steamed Jasmine Rice (page 286)

Tomato Egg (page 30)

Tried-and-True Gai Lan with Oyster Sauce (page 119)

NOODLE NIGHT

Saucy Black Bean Noodles (page 92)

Kohlrabi and Radish Salad with Chili Crunch (page 111)

MEATBALL MONDAY

Gingery Brown Rice (page 290)

Miso Pork Meatballs (page 58)

Saucy Sesame Long Beans (page 123)

DINNER FOR FOUR

SORT OF ALL-AMERICAN

Country Ham and Corn Egg Drop Soup (page 297)

Shacha Roast Chicken (page 193)

Numbing Smashed Potatoes (page 139)

Soy Caramel Apple Crisp* (page 342)

HELLA BAY AREA

San Francisco Garlic Noodles (page 90)

Steamed Dungeness Crabs with Tomato Butter (page 216)

Chrysanthemum Salad with Lap Cheong Vinaigrette (page 116)

Fruit on Ice (Lime Granita) (page 317)

GRILL OUT

Lemon Togarashi Grilled Chicken (page 181)

Oysters with Mandarin Mala Mignonette (page 149)

Coconut Crunch Coleslaw (page 168)

Grilled Peaches and Coconut Sticky Rice (page 336)

DINNER FOR SIX

SUMMER SHINDIG

Momma Cho's Fried Chicken (page 174)

Char Siu Mushrooms (page 172)

Smashed Ranch Cucumbers* (page 115)

Garlicky Whipped Tofu Dip* (page 161)

Banh Mi Pasta Salad* (page 164)

Passion Fruit and Hojicha Icebox Cake* (page 334)

VEGETARIAN'S DREAM

Mapo Tofu Wontons* (page 245)

Wispy Mushroom Chow Mein (page 95)

Daan Bing Egg Rolls* (page 269)

Basil Lime Eggplant (page 131)

Pistachio Pear Baked Nian Gao* (page 340)

IT'S FRYDAY

Orange Pepper Popcorn Chicken (page 44)

Whitefish Rangoon* (page 258)

Salted Egg Yolk Squash Rings (page 142)

Tingly Instant Ramen Salad* (page 73)

Mango Pomelo Sago* (page 320)

HOLIDAY AT HOME

XO Scallop Jook (page 210)

Red-Braised Lamb (page 202)

Chicken and Cabbage Spring Rolls* (page 263)

Crispy Brussels Sprouts with Sriracha Mayo (page 136)

Sesame Persimmon Galette* (page 338)

DINNER FOR EIGHT

THE ULTIMATE LUNAR NEW YEAR

Everyday Tong (page 294)

Perfect Steamed Jasmine Rice (page 286)

Cho Family Dumplings* (page 229)

Chop Shop Pork Belly (page 195)

Oxtail and Daikon Stew (page 205)

Extra-Special XO Nian Gao (page 99)

Chow Mein Pancake (page 96)

Fiery Garlic Chives and Summer Squash* (page 128)

Lucky Cheesecake with Kumquats* (page 347)

MY DREAM BIRTHDAY

Hot-and-Sour Soup (page 298)

Gingery Brown Rice (page 290)

Party Pickles* (page 309)

Tea-Brined Duck Breast (page 198)

Welcome Home Steak (page 54)

Sizzle Sauce Noodles (page 81)

Wood Ear Mushroom Salad* (page 112)

Cleveland-ish Cassata Cake* (page 351)

RESOURCES

Sauces

Fly By Jing | Chili crisp | flybyjing.com

Lao Gan Ma | Chili crisp | laoganmausa.com

Lee Kum Kee | Soy sauces and Asian prepared sauces | usa.lkk.com

Red Boat | Fish sauce | redboatfishsauce.com

Squid Brand | Fish sauce | squidbrand.com/en/home-en

Yun Hai | yunhai.shop

Rice + Noodles

Koda Farms | Mochiko sweet rice flour | kodafarms.com

Mama | Instant ramen | mama.co.th/en/products-export-cate-list/20/17/Pack-55g-60g

Nongshim | Instant ramen | nongshimusa.com

Sapporo Ichiban | Instant ramen | sanyofoodsamerica.com

Three Ladies Brand | Jasmine rice, rice noodles, and rice flours | vinhsanh.com/three-ladies-brand-m-98.html

Twin Marquis | Noodles and wonton wrappers | twinmarquis.com

Tofu

Hodo | Tofu | hodofoods.com

House Foods | Tofu | house-foods.com

Wo Chong Company | Tofu | wochong.com

Spices + Preserved Goods

KamYenJan | Lap cheong (Chinese sausage)

Oaktown Spice Shop | Spices and teas | oaktownspiceshop.com

Yang Jiang | Salted black beans with ginger

Oils

California Olive Ranch | Olive oil | californiaoliveranch.com

Chosen Foods | Avocado oil | chosenfoods.com

La Tourangelle | Avocado and grapeseed oils | latourangelle.com

Home + Kitchen Wares

All-Clad | all-clad.com

Breville | breville.com

Crate & Barrel | crateandbarrel.com

Dansk | dansk.com

Earlywood | earlywooddesigns.com

East Fork | eastfork.com

Field Company Cast Iron | fieldcompany.com

Food52 | food52.com

GIR | gir.co

Hawkins New York | hawkinsnewyork.com

Heath Ceramics | heathceramics.com

KitchenAid | kitchenaid.com

Le Creuset | lecreuset.com

Lulu and Georgia | luluandgeorgia.com

Made In | madeincookware.com

Material Kitchen | materialkitchen.com

Stina Ceramics | stinaceramics.com

Williams Sonoma | williams-sonoma.com

ACKNOWLEDGMENTS

Bringing this cookbook into existence was such an enormous group effort, and I wouldn't have been able to do it without the help of the amazing people in my life.

Thank you to my loving family. Reuben, I'm so grateful to you for being the most supportive partner and for designing and managing the construction of our kitchen and house while I was in the thick of recipe writing and cookbook shoots. Mom and Dad, everything that I am and have been able to accomplish in this life is because of the both of you and your selfless spirits. Wai, you're the best little brother, and I'm honored to be able to reminisce about our youthful restaurant days and exploring Hong Kong together. Olive Loaf, thank you for always curling up with me while I worked on my manuscript for countless hours and for never eating the food I made without permission.

I'm so honored to work with the thoughtful and incredible team at Artisan Books. Thank you to my amazing editor, Judy Pray, for pushing me to be a better writer and to Lia Ronnen for passionately believing in this book.

Kitty Cowles, my literary agent, you already know I owe so much of my career to you. Thank you for always having my back and being one of my greatest advocates. I feel like I'm in such good hands with you in my corner.

Thank you to Ellen Morrissey for being such a meticulous recipe tester and gently teaching me how to write the clearest and most efficient recipes. These recipes wouldn't be as streamlined and easy to follow without your attentive touch.

To our incredibly kind and talented contractors, José and Eduardo of Ayala Construction, thank you for building the kitchen of my dreams and being so patient with me as I was cooking all my recipes in it while it was still an active construction site. I loved seeing you both and your crew every day and having you all as taste testers.

An extra-special thanks to all the people who opened their homes to me to cook and photograph in, stepped in as hand models, created custom linens and ceramics, and overall kept me sane during the photography process: Susanna, Toshi, Alex,

Rebecca, Frances, Eugene, Barbara, Brianna, Martin, Jessica, Alex, Lauren, Christina, Ryan, and Johnny.

A major thank-you to Arlene Easterwood for photographing some special meals and moments cooking with the people I love. You have the amazing ability to capture the spirit of a moment, and I'm going to cherish these photos forever. I'm so glad many of them are in this book.

And last but certainly not least, thank you to all my readers and supporters of Eat Cho Food. Your enthusiasm, kindness, and friendship make writing and developing meaningful recipes worthwhile. I love being able to share this part of my life and love with you.

INDEX

Page numbers in *italics* refer to photographs.

KRISTINA CHO is a James Beard Award–winning cookbook author and the creator of @EatChoFood. Her food is influenced by her Chinese heritage, Midwestern upbringing, and sunny life in California. *Mooncakes & Milk Bread* (2021) was Kristina's groundbreaking debut cookbook, and you'll find many of her recipes featured in *Food Network Magazine*, *Food & Wine*, and the *New York Times*. She lives and cooks in the San Francisco Bay Area with her husband, Reuben, and rescue dog, Olive.